Boasian Verse

Boasian Verse explores the understudied poetic output of three major twentieth-century anthropologists: Edward Sapir, Ruth Benedict, and Margaret Mead. Providing a comparative analysis of their anthropological and poetic works, this volume explores the divergent representations of cultural others and the uses of ethnographic studies for cultural critique. This volume aims to illuminate central questions, including:

- Why did they choose to write poetry about their ethnographic endeavors?
- Why did they choose to write the way they wrote?
- Was poetry used to approach the objects of their research in different, perhaps ethically more viable ways?
- Did poetry allow them to transcend their own primitivist, even evolutionist tendencies, or did it much rather refashion or even amplify those tendencies?

This in-depth examination of these ethnographic poems invites both cultural anthropologists and students of literature to reevaluate the Boasian legacy of cultural relativism, primitivism, and residual evolutionism for the twenty-first century. This volume offers a fresh perspective on some of the key texts that have shaped twentieth- and twenty-first-century discussions of culture and cultural relativism, and a unique contribution to readers interested in the dynamic area of multimodal anthropologies.

Philipp Schweighauser is Professor of North American and General Literature at the University of Basel, Switzerland. He received his PhD in Anglophone literary studies from the same university. After a research stay at the University of California, Irvine (2000–2001), a postdoc position at the University of Berne (2003–2007), and an assistant professorship at the University of Göttingen (2007–2009), he returned to the University of Basel in 2009. From 2012 to 2020, Schweighauser served as the president of the Swiss Association for North American Studies. He is the co-editor of eight edited volumes or special issues, and the author of two monographs: *Beautiful Deceptions: European Aesthetics, the Early American Novel, and Illusionist Art* (U of Virginia P, 2016) and *The Noises of American Literature, 1890–1985: Toward a History of Literary Acoustics* (UP Florida, 2006).

Routledge Studies in Twentieth-Century Literature

Exile as a Continuum in Joseph Conrad's Fiction
Living in Translation
Ludmilla Voitkovska

Ernest Hemingway and the Fluidity of Gender
A Socio-Cultural Analysis of Selected Works
Tania Chakravertty

The Life and Works of Korean Poet Kim Myŏng-sun
The Flower Dream of a Woman Born Too Soon
Jung Ja Choi

Boasian Verse
The Poetic and Ethnographic Work of Edward Sapir, Ruth Benedict, and Margaret Mead
Philipp Schweighauser

Valencian Folktales
Enric Valor
Translated by Paul Scott Derrick and Maria-Lluïsa Gea-Valor

The Postwar Counterculture in Novels and Film
On the Avenue of the Mystery
Gary Hentzi

Authors and Art Movements of the Twentieth Century
Painterly Poetics
Declan Lloyd

For more information about this series, please visit: www.routledge.com/Routledge-Studies-in-Twentieth-Century-Literature/book-series/RSTLC

Boasian Verse
The Poetic and Ethnographic Work of Edward Sapir, Ruth Benedict, and Margaret Mead

Philipp Schweighauser

NEW YORK AND LONDON

First published 2023
by Routledge
605 Third Avenue, New York, NY 10158

and by Routledge
4 Park Square, Milton Park, Abingdon, Oxon, OX14 4RN

Routledge is an imprint of the Taylor & Francis Group, an informa business

© 2023 Philipp Schweighauser

The right of Philipp Schweighauser to be identified as author of this work has been asserted in accordance with sections 77 and 78 of the Copyright, Designs and Patents Act 1988.

All rights reserved. No part of this book may be reprinted or reproduced or utilised in any form or by any electronic, mechanical, or other means, now known or hereafter invented, including photocopying and recording, or in any information storage or retrieval system, without permission in writing from the publishers.

Trademark notice: Product or corporate names may be trademarks or registered trademarks, and are used only for identification and explanation without intent to infringe.

ISBN: 978-1-032-21141-1 (hbk)
ISBN: 978-1-032-21142-8 (pbk)
ISBN: 978-1-003-26694-5 (ebk)

DOI: 10.4324/9781003266945

Typeset in Sabon
by Apex CoVantage, LLC

Für Marianne

Contents

	List of Figures	viii
	Acknowledgments	ix
	Introduction	1
1	**Soothing Blindness, Piercing Insight: Ruth Benedict's Verse**	16
	Concealing Disclosures 17	
	Yearning for Lost Plenitude 32	
	Of Syncretisms, Foils, and Cautionary Examples 39	
2	**Margaret Mead: How to Make It New, Differently**	56
	Reinventing the Social World 57	
	Toward an Anthropology of the Senses 76	
	The Public and the Private, In and Out of Verse 83	
3	**Exerting Poetic License: Edward Sapir's Poetry**	100
	Little Canadian Flowers 101	
	Poetry Magazine 108	
	Playing Seriously With Genres 120	
	Of Desert Sirens 134	
	Conclusion	144
	Works Cited	156
	Index	179

Figures

2.1	Pablo Picasso, *Les demoiselles d'Avignon* (1907)	64
2.2	Margaret Mead with her trademark cape and walking stick	84
3.1	Photograph of Tom Sayach'apis in Edward Sapir, "The Social Organization of the West Coast Tribes" (1915)	121
4.1	Plate thirty-eight in Gregory Bateson and Margaret Mead, *Balinese Character* (1942)	145
4.2 and 4.3	Details of plate thirty-eight in Gregory Bateson and Margaret Mead, *Balinese Character* (1942)	146

Acknowledgments

It is customary to thank one's beloved last. So let me thank you, Marianne, my love, first. Friends and family who also stuck with me through good times and bad include our daughter Lia, Ueli and Trudi Weisskopf, Daniel and Nina Schweighauser, Rosemarie Schweighauser, Damian Schweighauser, Levin Schweighauser, Barbara Weisskopf and Christoph Heer, Peter Burleigh and Sophie Jung, Hannes Nüsseler and Rebekka Basler, Daniele Ganser and Bea Schwarz, Laurenz and Wiebke Bolliger, Roger and Nadine Eicher, Thomas Zajac and Ayesha Curmally, Andreas and Anne Sudmann, and Arabelle Pfrunder and Tobias Pauli. I thank them all, with all my heart.

At my place of work, the Department of English of the University of Basel, I would like to express my gratitude to Ridvan Askin, whose incisive feedback on large parts of the manuscript has helped make this a better book. I am also indebted to Joana Gut and Andrea Wüst, who proofread and formatted the whole manuscript. Together with Alexandra Grasso, Joana also did an excellent job transcribing the letters Edward Sapir sent to Harriet Monroe, the editor of *Poetry* magazine, and scanning biographies of the Boasians for discussions of their poetry. Kathrin Eckerth deserves extra thanks for securing permissions for images and poems. At Basel, I also profited from the feedback given to me by the participants in our departmental research colloquium, among them Ina Habermann, Miriam Locher, and Heike Behrens. Further important input came during the question-and-answer sessions of talks I have given about 'my literary anthropologists' at the Universities of Fribourg (where, in 2004, I gave my first talk on the topic—on Ruth Benedict's poem "Unshadowed Pool"), Berne, Strasbourg, Munich, Harvard, Freiburg im Breisgau, Hannover, FU Berlin, and the Collegium Helveticum in Zürich.

This book grows out of the Swiss National Science Foundation research project "Of Cultural, Poetic, and Medial Alterity: The Scholarship, Poetry, Photographs, and Films of Edward Sapir, Ruth Fulton Benedict, and Margaret Mead" (2014–17) which I directed, as principal investigator, together with cultural anthropologist Walter Leimgruber (University of Basel) and fellow literary scholar Gabriele Rippl (University of Berne). The project members were A. Elisabeth Reichel (in literary studies) and Silvy Chakkalakal (in cultural anthropology). All members of the project team gave me much food for thought, for which I am very thankful. I also want to express my gratitude to Samira Lütscher and Simon Reber, two young researchers in literary studies who made important early contributions to the formulation of the original research project but, for various reasons, decided not to pursue doctoral dissertations. At Routledge, Michelle Salyga and Bryony Reece believed in and supported this project from the start and the two external readers, one anonymous, the other Richard Handler, helped me improve this book.

Selected poems by Edward Sapir, Ruth Benedict, and Margaret Mead are reprinted courtesy of the American Philosophical Society; the Archives and Special Collections, Vassar College Library; and the American Anthropological Association.

Parts of this book have already appeared in other places. I am grateful for permission to reprint parts of the following essays: "An Anthropologist at Work: Ruth Benedict's Poetry," *American Poetry from Whitman to the Present*, eds. Robert Rehder and Patrick Vincent. SPELL: Swiss Papers in English Language and Literature 18. Tübingen: Gunter Narr, 2006. 113–25; "Playing Seriously with Genres: Sapir's 'Nootka' Texts and Mead's Balinese Anthropology," *RANAM: Recherches anglaises et nord-américaines* 50 (2017): 107–21; (with A. Elisabeth Reichel) "Folk Communities in Translation: Salvage Primitivism and Edward Sapir's French-Canadian Folk Songs," *American Communities: Between the Popular and the Political*, eds. Julia Straub and Lukas Etter. Tübingen: Gunter Narr, 2017, 61–83; (with Gabriele Rippl, A. Elisabeth Reichel, and Silvy Chakkalakal), introduction to *Boasian Aesthetics: American Poetry, Visual Culture, and Cultural Anthropology*, eds. Schweighauser, Rippl, Chakkalakal, Reichel, special issue, *Amerikastudien/American Studies* 63.4 (2018): 431–40; "Ways of Knowing: The Aesthetics of Boasian Poetry," *Boasian Aesthetics: American Poetry, Visual Culture, and Cultural Anthropology*, eds. Schweighauser, Rippl, Chakkalakal, and Reichel, special issue, *Amerikastudien/American Studies* 63.4 (2018): 541–56; "Faire du neuf, autrement: la poésie de Margaret Mead," trans. Éléonore Devevey, *Anthropologie et poèsie*, eds. Vincent Debaene and Nicolas Adell, special issue, *Fabula LHT* 21 (2018); "Of Syncretisms, Foils, and Cautionary Examples: Ruth Fulton Benedict's Ethnographic and Poetic Styles," *Revisiting Style in Literary and Cultural Studies: Interdisciplinary Articulations*, eds. Jasmin Herrmann et al. New York: Peter Lang, 2019.193–205.

Open access publication was made possible by generous funding from the Swiss National Science Foundation.

Introduction

This book is concerned with one of the less explored outputs of three major Boasian anthropologists: the over one thousand poems written by Edward Sapir, Ruth Fulton Benedict, and Margaret Mead. It is well known that, schooled by their academic teacher Franz Boas, the German-American founder of U.S. cultural anthropology, the Boasians were instrumental in putting forward the concept of 'culture'—a key concept in the twentieth- and twenty-first-century social sciences and humanities. The Boasians also played the major role in shaping the public discussion of 'culture' and in introducing cultural relativism into the social sciences as an important tool for grasping the diversity and equality of cultures, or "the coexisting and equally valid patterns of life which mankind has created for itself from the raw materials of existence" (Benedict, *Patterns* 278).[1] About her instructor, colleague, and intimate friend Benedict's best-selling *Patterns of Culture* (1934), Mead rightly said,

> That today the modern world is on such easy terms with the concept of culture, that the words 'in our culture' slip from the lips of educated men and women almost as effortlessly as do the phrases that refer to period and to place, is in very great part due to this book.
> ("Preface" xixi)

The Boasians were also key in pushing back the social evolutionist model of anthropological research and in countering scientific racism—an endeavor in which Boas played a particularly prominent role, from his 1887 challenge to Otis T. Mason's evolutionist scheme of classification for the U.S. National Museum onward (Boas, "Occurrence").[2] Arguably, Mead was the first American anthropologist who conducted fieldwork in Bronisław Malinowski's sense of participant observation[3]—work that resulted in her influential and controversial first book, *Coming of Age in Samoa: A Psychological Study of Primitive Youth for Western Civilization* (1928).[4] Mead's pioneering contributions to visual anthropology[5]—her experiments with forms other than conventional ethnographic writing, in

DOI: 10.4324/9781003266945-1

particular photography and film, and her published reflections on those practices—have also received much scholarly attention.[6]

What is far less well known is that Mead wrote over 190 poems. Mead is in good Boasian company here. Her close collaborators Sapir and Benedict also wrote and published a great deal of verse, some of it in renowned magazines such as *Poetry*, *The Dial*, *The Measure*, *The Nation*, and *The New Republic*. Between 1919 and 1931, Sapir alone was able to place no less than twenty-three poems in *Poetry*, the flagship little magazine of the modernist movement. Out of the three, Sapir was the most productive, publishing over three hundred of his poems and writing over three hundred additional, unpublished ones. But Benedict's and Mead's poetic oeuvres are substantial too. By A. Elisabeth Reichel's count, this corpus of Boasian verse encompasses 1,015 texts, including "318 published and 345 unpublished poems written by Sapir, 61 published and 96 unpublished poems written by Benedict, and 22 published and 173 unpublished poems written by Mead" (*Writing* 6). Sapir, Benedict, and Mead read each other's poems, collected them, commented on them, and dedicated poems to one another.[7] *An Anthropologist at Work* (1959), an anthology of Benedict's writings edited by Mead, provides a glimpse into the importance they attributed to each other's lyrical work: Next to letters by Sapir that provide detailed responses to Benedict's verse, the volume contains in full the selection of poems that Benedict made for Mead in 1941 and presented to her as a gift in a hand-bound book.

This prolific poetic output makes Sapir, Benedict, and Mead a unique group in the history of twentieth-century cultural anthropology: they were the only anthropologists of the era that left a sizeable body of poetry, much of which deals with the objects of the writers' anthropological investigations. In this rich yet sorely understudied corpus of Boasian poetic production,[8] those texts that I call 'ethnographic poems' are of particular interest to me: that part of Sapir's, Benedict's, and Mead's poetic oeuvre which engages with subjects and issues that they encountered in their ethnographic work. In many cases, these poems stage in-depth explorations of issues at the heart of our anthropologists' ethnographic writings: the inescapably evaluative dimension of cultural description, the search for adequate ways of representing the cultural other, and the ethical implications of cultural relativism. In Mead's case, it is no coincidence that she wrote some of her early poems during her fieldwork in American Samoa (1925–26) and Papua New Guinea (1928–29), where she had her most productive period as a poet.[9] Reading these poems and those by her fellow Boasians, one question that immediately imposes itself is this: What difference does it make when anthropologists decide to write about another culture in verse instead of ethnographic prose? This is the most general question this book asks—a question that is simultaneously aesthetic (since it inquires into the specific functions of specific genres), epistemological (since it asks about the different kinds of knowledge enabled by different generic choices), and ethical (since it invites us to think about what constitutes 'good' representations of ethnic others).

What *Boasian Verse* probes, then, is the intersection of cultural alterity (the otherness of the cultures anthropologists study) and poetic alterity (the use of a different language—the language of poetry—in ethnographic investigation, a practice that has become quite common in today's multimodal anthropologies). Drawing on Alexander Gottlieb Baumgarten's original definition of 'aesthetics' as "the science of perception" (*Reflections* §116, 78) and "the science of sensuous cognition" (*Aesthetica* I: §1, 10), I understand the Boasians' ethnographic and poetic interventions as aesthetic and aisthetic practices, i.e., as artistic practices and negotiations of sensuous perception. This attunement to the sensory in aesthetics is closely connected with cultural anthropologists' turn to the senses since Helmuth Plessner initiated the anthropology of the senses in the 1970s and characterized it as a subfield of cultural anthropology that probes the intersection of sensual impression, body, reason, and reflection.[10] While cultural anthropologists most commonly discuss sensory practices in ethnographic work under headings such as 'the anthropology of the senses,' 'sensory anthropology,' or 'sensory ethnography,' they share with recent returns to aesthetics a sustained interest in the epistemic dimensions of *aisthēsis* (sense perception, sensation, feeling). In philosophy and literary studies, this earliest meaning of aesthetics has received much attention in recent decades. Today, Gernot Böhme (*Atmosphäre; Aisthetik*) and Wolfgang Welsch (*Aktualität*; "Aesthetics Beyond Aesthetics"; *Ästhetisches Denken*) are among the most prominent advocates for understanding aesthetics again as a theory of sensuous cognition, seeking to "bring about an aesthetics which manages to cover the full range of the expression 'aesthetic' and the various domains and states of *aisthesis*" as "[t]here are no good reasons for aesthetics to restrict itself to artistics. . . . *[A]s a discipline* aesthetics should comprehend the *full* range of such endeavours" (Welsch, "Aesthetics Beyond Aesthetics" 14–15; emphasis in original). Jacques Rancière has given this original notion of aesthetics a political twist that is also relevant to *Boasian Verse*. Rancière redefines 'aesthetics' as a site that explores the 'distribution of the sensible' in social space to probe "aesthetic acts as configurations of experience that create new modes of sense perception and induce novel forms of political subjectivity" (9). From this perspective, aesthetics is a decisively political notion in the sense that "[p]olitics revolves around what is seen and what can be said about it, around who has the ability to see and the talent to speak" (13).[11]

It is, I believe, with this broad understanding of aesthetics—an understanding that is attuned to both the sensory and the political dimensions of artistic and scientific practices—that we need do approach sensuously rich passages in Boasian ethnography such as Mead's description of life on the island of Ta'ū, American Samoa, around midday:

> As the sun rises higher in the sky, the shadows deepen under the thatched roofs, the sand is burning to the touch, the hibiscus flowers wilt on the hedges, and little children bid the smaller ones, "Come out of the sun." Those whose excursions have been short return to the village, the women with strings of crimson jelly fish, or baskets of shell fish, the men with cocoanuts, carried in baskets slung on a shoulder pole. The women and children eat their breakfasts, just hot from the oven, if this is cook day, and the young men work swiftly in the midday heat, preparing the noon feast for their elders.
> (*Samoa* 13–14)

For this early anthropologist of the senses, the cultures she studied should be perceived not only through sight and hearing but also through touch, smell, and taste. Mead's decision to provide a multi-sensorial account of Samoan culture constitutes not only a disciplinary intervention (because it exposes the limitations of a research field that Mead dubbed a 'discipline of words' in her programmatic essay on visual anthropology) but also a political intervention in that it evokes, in primitivist fashion, the sensuous fullness of a culture that she would, in the two final chapters of *Coming of Age in Samoa*, favorably compare to her own.

Such turns to the sensory, which characterize both Mead's brand of Boasian anthropology and recent returns to the aesthetic, were also crucial in the development of modern literary theory which, arguably, began with the Russian Formalists' exploration of what makes literature literature in the first three decades of the twentieth century. For Victor Shklovsky, literature speaks in a recalcitrant language that resists ready absorption and breaks with habitualized forms of perception in order to refresh our sensuous experience of the world:

> And so, in order to return sensation to our limbs, in order to make us feel objects, to make a stone feel stony, man has been given the tool of art. The purpose of art, then, is to lead us to a knowledge of a thing through the organ of sight instead of recognition. By 'enstranging' objects and complicating form, the device of art makes perception long and 'laborious.' The perceptual process in art has a purpose all its own and ought to be extended to the fullest. *Art is a means of experiencing the process of creativity. The artifact itself is quite unimportant.*
> (6; emphasis in original)

Shklovsky formulated these thoughts in 1917, at the height of the modernist movement in literature and the arts. This is no coincidence. His conviction that literature is an obstinate form of language use that slows down perception fits the difficult, experimental texts written by the modernists particularly well. At the same time, what Shklovsky develops here is a general theory of literature of all ages,[12] a theory that reminds us to pay close attention to the specific forms of specific literary texts written in *any* literary period. For the purposes of the present inquiry, the fact that Shklovsky's reflections on literariness—which serve as a lodestar for this book—propose a theory of literature in general (rather than a theory of literary modernism) is crucial since, even as Benedict and especially Sapir were aware of contemporaneous developments in poetry,[13] the three Boasians under consideration in this book wrote verse that for the greatest part has a decidedly nineteenth-century ring to it. So let me ask again: Why did they choose to write poetry about their ethnographic endeavors, and why did they choose to write the way they wrote? Could it be that this influential group of early twentieth-century anthropologists turned to poetry as a special form of language use that allowed them to approach the objects of their research in different, perhaps ethically more viable ways? Did poetry allow them to transcend their own primitivist and, yes, evolutionist tendencies,[14] or did it much rather refashion or even amplify those tendencies? These questions invite me to read Sapir's, Benedict's, and Mead's poetic negotiations of cultural alterity as reflections on their ethnographic practice that have important aesthetic/aisthetic, epistemological, and ethical ramifications.

In exploring these ramifications, the Boasians' roles as cultural critics needs to be kept in focus. Out of the three anthropologists treated in this book, it was Mead who most consistently used "anthropology as a weapon in the attack upon 'Americanism'" (Matthews 17). While twenty-first-century proponents of cultural relativism emphasize that "fundamentally different standards of morality, practices and belief systems operate in different cultures and cannot be judged with regard to their worth from a standpoint exterior to them" (Sedgwick 99), Boasians like Mead and Benedict explicitly brought their positive valuations of other cultures (e.g. Mead's lusty Samoans; Benedict's 'Apollonian' Zuni) to bear on a enstranging critique of their own culture, thus testifying to Bernhard Waldenfels's insight that the othering of the cultural other often results in the othering of the self. Already in the two final chapters of *Coming of Age in Samoa*, Mead used the insights she gained while studying Samoan culture to question dominant American child-rearing practices and the sanctity of the nuclear family.[15] As we shall see, even as we appreciate our three Boasians' emancipatory uses of ethnographic knowledge for cultural critique, we need to remain aware that this political engagement comes with its own liabilities in that it bears witness to primitivism's "urge toward deliberate regression combined with an even more compelling desire for rejuvenation" (Connelly 35).[16] Contrary to Benedict's claim that she avoids romantic utopianism and any "romantic return to the primitive" (*Patterns* 19), her poetry as well as that of her colleagues in many ways seems a primitivist attempt to counterbalance the demystification and rationalization of the Western world that they disapprove of. Clearly, the Boasians' adherence to more traditional poetic forms (rhymes, regular meter, conventional tropes) is related to their privileging of holism, form, and integration in their ethnographic writings.[17] At the same time, what may seem like an idealized depiction of primitive cultures can, upon closer examination, reveal itself as a sophisticated negotiation of cultural alterity. Thus, Benedict's poetic reflections on the destruction of sacred objects through the anthropologist's gaze in "Countermand" (1930), "Unshadowed Pool" (1930), and "Moth Wing" (n.d.) as well as Mead's ruminations on the effects of colonization in "Monuments Rejected" (1925) demonstrate a keen awareness that ethnographers are more than keepers of older, more harmonious ways of life. Even in Sapir's writings, there is a tension between his politically conservative resistance to changes of social forms—his essay "Observations on the Sex Problem in America" (1928) is a particularly egregious example whose critiques of female sexual and economic liberation, promiscuity, and homosexuality enraged Benedict and Mead[18]—and his willingness to experiment with various poetic forms.

Compared with the primitivism that European and American modernist writers and artists ranging from Pablo Picasso and Emil Nolde in painting to Tristan Tzara and T. S. Eliot in poetry engaged in, the Boasians stressed the critical over the therapeutic function of Western subjects' engagement with 'primitive' peoples and their cultures. As I will elaborate in my discussion of Benedict's poetry in Chapter 1, the Boasians often used foreign, supposedly simpler cultures as either foils or cautionary examples to critique what they felt was wrong about their own culture. Mead famously used her research on adolescence in American Samoa to stage a critique of American sexual morality and of "the evils inherent in the too intimate family organisation" (*Samoa* 149); Benedict saw contemporary U.S. society beset by something akin to the fierce competitiveness she found in the 'Dionysian' Kwakiutl of the Pacific Northwest (*Patterns*); and for Sapir, present-day America was a 'spurious' culture beset by "a chronic state of cultural maladjustment" that has "reduced much of our higher life to sterile externality" while "[it] is easier, generally speaking, for a genuine culture to subsist on a lower level of civilization" ("Culture, Genuine and Spurious" 413).[19] Mead, Benedict, and Sapir inherited this critical strain from their academic teacher Boas, who deeply impressed W.E.B. Du Bois when, as early as May 31, 1906, he commented on racial inequality and evoked the glories of ancient African kingdoms south of the Sahara in his commencement address at Atlanta University ("Commencement Address").[20] Of course, from a twenty-first-century perspective, such returns to supposedly simpler cultures are deeply problematic even if they are put in the service of a critique of the anthropologist's own culture.

In their ethnographic writings, the Boasians under consideration in this book both represent cultural others—Mead's Samoans, Benedict's Kwakiutl, Sapir's Native Americans, and many other others—and reflect on adequate ways of representing foreign subjects and cultures. It is particularly this self-reflexive dimension of Boasian ethnography that invites me to probe its practitioners' exploration of alternative, poetic forms of representation. As I explore the differences and convergences between the Boasians' ethnographic and poetic verbalizations of cultural alterity, I probe the epistemological, ethical, and aesthetic/aisthetic valences of the generic choices Sapir, Benedict, and Mead make. What emerges from these probes is no neat distinction between 'good' (say, ethically sound and aesthetically satisfying) poetic representations and 'bad' (say, primitivist and/or evolutionist) ethnographic representations of cultural others but an awareness that generic differences make a difference. It is that difference that I wish to explore in my attempt to do justice to a sorely understudied corpus of modern American poetry.

Entitled "Soothing Blindness, Piercing Insight: Ruth Benedict's Verse," the first chapter begins with a literary-historical assessment of Benedict's poetry that places its probing of the relations between cultural and poetic alterity right at the intersection of nineteenth- and twentieth-century aesthetics. Taking issue with both Margaret Mead's characterization of her friend's poetry as little more than a psychological crutch and her insistence that Benedict resolutely kept anthropology and poetry apart, I propose to read her verse both biographically and ethnographically, as forms of 'concealing disclosure.' Even as poems such as "Unshadowed Pool" and "In Parables" probe the ethics of making visible both the self and the cultural other, many a poem by Benedict uses foreign cultures as foils to enable a sharper perspective on the author's own culture that renders the familiar strange again. Thus, Benedict the poet joins Benedict the anthropologist in staging a countercultural critique that is energized by the author's experience of foreign cultures. As a close reading of Benedict's unpublished poem "Myth" makes clear, though, much of her poetry stages that critique in ways that differ from her ethnographic writings. While Benedict's scholarly work embraces a strong variety of cultural relativism according to which different cultures are incommensurable, her verse tends to revel in the syncretistic fusion of cultures.

The second chapter, "Margaret Mead: How to Make It New, Differently," shows how, energized by progressivist convictions and a profound distrust in the epistemic value of words (expressed most forcefully in her 1924 poem "Warning"), Mead—who had been writing poetry since the age of nine—did not join the modernists in striving to 'make new' literary language but sought to reinvent, first, her discipline and, second, the social world. What comes into view as I compare Mead's poetry to Eliot's *The Waste Land* is divergent forms of literary primitivism that are fed by different conceptualizations of foreign cultures: social evolutionist in

Eliot's case; cultural relativist in Mead's. As a result, while both Eliot and Mead draw on foreign cultures to stage a cultural critique of modernity, they employ other cultures differently: as sources of cultural rejuvenation in the former; as vanishing cultural forms and practices in the latter. Taking a close look at Mead's letters from Samoa and several of her ethnographic poems also reveals that she reflected on the epistemic valence of sensory perception in her poetry and field notes long before she made her pioneering contributions to the anthropology of the senses in the 1950s. What we also encounter in lyrical ethnographic poems of Mead's such as "The Need That Is Left"—poems that both give expression to feelings and ponder anthropological subject matters—is a subtle and intriguing troubling of the private-public divide that this eminently public intellectual negotiated in her life and work.

My third and final chapter, titled "Exerting Poetic License: Edward Sapir's Poetry," begins with a consideration of what looks like an oddity at first sight: Sapir's publication of four translated Québécois folk songs in the July 1920 issue of *Poetry*, the major little magazine that promoted modernism in the Anglophone world. A closer look at these poems and the texts that surround them reveals that, far from being an exception, the publication of these poems testifies to Harriet Monroe and her fellow editors' keen interest in both 'folk poetry' and fairly traditional verse. That there is a crucial ethical dimension to Sapir's poetic treatment of 'folk' materials becomes even more evident as we consider a long poem based on his most extensive research effort. In "The Blind, Old Indian Tells His Names," Sapir plays fast and loose with stories and people he encountered during his field work among the First Nations community Nuu-chah-nulth, raising the question of an anthropologist-poet's ethical obligations toward the subjects of his research. In view of the *Writing Culture* debate's call to probe the politics of ethnographic representation, when does poetic license lose its sway in the making of ethnographic poems? What do I, as a literary scholar, do when concepts dear to my discipline such as poetic license begin to ring of ethnocentrism? In concluding this chapter, I turn to "Zuni," another ethnographic poem that Sapir managed to place in *Poetry*, to show how he uses poetry to give professional advice to Benedict and, in doing so, evokes the sensuous plenitude of another culture, even as he calls upon his fellow Boasian to detach herself from that culture's allure. In returning us to the conjoint issues of cultural alterity, representation, and sensory perception, "Zuni" once more invites us to consider the question that is at the heart of the present book: What aesthetic/aisthetic, epistemological, and ethical difference does it make whether one represents cultural others in ethnographic prose or in the language of Dickinson, Millay, and Pound?

In my conclusion, I start by considering Mead's dismissal of a Balinese artist's intention in her and Gregory Bateson's *Balinese Character*. This leads me into a discussion of the ways in which European literary-critical concepts such as 'intentional fallacy' and 'enstrangement may ring false when applied to other cultures. By way of concluding this book, I review three recent reappraisals of Boasian liberalism before I explain why my own take on the Boasians' ethnographic and poetic work is by and large appreciative. First, because my own account of Sapir's, Benedict's, and Mead's work follows a largely implicit liberal trajectory; second, because in evaluating the politics of the Boasians' work I try to stay clear of presentism; third and finally, because in my book, calling someone a 'liberal' does not necessarily amount to passing a negative judgement.

Notes

1. The account in this paragraph of the Boasians' place in the history of anthropology relies on George W. Stocking's seminal contributions to the history of the discipline, particularly *Race, Culture, and Evolution: Essays in the History of Anthropology* (1968), *Victorian Anthropology* (1987), *Romantic Motives: Essays on Anthropological Sensibility* (1989), "Paradigmatic Traditions in the History of Anthropology" (1989), "The Ethnographic Sensibility of the 1920s and the Dualism of the Anthropological Tradition" (1992), and *American Anthropology, 1921–1945: Papers from the American Anthropologist* (2002). See also Marvin Harris's *The Rise of Anthropological Theory: A History of Theories of Culture* (2001), Fred W. Voget's "History of Anthropology" (1996), and Sydel Silverman's "The Boasians and the Invention of Cultural Anthropology" (2005).
2. Positing a later date for Boas's first engagement with scientific racism—his 1906 commencement address at Atlanta University—Sydel Silverman notes that "Boas began making public statements on race as early as 1906, and it is said that his last words as he collapsed and died in Claude Lévi-Strauss's arms were about race" (269).
3. As Silverman notes, "Mead's Samoan work was probably the first American ethnography in the holistic, Malinowskian sense, based upon participant observation" (268).
4. The two most prominent and forceful critiques of Mead's Samoan ethnography were published after Mead's death: Derek Freeman's *Mead and Samoa: The Making and Unmaking of an Anthropological Myth* (1983) and his follow-up book *The Fateful Hoaxing of Margaret Mead* (1999). In *Mead and Samoa*, Freeman's main charges were that Mead blindly followed her teacher Boas in privileging cultural over biological determinism and that she ignored less sanguine aspects of Samoan culture, in particular its intense competitiveness and violent side, that did not fit her preconceived romantic ideas. In *The Fateful Hoaxing of Margaret Mead*, he added that she was deceived and made fun of by two of her major indigenous informants, which led to falsehoods and overstatements concerning Samoan girls' sexual liberty. The Mead-Freeman debate took off after her death in 1978, receiving attention and coverage well beyond anthropological circles. Paul Shankman's *The Trashing of Margaret Mead: Anatomy of an Anthropological Controversy* (2009) provides a balanced account of the debate. Peter Hempenstall's intellectual biography of Freeman, *Truth's Fool: Derek Freeman and the War over Cultural Anthropology* (2017) is also helpful to understand the ferocity and persistence of his critique of Mead and U.S. cultural anthropology more generally.

10   *Introduction*

5. Mead and her collaborators' most significant pioneer work includes Gregory Bateson and Mead's *Balinese Character: A Photographic Analysis* (1942), ethnographic films of theirs such as *Trance and Dance in Bali* (1952) and *Bathing Babies in Three Cultures* (1954), Mead and Frances Cooke Macgregor's *Growth and Culture: A Photographic Study of Balinese Childhood* (1951), Mead and Rhoda Métraux's *The Study of Culture at a Distance* (1953), Mead's "Anthropology and the Camera" (1963), and her "Visual Anthropology in a Discipline of Words" (1975).

6. One indicator of this is that Paul Hockings' standard anthology of the subfield, *Principles of Visual Anthropology*, now available in its third edition, begins with Mead's classic essay "Visual Anthropology in a Discipline of Words" (1975). For an assessment of Mead's and Gregory Bateson's roles in the development of visual anthropology, see also Ira Jacknis's "Margaret Mead and Gregory Bateson in Bali: Their Use of Photography and Film" (1988), David MacDougall's "The Subjective Voice in Ethnographic Films" (1995), Anna Grimshaw's *The Ethnographer's Eye: Ways of Seeing in Modern Anthropology* (2001), Jay Ruby's "The Professionalization of Visual Anthropology in the United States—1960s and 1970s" (2002), Ute Holl's *Kino, Trance & Kybernetik* (2002), Karl G. Heider's *Ethnographic Film* (2006), Sarah Pink's *Doing Visual Ethnography: Images, Media and Representation in Research* (2007), and Silvy Chakkalakal's "Sensible Ethnographien—Modernistische Empfindsamkeit als Modus einer ethnographischen Ästhetik" (2015) and "Ethnographic Art Worlds: The Creative Figuration of Art and Anthropology" (2018).

7. As Mead remembers,

> Chief among these relationships which, for the first time, made her interest in writing poetry a lively, shared preoccupation was her friendship with Edward Sapir, which began in formal anthropological terms but soon overflowed into an interchange of poems and discussions of poetry. As she came to know Léonie Adams and Louise Bogan and Eda Lou Walton, she had their poems, too, to enjoy in manuscript and as part of the lives of people she knew. . . . Many of our poems grew out of our relationships to one another, and the intensities of the contemporary human plots were discussed and rediscussed against the background of the childhood experience and special temperament of each. Sapir dedicated "Zuñi" and "Signal" to Ruth Benedict, and "Ariel" to me. She wrote "Lift Up Your Heart" and "This Gabriel" for me. I wrote "Misericordia" and "Absolute Benison" for her, and "For a Proud Lady" for Louise Bogan.
>
> (Benedict, *Anthropologist* 87–88)

Hilary Lapsley notes that, in publishing "Misericordia" in *An Anthropologist at Work*, Mead omitted the two final lines ("Hearts that are human were born with no defense / Against this beauty unconfused by sense"), speculating that including them would have "perhaps" been "too revealing of her attachment to Ruth" (170).

8. To this date, only one monograph has been dedicated to the poetry of the Boasians under consideration in the present book: A. Elisabeth Reichel's *Writing Anthropologists, Sounding Primitives: The Poetry and Scholarship of Edward Sapir, Margaret Mead, and Ruth Benedict* (2021), which "analyze[s] poetic and scholarly treatments of sound and music, alphabetic writing, and photography and film as part of an investigation into the political and epistemological ramifications of the representation of cultural alterities in Sapir, Benedict, and Mead" (8), and pays particular attention to the "inter- and plurimedial" (9) nature of these anthropologists' negotiations

of cultural alterity and their "discursive treatment of media and signs other than and including written words" (9). Reichel is, in other words, interested in both the different *forms* that Sapir's, Benedict's, and Mead's negotiations of other cultures take and in the *values* that these negotiations attribute to various media and sign systems. Most importantly, in probing the Boasians' politics of representation, she shows the extent to which Sapir, Benedict, and Mead engage in evaluating (and often devaluing) other forms of being, communicating, and sounding. In Reichel's readings, Boasian ethnographies and poems—most prominently Mead's—often bear testimony to strong evolutionary residues in these cultural relativists' work.

Before Reichel's excellent literary-critical study, the cultural anthropologist Richard Handler has produced the most substantial body of work on Boasian verse. His *Critics against Culture: Anthropological Observers of Mass Society* (2005) contains three of his pioneering essays on Sapir's and Benedict's verse. For further substantial journal articles and book chapters on the poetry of Sapir, Benedict, and Mead, see the entries for Schweighauser, Reichel and Schweighauser, Susan Hegeman, Marc Manganaro, Eric Aronoff, Karin Roffman, and James Dowthwaite in the list of works cited. For early, cursory and largely biographical treatments of the Boasians' poetry—much of it revolving around the intertwinement between Benedict's and Mead's intimate relationship and some of their poems—see Mead's discussion of Benedict's verse in *An Anthropologist at Work* (1959, 5–6, 83–96, 562–63n.1), Jane Howard's *Margaret Mead: A Life* (1984; 13–15, 29, 51–52, 57–58, 73–74), Judith Modell's *Ruth Benedict: Patterns of a Life* (1984; 3, 8, 10, 99, 128–29, 134–42), Mary Catherine Bateson's *With a Daughter's Eye: A Memoir of Margaret Mead and Gregory Bateson* (1984; 113–14, 124–27, 223), Toni Flores's "The Poetry of Edward Sapir" (1986), Margaret M. Caffrey's *Ruth Benedict: Stranger in This Land* (1989; 167, 169–70, 178–79, 180–81, 183–85, 192–96), Regna Darnell's *Edward Sapir: Linguist, Anthropologist, Humanist* (1990; 133, 135–36, 159–60, 164, 173–75, 181, 183, 187), Hilary Lapsley's *Margaret Mead and Ruth Benedict: The Kinship of Women* (1999; 51–52, 64–65, 72, 85, 87–89, 90–91, 94–96, 98–100, 110–11, 113–14, 115–16, 121–22, 131–32, 135–36, 159–60, 169–70, 179–80, 184–85), and Lois W. Banner's *Intertwined Lives: Margaret Mead, Ruth Benedict, and Their Circle* (2003; 51–52, 82, 136–37, 141, 208–11, 223–26, 249–50, 259–62, 273, 275–76, 490n.40).

9. To give but two examples: at the bottom of the typescript of her unpublished poem "Monuments Rejected" (which I discuss in Chapter 2), Mead writes:

Pago Pago,
September 1, 1925.

Pago Pago is the territorial capital of American Samoa, where, in September 1925, Mead was preparing for the fieldwork that she was about to conduct on the island of Ta'ū. Mead's first book *Coming of Age in Samoa* (1928) reports on this fieldwork. The second example concerns Mead's poem "Art Deserted," another unpublished poem whose spatial and temporal origin she notes, again at the bottom of her typescript:

July 15, 1929
Sumsum, New Britain.

Sumsum (or Sum Sum) was a plantation located in New Britain in Papua New Guinea. In Papua New Guinea, Mead would study the Manus—research that she would present in *Growing up in New Guinea: A Comparative Study of Primitive Education* (1930).

12 Introduction

10. For more recent outlines of the anthropology of the senses, see David Howes's "Controlling Textuality: A Call for a Return to the Senses" (1990) and *Sensual Relations: Engaging the Senses in Culture and Social Theory* (2003), Constance Classen's *Worlds of Sense: Exploring the Senses in History and across Cultures* (1993) and "Foundations for an Anthropology of the Senses" (1997), Michael Taussig's *Mimesis and Alterity: A Particular History of the Senses* (1993), C. Nadia Seremetakis's *The Senses Still: Memory and Perception as Material Culture in Modernity* (1994), Regina Bendix's "Was über das Auge hinausgeht: Zur Rolle der Sinne in der ethnographischen Forschung" (2006), and Sarah Pink's *Doing Sensory Ethnography* (2009).

11. In his study of sense perception in the British novel of the 1980s and 1990s, Ralf Hertel concretizes Rancière's reflections on the 'distribution of the sensible' (without referring to him):

> Although it is not easy to name a single reason why writing about the senses often carries social implications, one could speculate that the fact that we define our position in, and relation to, society through our senses is crucial in this regard. . . . [T]he senses . . . are our windows on the world, the tools by which we interact with it. Our relationship with our surroundings and our position within society are crucially defined by our perception, and acts of sensation show what stance we adopt. . . . Whether a literary figure greedily woolfs down food or is on an ascetic diet, stares intensely at others or constantly averts his eyes, indulges in sweet smells or avoids the touch of others can all be significant in subtly characterising him and his attitude.
>
> (203)

While Rancière studies the social and Hertel the literary, and while Hertel's book does not pursue a political purpose the way Rancière does, their projects converge to a certain extent, as Hertel's characterization of his book makes clear:

> [W]e will have to trace literary markers of sensuousness. . . . [M]y study . . . is . . . neither a study in the phenomenology of reading nor in aesthetics; rather, it is an *aisthetics* of the contemporary novel in the true sense of the word: a study in the sensuous perception of literature.
>
> (Hertel 26; emphasis in original)

12. Toward the end of "Art as Device," Shklovsky sketches a literary history based on his key conviction that literature deviates from conventionalized ways of speaking and writing. For Shklovsky, literary devices too can become conventional and habitual, which generates a need for the literary system periodically to renew itself (12–14). See Yuri Tynianov's "On Literary Evolution" (1927) for the classic Russian Formalist account of literary history as intra-systemic evolution.

13. Apart from a host of book reviews of poetry collections penned by writers ranging from Emily Dickinson to H. D., Sapir also wrote a considerable number of literary-critical and cultural essays, among them "The Twilight of Rhyme" (1917), "Realism in Prose Fiction" (1917), "The Heuristic Value of Rhyme" (1920), "The Musical Foundations of Verse" (1921), and "Culture, Genuine and Spurious" (1924).

14. For critical accounts of the Boasians' primitivism and (residual) evolutionism, see Johannes Fabian's *Time and the Other: How Anthropology Makes Its Object* (1983), Karl-Heinz Kohl's *Abwehr und Verlangen: Zur Geschichte der Ethnologie* (1987), Marianna Torgovnick's *Gone Primitive: Savage Intellects, Modern Lives* (1990), Stocking's "The Ethnographic Sensibility of

the 1920s and the Dualism of the Anthropological Tradition" (1992), Fred Myers's "'Primitivism,' Anthropology, and the Category of 'Primitive Art'" (2006), James Clifford's "Histories of the Tribal and the Modern" (2006), and Tisa J. Wenger's "Modernists, Pueblo Indians, and the Politics of Primitivism" (2006).

15. In his contribution to the *Writing Culture* volume, Michael M.J. Fischer notes that what Mead does in *Coming of Age in Samoa*

> has always been part of the anthropological rationale: seeing others against a background of ourselves, and ourselves against a background of others. The juxtaposing of exotic customs to familiar ones, or the relativizing of taken-for-granted assumptions, has always been the kind of cultural criticism promised by anthropology.
>
> (199)

16. See also Stocking's characterization of Mead's interest in the 'primitive':

> From the time that Captain Cook returned from Tahiti, the focal ganglion in the world geography of European primitivistic longing was the islands of the 'South Seas,' where handsome brown-skinned natives led untroubled lives, finding ready sustenance in the fruit of palm trees under which they made a free and easy love. . . . In a postwar context of cultural criticism, moral questioning, and sexual experimentation, it is scarcely surprising that this anthropological interest became entangled, in the work of Margaret Mead, in 'invisible threads' [D. H. Lawrence's phrase] of primitivist consciousness.
>
> ("Ethnographic Sensibility" 307)

17. For a good discussion of convergences between the Boasians' holistic vision of culture, Benedict's poetry, and the New Critical organic unity doctrine, see Marc Manganaro's *Culture, 1922: The Emergence of a Concept* (151–74). Manganaro's comparison between Benedict's configurationist, holistic anthropology and the New Critics' notion of poetry is illuminating because it helps us put Benedict's preference for whole, integrated, and harmonious cultures in its historical contexts. In Manganaro's reading, Benedict and the New Critics share a distaste for the fragmented nature of the modern, industrialized and rationalized world that they answer with a turn to a more harmonious, integrated other: the unified, Apollonian culture of the Zuñi Pueblo in Benedict's case, the organic unity of the poem in the Southern agrarian New Critics' case.

    I should, however, note that several of the analogies Manganaro draws between the two are nothing more than that: analogies. Consider, for example, the following passages:

> Another of the New Critics' keywords also points to the filiation of Benedict to the New Critics. Brooks defines irony as "the most general term . . . for the kind of qualification which the various elements in a context receive from the context." . . . As such, irony functions as a rhetorical equivalent to cultural relativism as the latter operates in *Patterns of Culture*: as that which qualifies, reconfigures, attitudes but only according to, within, a contextual or relational framework. The "sense" of a poem, then, is that readjustment, "qualification," or broadening of mind that comes with a resolutely contextual approach.
>
> (169–70)

> [The New Critic Cleanth] Brooks says it perhaps most tellingly in *Modern Poetry and the Tradition* when, opposing what he sees as the Romantic critical tradition, he argues the need "to shift the matter at issue from a

14 Introduction

> consideration of the truth of the poem's doctrine to the poem's structure—from what the poem means to what it says." . . .
>
> As a version of Archibald MacLeish's famously poetic pronouncement on poetics, "a poem does not mean, but be," Brooks's statement amounts to an argument for the lived experience of the poetic, much as Malinowski argued for the lived experience of the ethnographer among the natives.
>
> (172)

In these two examples, Manganaro confounds four levels of analysis: a) New Critics' notion of poems as organic unity, b) Benedict's notion of cultures as coherent wholes, c) poems (modernist and not), and d) cultures (Western and non-Western). All too often, those categories are conflated, for instance when, in the first example, New Critics' identification of irony as a key feature of poetic language is taken to be analogous to anthropologists' cultural relativism. In the former case, we are talking about a feature of the research object; in the latter, we are talking about a scientific method. The same applies to my second example: while the New Critics ask us to focus on the research object itself (the literary text), early twentieth-century anthropologists ask us to focus on the *experience* of the research object (the anthropologists' sensuous experiences in the field).

The limits of Manganaro's analogies between New Critics' understanding of poetry and Benedict's of culture come into even sharper focus when we consider the poetry Benedict actually wrote. Much of the poetry she penned is not 'good' poetry in a New Critical sense: a lot of it has closer affinities with the nineteenth-century poetry the New Critics generally disliked than with the iconoclastic experiments of an Eliot or a Pound that they embraced.

18. Note that the essay takes explicitly aim at Mead, who was Sapir's lover before she departed for Samoa, when he dismisses "excited books about pleasure-loving Samoans and Trobriand Islanders" (523). Homosexuality he judges to be "unnatural" (529). Benedict may have also read Sapir's assertion that "the 'free' woman . . ., whether poetess or saleslady, has a hard job escaping from the uncomfortable feeling that she is really a safe, and therefore a dishonest, prostitute" (533) as a personal attack on her. In any case, Sapir felt he had to dispel such a reading of his essay in a letter he wrote to Benedict on April 29, 1929:

> That you would not care for my sex article, I took for granted, hence was not interested in sending you a copy, as I do not wish to have our relations unnecessarily muddied by irreconcilable differences, but that you were outraged by a supposed quotation shocked as few things have shocked me. . . . You will not believe me—and yet it is the sober truth—when I say that you were never once in my thoughts when I wrote the paper on sex, which I did, by the way, rather reluctantly at the request of Harry Stack Sullivan.
>
> (Benedict, *Anthropologist* 195)

19. Providing the first phrasing of the Boasian idea of cultural integration, Sapir characterizes a 'genuine culture' thus:

> The genuine culture is not of necessity either high or low; it is merely inherently harmonious, balanced, self-satisfactory. It is the expression of a richly varied and yet somehow unified and consistent attitude toward life, an attitude which sees the significance of any one element of civilization

in its relation to all others. It is, ideally speaking, a culture in which nothing is spiritually meaningless, in which no important part of the general functioning brings with it a sense of frustration, of misdirected or unsympathetic effort. It is not a spiritual hybrid of contradictory patches, of water-tight compartments of consciousness that avoid participation in a harmonious synthesis.

("Culture, Genuine and Spurious" 410)

Handler aptly captures the sources of Sapir's discontent with an American culture he perceives as far from genuine:

> We can place Sapir's cultural criticism in a tradition that includes Matthew Arnold's *Culture and Anarchy* (1868)—which Sapir certainly knew well—as well as Tocqueville's *Democracy in America* (1835–1840) and Weber's *The Protestant Ethic and the Spirit of Capitalism* (1905). Like Sapir, all these thinkers were troubled by the secularization of Protestant individualism, which entailed the rationalization of unlimited economic growth accompanied by an emphasis on self-development that was ultimately self-defeating. Sapir's critique of the culture of self-development grew out of his conception of the genuine culture as one endowed with rich aesthetic resources.
>
> ("Introduction" 742)

Note that Sapir's reference to "a lower level of civilization" betrays the evolutionist residues of his *"critical nostalgia"* (Clifford, "On Ethnographic Allegory" 113–14; emphasis in original)—residues that beset, as we shall see throughout, the work of his Boasian colleagues Benedict and especially Mead too.

20. Here is how Du Bois remembers Boas's commencement address,

> Franz Boas came to Atlanta University where I was teaching History in 1906 and said to the graduating class: You need not be ashamed of your African past; and then he recounted the history of black kingdoms south of the Sahara for a thousand years. I was too astonished to speak. All of this I had never heard and I came then and afterwards to realize how the silence and neglect of science can let truth utterly disappear or even be unconsciously distorted.
>
> (Du Bois, qtd. in Baker 121–22)

1 Soothing Blindness, Piercing Insight
Ruth Benedict's Verse

It is a well-known story: "on or about December 1910 human character changed" (Woolf 38). Virginia Woolf's assertion of a radical break between nineteenth- and early twentieth-century aesthetics—or, as she puts it, between Edwardian and Georgian aesthetics—is echoed both by proponents of modernism and by those who mourn the displacement of an earlier literary tradition that included, in poetry, the work of the so-called fireside poets and the once immensely popular verse of women writers such as Lydia Huntley Sigourney, Ella Wheeler Wilcox, or Celia Thaxter, now denigrated as sentimental poetesses by many.[1] Yet when we take a closer look at some of the canonical critical pronouncements asserting that both of these groups claimed a break and, by claiming it, constructed it, we find that their affirmation of a rupture in literary and cultural history is more qualified than we tend to remember it. George Santayana's indictment of what he has termed the 'genteel tradition,' for example, does not consign that tradition to the past, but emphasizes that it survives into the twentieth century to co-exist with a younger, more aggressive and more energetic vision of America. Speaking before the Philosophical Union of the University of California in 1911, Santayana in fact held that "[i]n all the higher things of the mind—in religion, in literature, in the moral emotions—it is the hereditary spirit that still prevails" ("Genteel Tradition" 188). And when we read in his 1930 essay "A Brief History of My Opinions" that "every impulse or indulgence, including the aesthetic, is evil in its effect, when it renders harmony impossible in the general tenor of life, or produces in the soul division and ruin" (20), we hear a distinctly nineteenth-century voice.

Amy Lowell's narrative of rupture in her essay "Two Generations in American Poetry" (1923) is more pertinent still to the concerns of the present book. While Lowell does disparage Wilcox, Thaxter and other nineteenth-century women poets as "caged warblers" whose "chaste and saccharine music wander[ed] through the ambient air of current periodicals," the two generations Lowell's title refers to are not divided by the turn of the previous century (111–12). Lowell's main concern is with two generations of *twentieth-century* poets. Lowell distinguishes between the

DOI: 10.4324/9781003266945-2

early, iconoclastic and experimental modernism of H. D., Pound, and Sandburg and a second generation of modernist poets emerging in the 1920s. That younger generation of American modernists, Lowell submits, can itself be divided into two groups: the "Secessionists" and the "Lyrists" (121). About the secessionists, Lowell writes that "to them art is akin to mathematics," and she wonders "whether a movement which concerns itself more with statements about poetry than with the making of poetry itself is ever going to produce works of art of a quality to justify the space taken up by the pronunciamentos" (121).[2] The lyrists, a term Lowell herself coins, are an entirely different group. Less experimental than either the secessionists of the 1920s or the modernists of the first decade of the twentieth century, they wrote highly personal poetry that combines emotion with intellect to produce work of a more conventional poetic diction. In Lowell's estimation, "the lyrists are unquestionably doing the better work" than the secessionists (119–20). Lowell names Edna St. Vincent Millay and Elinor Wylie as the chief representatives of the group, which she identifies as "a feminine movement" (121).

In organizing his selection of poems for his prestigious anthology *Modern American Poetry*, Louis Untermeyer in the 1920s and early 1930s adopted Lowell's term and changed it to 'the new lyricists'—a group that included Millay, Sara Teasdale, Elinor Wylie, Louise Bogan, and Léonie Adams among others and which produced "poetry that was both sensuous and cerebral" (Untermeyer 31). Another member of that group is Anne Singleton, who contributes two poems to the fourth edition of Untermeyer's anthology, "But the Son of Man" (1930) and "Unshadowed Pool" (1930). Anne Singleton is one of the pseudonyms under which Ruth Fulton Benedict published several of her poems.[3] As a student of Boas and one of the preeminent cultural anthropologists of the early twentieth century, Benedict established the culture-and-personality school of anthropology together with Margaret Mead, Irving Hallowell, and Clyde Kluckhohn (Silverman 267). Her book *Patterns of Culture* (1934) is one of the classics of the field, and, according to Sylvia Schomburg-Scherff, "the best sold and most influential work in twentieth-century cultural anthropology" (41; my translation).[4] Written in the mid-1930s, Benedict's book was instrumental in shifting the discussion within anthropology from biology to culture and, in its multiple challenges to many a contemporary ethnographer's desire "to identify our local ways of behaving with Behaviour, or our own socialized habits with Human Nature" (*Patterns* 7), contributed significantly to the dissemination of ideas about cultural pluralism and relativism.

Concealing Disclosures

Benedict's poetry is not modernist in any straightforward sense even though, in an undated journal entry, Benedict makes a remarkable observation concerning the importance of the medium of art that not only anticipates Marshall McLuhan's famous assertion that "the medium is the message" (24), but in its insistence on the self-reflexivity of great art and its focus on its own materiality and mediality, also links her understanding of art to that of the modernists:

> The secret of art is a love of the *medium*. The medium is only the outwardness thru' which the spirit at the moment works, yet to love it in itself and for itself is the indispensable prelude to achievement. It must be a love for it that makes easy submission to its limitations and insight into its possibilities. So that a wood-cut page from an old 15th century Book of Hours, with its honest limitation to the nature of the wood it worked in, can give us a quality of pleasure which the superfluous craftsmanship of Timothy Cole can never touch. And a dozen lines of an etching by Rembrandt, each line bitten visibly into the metal, conjures up a joy and a sense of finality that the whole 19th century does not communicate.
>
> So with words.
>
> (Anthropologist 153)

Yet when we turn to close readings of her poems, we find verse that is quite different from that of her modernist contemporaries. Benedict's "Unshadowed Pool," for instance, uses comparatively conventional imagery, a regular rhyme scheme, and lacks the fragmented linguistic surface we have come to associate with modernist poetry:

> You are a pool unshadowed by cast lustre,
> Crystal as air, having no skill to hold
> Skies that are cloudy-petaled, and the rushes blowing,
> Intricate patterns and sun-aureoled.
>
> Pools should be spread with design caught at heaven,
> Laced by near stems and taking the quick bird.
> They should be garmented with far-sought garments
> Lest any come there and find the pool unstirred;
>
> Lest, at arm's length, pebble to pebble lying,
> Life's farthest depths show clear as whitened bone,
> Nothing be water-misted, nothing secret,
> Past the rent altar-veil, the common stone.

With Lowell and Benedict's biographer Margaret M. Caffrey, we could argue that, in its focus on the personal and emotional and in its reliance on more traditional poetic forms, "Unshadowed Pool" belongs to the lyrist school of poetry which subsequent literary criticism has—unfairly or not—relegated to the margins and, indeed, beyond the pale of the modernist enterprise (162–82). In this reading, "Unshadowed Pool" is, in Judith Modell's words, a poem about "the dangers of exposure to truth" in the most personal terms, the repeated "lest" indicating the poetic speaker's apprehension that, without a veil of secrecy, the world may peer into the very depths of one's soul—a pool being, of course, a conventional symbol of the soul (Modell 231). This apprehension is formulated as a warning to the poem's addressee, but it is an apprehension that Benedict, for whom the choice of pseudonyms was an important protective measure when she started publishing her poetry, shared.[5] In this reading, then, "Unshadowed Pool" belongs to the lyrist (or 'lyricist') variety of modernist poetry at its farthest remove from T.S. Eliot's impersonal theory of poetic production.

This assessment is, I think, correct to a certain extent, as is Richard Handler's assessment of two of Benedict's major themes:

> Aside from metaphysical despair, the dominant theme of Benedict's poetry is passion—suppressed or uncontrollable, sated or unfulfilled, but above all, passion confined to the self, passion without reply.
> ("Vigorous" 140)

Other verse by Benedict is nature poetry (e.g., "Sleet Storm," "Countermand," "November Burning," "Dedication," "Brook Turning"); religious poetry (e.g., "Resurgam," "Resurrection of the Ghost," "Annunciation," "Price of Paradise," "This Is My Body"); and love poetry (e.g., "Love that is Water," "Withdrawal," "Lovers' Wisdom"). Still other poems revolve around transience (e.g., "This Breath," "In Praise of Life"); death (e.g., "Burial," "There Is no Death," "Death is the Citadel," "Rupert Brooke, 1914–1918," "Lost Leader," "Sepulchre"); Greek mythology (e.g., "Another Theseus," "Sirens' Song," "Verses for One Dancing"); and dreams ("As a Dream," "The Dream," "Profit of Dreams").

While few of these poems are characterized by the linguistic experiments we associate with modernism, I would argue that Benedict's poetry belongs to modernism for a different reason. As a poet *and* an anthropologist, Benedict was crucially interested in two types of alterity that modernist artists have been bringing into a dialogue since the earliest stages of the movement in the United States and elsewhere: cultural and poetic alterity, i.e. the otherness of other cultures, on the one hand, and the otherness of poetic language on the other. Think, for instance, of the well-known primitivism of some of Tristan Tzara's Dadaist poems, Langston Hughes's "Danse Africaine," or T.S. Eliot's 1919 review essay "War-Paint and Feathers," in which he proclaimed that one could no longer understand the cultural present without knowing "something about the medicine-man and his works" and added that "it is certain that primitive man and poetry help our understanding of civilized art and poetry. Primitive art can even, through the studies and experiments of the artist or poet, revivify the contemporary activities" (138). Alternatively, consider the fact that Harriet Monroe's *Poetry* magazine—the preferred publishing venue for the likes of H. D., Pound and Eliot—in 1917 devoted a special issue to so-called "aboriginal poetry," i.e., reinterpretations and imitations of Native American verse by European and Anglo-American poets such as Constance Lindsay Skinner, Mary Hunter Austin, Alice Corbin Henderson, Frank S. Gordon, and Edward Eastaway (Castro 16–19).

Poetry was also the magazine in which Benedict published no less than twelve of her own poems, most of them under her most frequently used pen name Anne Singleton. Other verse of hers was published in *Palms* (seven poems), *The Measure* (six), the *New York Herald Tribune Books* (four), and *The Nation* (three). Today, a good number of her poems are accessible via *An Anthropologist at Work: Writings of Ruth Benedict*, Mead's tribute to her colleague, which she edited to make accessible "Ruth Benedict's published and hitherto unpublished short papers" (Benedict, *Anthropologist* xvi). Among the fifty-one poems included therein are the thirty-three poems reproduced in the separate section "Selected Poems: 1941," which, Mead tells us in a note, is a selection Benedict made herself in 1941 and gifted to her in "a little hand-bound book" (563n1). Since, to date, *An Anthropologist at Work* is the most readily available source of just under a third of Benedict's 157 poems, Mead has rendered lay readers, biographers and cultural anthropologists who have an interest in her poetry, and literary scholars a great service. Yet the way Mead frames these poems creates problems. This is primarily so because the place Mead assigns to her friend's verse has paved the way for biographical kinds of readings that shortchange these poems. Mead assigns Benedict's verse an auxiliary function; they are there to give insights into Benedict's biography, which in turn enables readers better to understand some of her scholarship. Mead is explicit about this:

> She wrote so little and so infrequently that it would be hard for the student to piece together the background of each period—why certain problems were selected, why some point was stressed with seemingly undue emphasis, why sometimes boredom and sometimes laughter weigh down or lift a sentence or a paragraph. So I have interspersed through the papers background chapters which draw, especially in the earlier years, also on the parts of her thought which originally were kept separate from her anthropological work and were put instead into poems, some of which were published under the *nom de plume* of Anne Singleton. There will be least about the years of teaching and administration at Columbia University, between 1931 and 1939, for I was out of the country for five of those years and have only letters

to fill them in. Toward the end of her life her anthropological writing became a sufficient vehicle; there were no more poems, but unashamedly lovely passages of prose placed precisely as she felt and wished them to be. The need for describing the background of each paper grows less and less, until finally her last paper stands alone.

(Benedict, *Anthropologist* xvi)

Arguably, to write, as I do, that Mead gives Benedict's poems an "auxiliary function" is an understatement. In Mead's account, they are more like a psychological crutch that could be disposed of as Benedict grew to full intellectual and writerly maturity.[6] Mead's framing of Benedict's poetry creates an additional issue. For her, Benedict's poems are also there in *An Anthropologist at Work* to help explain, almost excuse, some of the obscurity or limitations of Benedict's early work ("why some point was stressed with seemingly undue emphasis, why sometimes boredom and sometimes laughter weigh down or lift a sentence or a paragraph"). I do not suggest that Mead intended to say this about her friend's literary output; but that is precisely what she does say in these words. The present book was written with the conviction that it is high time to liberate Benedict's and her fellow Boasians' poems from Mead's influence and from the biographical readings that Mead's comments on Benedict's work have prompted.

Of course, from a literary-critical perspective, Mead's assignment of a subservient role to Benedict's poetry is not the only objectionable move. Her suggestion that these poems are interesting first and foremost for the insights they provide into Benedict's life and work has had a more lasting and more detrimental effect on Benedict scholarship. For literary scholars, straightforward biographical readings of literary texts have been largely discredited since the mid-1940s, when William K. Wimsatt and Monroe R. published their influential essay "The Intentional Fallacy" (1946). This is not to deny that, under the heading of 'life writing,' there has been a resurgence of literary-critical interest in the (auto) biographical since the 1980s.[7] It is, moreover, also not do deny that early dismissals of authorial intention as the primary source of literary meaning such as "The Intentional Fallacy," Roland Barthes' "The Death of the Author" (1967), and Michel Foucault's "What Is an Author?" (1969) have been qualified in important ways.[8] But it is safe to assert that while the heuristic value of reading literary texts in the light of their author's biography is a matter of debate among literary critics, doing the reverse, i.e., interpreting an author's life in the light of the poems she has written tends to produce bad biography and quite simply does not constitute literary criticism.

Mead's account of how Benedict *herself* conceived of the relation between her literary and anthropological work has also had a detrimental influence on Benedict scholarship. Consider these remarks from one of Mead's chapter introductions in *An Anthropologist at Work*:

> She kept us all in separate rooms and moved from one to another with no one following to take notes. I visited her once at her summer home in New Hampshire, and I saw her husband three times. I never saw the family farm in the Shenango Valley. Before her death, I had met her mother and her sister only twice. Several of her closest friends I have never even seen. These all belonged in another part of life—as anthropology and poetry were separate worlds into which these others did not come in person.
>
> (Benedict, *Anthropologist* 3)

I am not contesting the accuracy of this account; Benedict herself may well have seen things exactly as Mead describes.[9] But, with the notable exceptions of Richard Handler, A. Elisabeth Reichel, and James Dowthwaite, Benedict scholarship has all too often taken Mead's account to suggest that there is little or no relationship between her poetic and scholarly output. Such a deduction, of course, constitutes a classic case of the intentional fallacy in Wimsatt and Beardsley's sense: Just because a writer considers her poetry unrelated to a given field of knowledge does not mean that her *writing* does not establish that relation. It is high time, then, to rescue Benedict's poetry from under Mead's spell.

In discussing Benedict's poetry, we can still start with Mead though, albeit not with what she has to say about her poetry. In her introduction to her *Letters from the Field, 1925–1975*, Mead hints at a nexus between poetic and cultural alterity that I consider to be at the heart of both Benedict's and her fellow Boasians' poetry:

> In fact, generation after generation, philosophers and educators, historians and naturalists, polemicists and revolutionaries, as well as poets and artists and storytellers, have drawn on the accounts of peoples who seemed more idyllic or more savage or more complexly civilized than themselves.
>
> (1–2)

Many years before Mead wrote those words—the *Letters* were first published in 1977, the year before she died—Mead herself had published poems in *The Measure* and *Poetry*, and so had Sapir, the anthropological linguist best known for his book *Language: An Introduction to the Study of Speech* (1921). Sapir, Mead, and Benedict not only wrote poetry and dedicated poems to one another; between 1922, when Sapir still addressed Benedict as "Mrs. Benedict" (Benedict *Anthropologist* 49), and 1938 (the year before Sapir's death), Benedict and Sapir exchanged a voluminous correspondence about their poems, submitting their work for comment and criticism and discussing plans for publishing their own volumes of collected verse—projects which, however, never materialized (Sapir's publication of *Dreams and Gibes* in 1917 predates his correspondence with Benedict). Unfortunately, Benedict's side of that correspondence has not survived, but a selection of Sapir's letters to Benedict is collected in *An Anthropologist at Work* (158–97).[10]

In the 1920s, their letters revolved mainly around each other's poetry, though scholarly and institutional matters as well as gossip also played their role. Judging from their correspondence, it is fair to say that their relationship was based primarily on their literary, and less on their anthropological aspirations. This changed toward the end of the decade, when Sapir renounced poetry writing. In a letter to Mead dated December 29, 1929, Benedict complains bitterly,

> He's singing hymns to the noble business man—four square and operating with the solid materials of existence. The way for us to follow in his footsteps is to serve on committees and importance will descend upon us. Why, THE AGE has no need of books of verse—that finished off poetry. It was pitiful.
>
> (*Anthropologist* 94–95)

Indeed, while Sapir, who had been publishing poetry since 1917, kept up a solid publishing regime of at least a dozen poems per year up to 1927, his literary output dwindled to two poems in 1928, five in 1929 and one in 1930.[11] In the November 1931 issue of *Poetry*, Sapir published his last three poems: "Autumn Raindrops," "Levels," and "God Blows a Message." From Sapir's letters to Benedict in the late 1920s, we can see that their relationship soured, not only because he had published "Observations on the Sex Problem in America" (1928), an article that gives expression to his less than progressive views on sexuality and gender relations, but also because he was turning his back on what had been the main source of their friendship and the *raison d'être* for their correspondence: poetry. A letter he wrote to Benedict on April 29, 1929 begins thus:

> Your letter of April 26th, with its strange misunderstanding moves me to an instant reply. But let me dispose of the lower toned matter first. I sent back the poetry volumes because I found I just wasn't in the mood to read poetry and wasn't likely to be for months to come, so there was no use holding on to the books any longer. I think the climax came one evening when I was feeling rather depressed and hoped Ransome's verse would be a relief. I came onto a run of what struck me as completely pusillanimous, perverted verse—a lot of strong blasphemy about items so dead to most of us that we've forgotten there is still a kick to be got out of the blasphemous exercise—and tangled, emotionally non-significant rhythm. So I chucked the

book on the floor and picked it up next morning with the determination to have done with it.

(Benedict, *Anthropologist* 195)

To the reticent Benedict, Sapir's abdication of poetry came as a shock not only because their relationship had been founded on it but also because they were each other's most astute readers and critics. Since only Sapir's letters have survived, we can gain the best insights into his responses to her poetry. What is most striking about those responses is their detailedness and frankness—qualities that testify to both Sapir's serious engagement with his colleague's literary work and to a paternalistic attitude that could not have escaped Benedict, who was painfully aware of gender inequality[12] and planned to write a volume of biographies of famous women—a project that was rejected by Houghton Mifflin (Handler, "Vigorous" 135) but resulted in an unpublished biographical sketch of the major early feminist thinker Mary Wollstonecraft (Benedict, *Anthropologist* 491–519) as well as "notebooks and dozens of partial drafts" (536n.7) on Margaret Fuller and Olive Schreiner. Sapir himself both affirms the power differential at work and ironizes it when he characterizes his detailed response as "professoring" in a letter dated November 15, 1924:[13]

> Thank you for the verses, which I have wanted to write you about for some time. I like the two sonnets the best of the five poems. "Discourse on Prayer" is extraordinarily fine, and poignant. Could you not give it a less drab title than "Discourse on Prayer"? "Lovers' Wisdom" is even better in idea, if anything, and very moving, but seems to me [to] have one or two purely technical shortcomings. The off rhymes (silence—incense, lovers—idolators, relinquishment—argument), with their weight or half-weight on unaccented syllables, do not strike me as happy, though they are perhaps not unsought, and "lovers—idolators" is a technically inaccurate couple because lovers is a feminine ending, while ídólátórs has a weak masculine ending. I should not be professoring if I heard a subtle harmony in these curiously humble rhymes, but I am afraid I don't. Such half lights do not seem to me to go with the great feeling and large seriousness of the sonnet. Then, "idolators of foulness"—is it not a little precious? Finally, "the corrupted urn" does not quite follow up "corrupted under earth the sweet limbs are." I should not be so detailed in my remarks if I did not think so highly of this fine sonnet as to wish you to make it perfect. Certainly these two sonnets show that you can easily master the form if you wish, and that you can inform the outlines with individual feeling and keenness and great beauty is already abundantly evident. I do wish you would persuade yourself

to apply yourself more continuously to verse. Your efforts would be more than repaid and you would soon find yourself one of a very distinguished group indeed.

(Benedict, *Anthropologist* 159–60)

At this point in time, Sapir was a forty-year-old author of eight books, including scholarly monographs, collections of texts in First Nations and Native American languages, and the influential *Language* (1921). When writing this letter to Benedict, he was Director of the Canadian Geological Survey's Anthropological Division and in that position charged with institutionalizing anthropology in Canada. Also, by 1924, he had been publishing poetry for seven years, some of it in well-respected poetry magazines such as *The Dial* and *Poetry*. He could even call a book of poetry his own, published with the vanity publisher The Gorham Press, *Dreams and Gibes* came out in 1917.[14] Only three years Sapir's junior, Benedict was a late starter in anthropology. Increasingly unhappy with her marriage to Stanley Rossiter Benedict, deeply distraught by her infertility, and feeling unfulfilled by charity work, she attended her first lectures on anthropology at the New School for Social Research in 1919, at the age of thirty-two (Benedict, *Anthropologist* 7). She published her first article, "The Vision in Plains Culture" (1922), only in the year that her correspondence with Sapir began. By 1924, none of her poems had appeared in print.

Sapir's greater experience in anthropology as well as in the writing and publishing of poetry help explain not only his often paternalistic tone but also why Benedict took his advice concerning her literary work seriously. The version of "Lovers' Wisdom" published in *An Anthropologist at Work* bears witness to this:

> Lovers have only bitterness of death.
> To all beside there is some chancelled silence
> In deep grief that still keeps faith with breath;
> From loss and loveliness some sudden incense
> Drifts voluptuous down their sorrow. Lovers
> Have nothing left, the incomparable worth
> Of flesh become a shifting ash that covers
> Love's utmost grief with characterless earth.
>
> Lovers have nothing left. Thereby they win
> Largess of wisdom in relinquishment:
> Never to dream that those things which have been,
> Imperishable still, are argument
> For eyes that fear the present; never turn
> From this one hour to the corrupted urn.

While Benedict keeps two of the "off rhymes" (silence—incense, relinquishment—argument) that Sapir censures, the one that he singles out for the most detailed criticism (lovers—idolators) has disappeared; the "precious" phrase "idolators of foulness" has been edited out; and the jarring imageries of "the corrupted urn" and "corrupted under earth the sweet limbs are" are emended as the former is retained and the latter dropped. "Lovers' Wisdom" is but one example that should guard us against dismissing Sapir's advice purely as patriarchal posturing. True, there is an often unbearable paternalistic ring to what he writes, but it is equally clear that Benedict respected his concrete suggestions as she did what is familiar to any scholar and any poet responding to requests for revision: She accepts some of those requests and denies others (in this case also Sapir's new piece of advice in his lackluster response of her revised version of "Lovers' Wisdom" in a letter dated December 20, 1924):

> I prefer the earlier version of "Lovers' Wisdom" in spite of my former criticism. I should not like to lose "plumb the mockery of God's mirth." In the later version the new image seems rather drab and I find the assonance "characterless earth" somewhat jejune.
> (Benedict, *Anthropologist* 168)

Moreover, while gauging the tone and extent of Benedict's criticism of Sapir's poems is difficult since her letters to him have not survived, Sapir's letters to her make clear that she gave him plenty of advice that he took seriously, too. As we read in a letter from February 7, 1925:

> Thank you very much for your very careful reading of the MS. As you may have noticed from my new table of contents, I followed all your suggestions in regard to order of pieces, exclusion and inclusion, and title (I changed "Tearless Memory" to "Quiescence," which is an improvement, I think). . . . Many thanks for the individual comments, from which I am sure to profit. . . . Don't take the new title, "Stars in the Sea," too seriously. It is an interim title and may be changed later. I am not much good at titles and would be glad to get further suggestions from you.
> (Benedict, *Anthropologist* 172)

Sapir here responds to what looks like extensive comments on Benedict's part on his second projected volume of poetry, which was never published. In other cases, Sapir's response to Benedict's criticism was more reserved. As we read in a letter from November 26, 1924:

> Your copy of "Time's Wing" must be blurred. The last lines read:
>
> Nor I can rùn
> Befòre your wíng

With ă cóolněss còme
And stráight swíng.

In other words, "nor is it I who can escape Time—no more than God himself—, as he comes ["come" is the participle] with the coolness, wing-beaten air, that warns of his impending presence and with the straight, unflinching, measured swing or flap of his wings." Others too find this last stanza difficult, so that I may try to change it, though to me it is so simple and transparent as can be. I had hoped you would like the poem, as it is perhaps the most authentic thing rhythmically I ever essayed.

(Benedict, *Anthropologist* 163)

Sapir appears reluctant to accept Benedict's criticism and it is unclear to what extent he assigns the blame for his frustrated hope that she "would like the poem" to himself or to her. Indeed, in the published version of "Time's Wing," Sapir retains the stanza Benedict critiqued:

Nor I can run
Before your wing
With a coolness come
And straight swing.

Apparently, in this case, Sapir took Benedict's advice seriously enough to reply to it in some detail but not seriously enough to change his verse. As this example demonstrates, Sapir's and Benedict's correspondence about their poetry is not quite an exchange among equals; but it is characterized by mutual respect. Moreover, it is remarkable how open Sapir appears to be to critique of his poetry. To Sapir the poet, Benedict is indeed a "dear and sweet counselor" (Benedict, *Anthropologist* 181). Finally, Sapir graciously supported Benedict's publication efforts in a glowing letter to Harriet Monroe, the editor of *Poetry*, in which he sends some of Benedict's poems for publication in the magazine and expresses his great admiration for them:

It seems to me that this verse is exceedingly strong, relentlessly sincere, very individual, and often of great beauty. Indeed I should not be in the least surprised if 'Alice Singleton' came to be looked upon as one of the four really important American poets writing now. I know of no one who has anything like her high and passionate seriousness. She knows how to use difficult words well, her imagery is bold, and her thought is never banal. Above all, every line of her work is sincere.

(Sapir, "Letter to Harriet Monroe of March 23, 1925")

As we have seen, *An Anthropologist at Work* contains Benedict's 1941 selection of her poetry, a fact that further attests to the high esteem in which Benedict's friends and fellow anthropologists held her literary endeavors. Why this interest in and dedication to poetry among a number of the leading anthropologists of the twentieth century? As students of other cultures, Mead, Benedict, and Sapir were keenly aware of not only the variety of language uses and the ways in which different language uses shape each linguistic group's understanding of the world, an insight most famously codified in the Sapir-Whorf hypothesis. As anthropologists, these scholars were also keenly aware of the ways in which Euro-American strategies of representing other cultures—including the scholarly monograph—threaten to distort their objects of representation and, indeed, destroy the very otherness of the other as they reduce the other to the cognitive and linguistic structures of the self and thereby efface it. In entering into a relation with the cultural other, anthropological discourse runs the risk of what Emmanuel Levinas calls totalization: the violent negation of alterity by way of "a reduction of the other to the same" (43). In Michael M.J. Fischer's words in his contribution to James Clifford and George Marcus's seminal *Writing Culture* volume, "one needs a check against assimilating the other to the self" (201). As anthropologists schooled by Boas in the self-critical reflection of their own methods of inquiry and the cultural situatedness of their own language uses, Mead, Benedict and Sapir already knew the importance of exploring alternative forms of representation. And explore they did, as they turned to poetry and, in Mead's case, to photography and film.

The idea that the language of literature *is* such an alternative form of representation has been a critical commonplace at least since Percy Bysshe Shelley's "A Defence of Poetry" and became a crucial tenet of the modernist program that centrally informs Theodor W. Adorno's reflections on the negativity of art in his *Aesthetic Theory* and whose main thrust is summed up in Georg Simmel's assertion that "[a]rt ... possesses that quality of distinctness from life itself, a release through contrast, in which the representation of things in their pure form makes any contact with our reality impossible" (66). Around the time Benedict began writing poetry, the otherness of poetic discourse was also stressed by Russian Formalist theorists like Shklovsky, whose "Art as Device" (1917), one of the classic statements on poetic alterity, was published in the same year as the 'aboriginal issue' of Monroe's *Poetry* magazine.

This nexus of poetic and cultural alterity is also at the heart of a number of Benedict's poems, including "Myth," "This Breath," and "Unshadowed Pool." Ostensibly lines about the dangers of personal revelation deeply felt by the reticent Benedict herself, "Unshadowed Pool" is also a poem about the dangers of exposing the cultural other to the world's gaze. With the altar, the "common stone" and the "whitened bones" in the final stanza, Benedict incorporates materials of her anthropological research. While the cultural references are not specific enough to attribute them to any particular culture Benedict studied, we know that, in her fieldwork in the Zuni Pueblo of New Mexico, she encountered the altar in the center of Zuni on which rests a stone in which, according to Zuni mythology, "beats the heart of the world" (Tedlock 501). Moreover, whitened bones spotting the Southwestern landscape regularly met Benedict's eyes when she conducted fieldwork among the Pima, the Cochiti Pueblo, and the Zuni Pueblo in the mid-1920s (Modell 231; Darnell, "Benedict" 46–47). In her poem, Benedict transposes all of those cultural markers from the surface of the land to the depths of a pool, as if to hide them from view. The poetic speaker's apprehension that the bones, the altar and the stone may be discovered by "any" who "come[s] there and find[s] the pool unstirred" bespeaks an awareness on the poetic speaker's as well as Benedict's part that the revelation of the cultural other may result in its annihilation.

This is an insight Benedict herself had to be reminded of at times, for instance by the linguist, ethnomusicologist, and novelist Jaime de Angulo, who wrote the following words to her in a letter dated May 19, 1925:

> As for helping you get an informant, and the way you describe it "if I took him with me to a safely American place" . . . "an informant who would be willing to give tales and ceremonials" . . . oh God! Ruth, you have no idea how much that has hurt me. I don't know how I am going to be able to talk to you about it because I have a sincere affection for you. But do you realize that it is just that sort of thing that kills the Indians? I mean it seriously. It kills them spiritually first, and as in their life the spiritual and the physical element are much more interdependent than in our own stage of culture, they soon die of it physically. They just lie down and die. That's what you anthropologists with your infernal curiosity and your thirst for scientific data bring about.
>
> Don't you understand the psychological value of secrecy at a certain level of culture? Surely you must, but you have probably never connected it with this. You know enough of analytical psychology to know that there are things that must not be brought to the light of day, otherwise they wither and die like uprooted plants.
> (Benedict, *Anthropologist* 296–97)

In her introduction to *An Anthropologist at Work*, Mead reminds the book's readers that Benedict's generation was less attuned to the ethnographers' ethical obligations toward the subjects of their research than present anthropologists:

> During the last quarter of a century, anthropologists have had to learn a great deal about how to combine descriptions of another culture with a due respect for the living and future members of the society who embodied that culture. . . . There are many references in

Ruth Benedict's letters from Zuñi to the Indians' distrust and reserve. It remained for us in later years to come fully to grips with the problem, and to realize that the description of any culture whose members had been identified as individuals involved writing a description to which they themselves would agree and which would not, furthermore, outrage the sensibilities of members of other cultures who would read the account.

(Benedict, *Anthropologist* xix–xx)

Mead's retrospective framing of Benedict's research and de Angulo's letter invite us to take another look at Benedict's poem and propose that the position it adopts toward revelation is more ambivalent than my reading so far has suggested. The "rent altar-veil" in the final line also belongs to Christian mythology, referring to the rending of the veil in the temple at the moment when Christ died on the cross (Matt. 27.51; Mark 15.38; Luke 23:45). According to scripture, the rending of the veil opened access to the holy of holies to all men and women (Heb. 10.19–20). Henceforth, direct communion with God would no longer be the prerogative of the high priests but an experience potentially available to every believer.[15] The rending of the veil, then, offers the promise of a mythical experience of the highest order, an experience desired by every true believer. And as the "common stone" in the final line suggests, that kind of experience as well as the search for it are shared across cultures.

In many a traditional account of the function of poetic discourse, moreover, poetry gives expression to a secularized version of this search. Shelley's reflections in "A Defence of Poetry," for instance, are shrouded in the metaphor of the veil and anticipate Shklovsky's observations in "Art as a Device" by a century:

Poetry lifts the veil from the hidden beauty of the world, and makes familiar objects be as if they were not familiar. . . . It creates anew the universe, after it has been annihilated in our minds by the recurrence of impressions blunted by reiteration.

(33, 56)

Benedict's poetry finds itself in a tension between this desire to rend the veil in search of experiences of a different, higher order—a desire that informs both the poet's and the anthropologist's work—and an apprehension that the object on the other side of the veil may shrivel and die beneath the observer's gaze. The stance "Unshadowed Pool" adopts toward revelation, then, is an ambivalent one: it is both to be feared and to be yearned for. Benedict's poem, in other words, gives expression to the modernist search for special moments of being, a search that finds its object in the epiphany, and at the same time registers the dangers of dragging into visibility things that may best be left hidden at the bottom of a shadowed pool.

In their yearning for the immediacy of mythical experience, the modernists were perennially in danger of locating the potential of that experience in other cultures they construed as more primitive than their own. This was a temptation Benedict herself was not immune to. Mead's account of Benedict's decision to enter anthropology under Boas's tutelage testifies not only to a desire on Benedict's part to locate aesthetic value in the differentness of the objects of her research, but also to a primitivist tendency:

> She had tried busy work that did not make sense to her; now she had found busy work with high standards set by someone for whom she had great respect, among materials that delighted her to the extent that they were bizarrely different and esthetically satisfying.
> (Benedict, *Anthropologist* 17)

Yet in her poetry, Benedict demonstrates a keen awareness of the possible ethical pitfalls of representing other cultures and channels that awareness into poetic forms that simultaneously disclose and hide the cultural other.

As the contributors to a *festschrift* for Martin Stern edited by Wolfram Malte Fues and Wolfram Mauser demonstrate, literature of all ages and in all genres is a practice of *verbergendes Enthüllen*, of concealing disclosure. In her poem "Little Girl-Mother—," an undated, unpublished companion piece to "Unshadowed Pool" that also thrives on pool, altar, and veil imagery, Benedict once more gives poetic expression to her preference for partially hidden, holy beauty:[16]

> Little girl-mother, with your candid eyes
> That open like clear pools
> Where one may tell each rainbow pebble at the utmost depth,
> Tell me, does life hold then no mysteries after all
> May one know love, and of it fashion in the flesh
> A thing so flower-like fair
> As that within your arms
> And draw no veil at all at any secret altar?

In "The Sense of Symbolism" (c. 1909), one of her sparse contributions to literary criticism, Benedict herself stresses that literature is—at its best—a form of concealing disclosure when she gives expression to her preference of symbolism over what she calls "extreme realism":

> The Modern Age . . . has turned from symbolism to extreme realism. In its nature there must be in symbolism revelation and yet

concealment. Our modern civilizations have lost, however, the charm of concealment—the aim of all effort, in science, in literature, in life is complete revelation.

(Benedict, *Anthropologist* 116)

Poetic alterity, then, is at least partly describable as an interplay or oscillation between masking and revelation. But an awareness of the ethical implications of that doubleness is thrust upon modernists fascinated by forms of cultural alterity to an unprecedented degree. Modernists are, in other words, faced with the question of what Wolfgang Iser calls 'translatability,' the question of how one may embark on a "translation of otherness without subsuming it under preconceived notions" given the fact that "the specificity of the [other] culture encountered can be grasped only when projected onto what is familiar" (5). It is in this respect that Benedict belongs to modernism. Hers is a self-reflexive modernism which draws much of its energy from the otherness of other cultures but which at the same time registers the dangers of normalizing and effacing the cultural other by assimilating it to the languages of the self. It is thus that Benedict's poetry links up with twenty-first-century concerns over the politics of ethnographic representations.

The two readings of the poem I have outlined, then—the psychological and autobiographical one that places Benedict firmly within the lyri(ci)st tradition on the one hand, and the anthropological reading on the other—do not exclude one another. "Unshadowed Pool" is precisely a poem about the self and the other, and the possible relations between the two. In her poem, Benedict stages an encounter of the self with the other that raises important questions concerning our responsibility toward other ways of speaking and being in the world. These questions continue to haunt literary studies, cultural studies, and aesthetics as much as they do the social sciences. They are, finally, questions that literary studies, concerned as it is with that *other* language use we call literature, is particularly well prepared to engage with.

Yearning for Lost Plenitude

The questions raised by "Unshadowed Pool" concerning the ethical valence of knowledge acquisition and the power of concealing disclosure receive a different twist in Benedict's "In Parables" (1926). In this poem, Benedict explores sightlessness in a mythological register:

> Once having sight, seek not
> Dear blindness any more.
> Our eyes are open; here
> Is the estranging door.

> Men have told long since
> This parable;
> Of the great darkness then,
> The merciful,
>
> When lay as lovers lie
> In passionate reach,
> The sweet-fleshed earth and sky
> Close-bosomed each to each.
>
> Light flowered that day
> The violent sea
> Drove salt between their lips'
> Idolatry.
>
> Cursed with unblinking light
> We too endure,
> They drink, men dreamed, this gall
> Of forfeiture.

Blindness, in this poem, is an epistemic condition. Published in the March 1926 issue of the poetry magazine *Palms*, "In Parables" frames the dialectic of blindness and (in)sight as a properly aesthetic issue not only because it is staged in a poem but also because the original, Baumgartian meaning of 'aesthetics'—the science of *aisthēsis*—firmly established the kind of intimate relation between the sensory and the cognitive that the poem takes for granted: Seeing is knowing.

Yet in the poem, blindness has an ambivalent valence. It is "[d]ear blindness" and "merciful" darkness that must not be sought anymore once sight is achieved. Blindness marks a state of blissful innocence—in both its moral and its noetic sense—that the inquisitive mind must overcome, though not without a sense of loss. Once knowledge is gained, the original state of innocence is no longer directly attainable, which renders (the final stanza makes clear) sight/knowledge a curse as well as a blessing. The poem frames this loss of innocence in two mythical registers—a duality that the poem's title announces through its plural noun. Its Biblical language ("blindness," "parable," "idolatry," "cursed") references the fall from innocence that Adam and Eve's tasting of fruit from the tree of the knowledge of good and evil brought about. In stanzas three to five, we enter, as Mead explains in a note added to the poem's reproduction in *An Anthropologist at Work*, a different mythical realm: "The central image in this poem derives from the Maori creation myth" (Benedict, *Anthropologist* 542n.8).[17]

In the New Zealand Māori version of this foundational myth, Rangi (Sky Father) and Papa (Earth Mother) are the primordial parents, the source of all living beings and things. Locked in a tight embrace, their many children—gods and goddesses themselves—live in the darkness between them. Yearning to escape from this dark and cramped condition as they grow up, they discuss various options, from killing their parents to prying them apart. It is Tāne-mahuta, the god of the forests, who manages to force his parents apart through sheer physical strength. To their great surprise and grief, Rangi and Papa are separated: While Rangi is pushed into the heavens, Papa remains on earth to nurture her children. Light pours into darkness so that the infantile gods and goddesses can see their parents' creation for the first time. Disagreeing about the means of escape and the outcome of their parents' separation, the children and their offspring wage war against one another. This combat changes the face of the earth, submerging a good part of it under water and creating today's world. Rangi and Papa continue to yearn and grieve for one another: The dew and rain that fall to earth are the tears that Rangi cries in the sky; the mists that rise from the lakes, mountains, and valleys are Papa's sighs. Eventually, Papa is turned over so that the lovers no longer have to endure the pain of facing each other.[18]

The analogy between the Biblical fall and the Māori creation myth seems clear. The coming to light/knowledge is a profoundly ambivalent event: Moral knowledge (of good and evil) is gained in one culture and the creation becomes visible in the other, but both processes are accompanied by a significant sense of loss (of innocence and paradise in Christian culture; of bodily warmth and intimacy in Māori culture). In her reading of the poem, Reichel (who also notes the text's ambivalence toward enlightenment and its use of Māori and Biblical mythology) makes an important point when she remarks that, in bringing together the two myths, Benedict's poem confuses the strict distinctions between cultures that are portrayed as radically different, even incommensurable in Benedict's ethnographic writing (*Writing* 213–18). I would, however, argue that, in the final analysis, the poem's use of another culture is not categorically different from Benedict's portrayal of 'Apollonian' Zuni culture as a more harmonious and balanced foil to Western social pathologies in *Patterns of Culture* or Mead's admonitory final two chapters in *Coming of Age in Samoa*. Like these, "In Parables" ultimately aims at a sharper perspective on the self by way of a detour through the other. This is how I read the "estranging door" of the poem's first stanza: This line literally marks the moment when the poem opens itself up to another culture. As its readers move from the first stanza to the second, they walk through an "estranging door" and what they encounter on the other side is a foreign culture's myth, knowledge of which allows for a heightened understanding of the culture of the self. The encounter with the other culture renders the familiar strange again.

That literary texts are privileged sites for such transformative experiences has become a commonplace in literary studies ever since the Russian Formalist thinker Victor Shklovsky argued, a decade before Benedict wrote her poem, "By 'enstranging' objects and complicating form, the device of art makes perception long and 'laborious.' The perceptual process in art has a purpose all its own and ought to be extended to the fullest" (6). A term that generations of Anglophone literary critics have translated as 'defamiliarization' but which Shklovsky's recent translator Benjamin Sher renders as 'enstrangement,'[19] *ostranenie* names the various devices through which literature and art refresh our experience and perception of the world. In this influential attempt to define the nature and function of art, it is seen as an antidote to the numbing of human experience through the repeated perception of the phenomenal world. In Shklovsky's account, repeated exposure to the world renders our perception of it so habitual that we hardly perceive the world anymore. The function of art is to jolt us out of our habitualized perception so that we can see the world anew, as if we saw it for the first time, as if we saw it through the eyes of a child. Art is there to 'enstrange' the world, to make it strange and exciting for us again.

The 'estranging' work that the cultural relativists did for their own, Western culture might not be entirely different from literature's work of 'e*n*strangement.' When Benedict writes that "here/Is the estranging door," she writes self-reflexively, betraying an awareness that the work of e(n)strangement happens precisely *here*, i.e., in and through poetry—a form of writing which, Shklovsky has taught us, has the power to render the familiar strange and new again so as to restore a sensual intensity to things (the stoniness of the stone) that has been lost due to habitualized, automatized perception. In Benedict's poem, e(n)strangement functions as an aesthetic phenomenon in the sense that it enhances our sensuous perception of the world. And indeed, the poem itself is an "estranging door." "In Parables" is self-reflexive to this extent: In it, blindness is not only a condition that is overcome in Christian and Māori myths; it is also the state of sensory attenuation that anthropologists seek to remedy as they introduce new ways of sensing and knowing into the world. Benedict's poem opens itself up to these new ways as it foregrounds sensory experiences beyond sight: the touch of bodies and the taste of salt on Papa's and Rangi's lips. As Susan Stewart notes,

> Of all the senses, touch is most linked to emotion and feeling. To be 'touched' or 'moved' by words or things implied the process of identification and separation by which we apprehend the world aesthetically. I have noted that we do not see our eyes when we see or hear our ears when we hear, but tactile perception involves perception of our own bodily state as we take in what is outside that state. The pressure involved in touch is a pressure on ourselves as well as on objects. Although the hand is paramount, no particular organ is exclusively associated with touch; rather, the entire surface of the body is touch's instrument.
>
> (Stewart 162)

Stewart uses 'aesthetics' as it is used in this book: as the theory of sensuous cognition. And in doing that, she draws our attention to the less-studied and reciprocal sense of touch, which Benedict powerfully evokes in "In Parables" next to taste and sight.

Shklovksy identifies several strategies through which art saves the world from the automatism of perception and renders it strange again, among them the choice of an unusual perspective (his most memorable example is from Tolstoy's story "Kholstomer," in which a horse reflects on the concept of 'property'), the use of archaic words of folk speech, and the placement of persons or objects in unfamiliar contexts. In challenging American parochialisms, Sapir, Benedict, and Mead repeatedly make use of the first of these strategies as they report on foreign cultures' astonishment at cultural practices that most Anglo-Americans consider natural. For instance, in her unpublished essay "Counters in the Game" (c. 1925), Benedict reports on the Ojibwas' amusement at White folks' exchange of "little metal disks" (*Anthropologist* 41) for land:

> To purchase land! The Brother-Gods of the Ojibwa were not above having their joke at the outlandish ways of the foreignborn. . . . Clearly there was no reasonableness in it. Did not the land belong to anyone who had the will or the need to work it? What had they to fear from that? Did they think anyone would insist on more than his share? But why would one seek to own more ground than one needed? Was it not enough to have land on which to plant the Indian corn and trap hare which one's own family could eat each year? Who would accumulate land he could not use? It was inconceivable. When one worked, one worked to some end; and here there was no end. . . . [H]ow could one become great through owning what was free as the water or the air?
>
> (40–42)

In this essay, Benedict's strategy cuts both ways: Just as the white practice of purchasing land is denaturalized, so is the Ojibwa practice of buying and selling visions: "[N]o man sees the logic of another's symbols" (43). Yet Benedict does not end her text on this cultural relativist note. Instead, in its final sentence, she resorts to sarcasm to stress the different real-world consequences of Ojibwa and Anglo-American cultural practices: "And if the red man's counters were harmless and dispossessed no one of food or shelter, on the white man's counters have hung progress, and the glories of civilization" (43). Such uses of cultural relativism are quite frequent in Benedict's writing. Many of her cross-cultural comparisons are based on a core tenet of cultural relativism: that cultures must be studied and judged on their own terms, not on the basis of the norms and values of the anthropologist's own culture. Yet the ultimate point—or punchline—of the comparison is often not a cultural relativist one. Instead, she makes the comparison useful for a sarcastic attack on 'Americanism' that judges American culture not by its own mainstream norms but by alternative, minoritarian ones that are external in the sense that they have been shaped at least partially by the anthropologist's experience of cultural alterity. This uneasy combination of cultural relativism and countercultural critique is most evident in her essay on "The Uses of Cannibalism," which, in true Montainesque fashion, contrasts American-style warfare with anthropophagy to asserts the "reasonableness" (Benedict, *Anthropologist* 44), "excellent ethical use" (45), and "serviceability" (48) of the latter. Benedict does not end her essay by asserting that war is as cruel as cannibalism; instead, she again employs sarcasm in asserting that the former is ultimately more harmful than the latter:

> Our well-proved methods of publicity give us a new assurance in the adoption even of unfamiliar programs; where we might at one time well have doubted the possibility of popularizing a practice so unused, we can now venture more boldly. While there is yet time, shall we not choose deliberately between war and cannibalism?
>
> (28)

In discussing *Patterns of Culture*, Marc Manganaro well captures what Benedict does here—and what unites her approach with Mead's

> what she shares with Mead in particular [is] the use of a comparative frame to either explicitly or implicitly compare exotic other cultures to our own and thereby to get us to think about the possible variability or less than naturalness of our own cultural values.
>
> (152)[20]

Lest we paint too rosy a picture of the work that ethnographers and writers do, we should, however, remember that, in Benedict's poem "In Parables," the transition from blindness to sight comes with a sense of bitterness and loss so profound that the poem's final words liken the salty sea that drives the lovers apart to "this gall/Of forfeiture." What is lost is a state of sensuous fullness beyond sight, a state of passion and physical intimacy of two bodies lying "as lovers lie/In passionate reach" while their children huddle in the dark yet warm enclosure between them. Who is it, then, that speaks "Idolatry"—a word foregrounded by the poem since it is the only one that takes up a full line—and what does it mean in this specific context? In its Judeo-Christian usage, the term denotes a pagan practice that must be overcome: "The worship of idols or images 'made with hands'; more generally, the paying or offering of divine honours to any created object" (OED). A cursory reading of "In Parables" may see in it a Christian observer's critique of a pagan myth, a reading that gains strength if we take into account an early, now obsolete sense of 'forfeiture': "Transgression or violation of a law; crime, sin" (OED). In this reading, the law that is transgressed would be the second commandment. Yet such a reading stands on shaky ground, for one simple reason: There are no idols in Benedict's poem. Thus, it is more likely that 'idolatry' is used in a broader, more secular sense, denoting an "[i]mmoderate attachment to or veneration for any person or thing; admiration savouring of adoration" (OED).[21] In this reading, it is Rangi and Papa's intimate embrace that qualifies as idolatry since their "immoderate attachment" obstructs their children's coming to light and knowledge of the creation. Crucially, the persona does not share the harsh judgment that "Idolatry" implies: She simultaneously channels and ironizes such a false indictment. After all, the poem's predominant attitude toward the primordial couple's violent separation is not jubilation but a sense of loss that is captured by the modern sense of 'forfeiture': "The fact of losing or becoming liable to deprivation of (an estate, goods, life, an office, right, etc.) in consequence of a crime, offence, or breach of engagement" (OED). What the poem ultimately stages is less an evolution from blindness to sight, from innocence to knowledge, than a temporary return to plenitude. As it takes us through its "estranging door," "In Parables" gives us a glimpse of a sensuous fullness that, the poem suggests, both the Christian and the Māori world once knew. In the final analysis, then, "In Parables" gives expression to a nostalgic longing for lost sensuous plenitude that also characterizes "Sacrilege," another of Benedict's ethnographic poems in which, in a "curious alien rite," an unnamed man breaks "strange boughs" and makes a fire in whose smoke he "read[s]/ Strange tongues/Whereof no living man/Shall testify." In both poems, enstrangement and exoticization go hand in hand. A similar dynamic is also at work in Benedict's and Mead's ethnographic work at its most primitivist, which we can see at work in Mead's introduction to the first part of *An Anthropologist at Work*:

> The anthropologist had no access to living events, for the actual life that the Indians were then living—as pensioners of the Federal government, casual crop-gatherers, followers of rodeos, or sellers of curios to tourists—held only fragments of the picture of life that could be reconstructed of earlier days when costume and house, the means of livelihood, and the ways of relating themselves to one another and to the universe were congruent and esthetically satisfying wholes.
>
> (Benedict, *Anthropologist* 15–16)

Mead here waxes nostalgic about the disappearance of what Sapir would call 'genuine cultures,' which have disappeared under the pressure of modernization. What none of the Boasians fully understood is that, in its primitivism, their search for "esthetically satisfying wholes" may not be categorically different from the experience "tourists" sought.

Of Syncretisms, Foils, and Cautionary Examples

Unpublished during her lifetime, Benedict's "Myth" is another poem that blends images and mythemes from two different cultures—Christian and Native American in this case—and, like "In Parables," taps into another culture to provide a revitalizing input to the culture of the self. More strongly than "In Parables," though, "Myth" shows that there are significant differences between Benedict's negotiation of cultural alterity in her poetry and ethnographic writing. While "Myth" is syncretistic in that it gives expression to a profound desire for the fusion of cultures, Benedict in ethnographic treatises such as *Patterns of Culture* stresses each culture's wholeness and difference, subscribing to a strong version of cultural relativism that proclaims cultures incommensurable (Silverman 268–69). Starting from Georges-Louis Leclerc, the Comte de Buffon's broad 1753 definition of 'style' as "nothing but the order and movement one gives to one's thoughts" (5; my translation),[22] my comparative reading of a sample of Benedict's texts show that this basic difference is inscribed in the specifics of her poetic and ethnographic styles.

In Benedict's ethnographic texts, claims for incommensurability do not amount to a complete disassociation of cultures. Early essays of hers such as "The Vision in Plains Culture" (1922) still firmly adhere to Boas's diffusionary paradigm, which calls for studies of the origin and cross-cultural dissemination of cultural traits by "painstaking attempts at reconstruction of historical connections based on studies of distribution of special features" (Boas, "Introduction" xix). In *Patterns of Culture* too, we find traces of the diffusionism Boas himself would abandon in his later work: "The extent of the primitive areas over which traits have diffused is one of the most startling facts of anthropology" (241). But in her ethnographic prose, Benedict's variety of cultural relativism entails that if cultures are connected and compared, one culture tends to become another's *foil* or *cautionary example*.

In *Patterns of Culture*, she portrays three widely divergent cultures: the Zuni of the U.S. Southwest, the Kwakiutl of the U.S. Pacific Northwest, and the Dobu of Papua New Guinea. Drawing on Friedrich Nietzsche's distinction, in *The Birth of Tragedy* (1872), between Apollonian and Dionysian types and forces in ancient Greek art and culture (Benedict, *Patterns* 78–79) and also on C.G. Jung's appropriation of Nietzsche's binary in *Psychological Types* (Stocking, "Ethnographic Sensibility" 298), Benedict conceives of whole cultures as "personality writ large" (Mead, "Preface" xi):[23] "A culture, like an individual, is a more or less consistent pattern of thought and action" (Benedict, *Patterns* 46). Thus, she describes the Zuni as a gentle, tranquil, harmonious, integrated, well-balanced, and modest Apollonian culture where "everyone co-operates, and no show of authority is called for" (100) and the Kwakiutl as an ecstatic, megalomaniac, intensely competitive, and violent Dionysian community where "[b]ehaviour . . . was dominated at every point by the need to demonstrate the greatness of the individual and the inferiority of his rivals" (214–15).[24] The Dobu do not fit Nietzsche's dichotomy but they, too, are personality writ large: A paranoid culture driven by treacherousness, misanthropy, and morbid fears. These three cultures, Benedict argues, are radically distinct expressions of specific psychological traits:

> The three cultures of Zuni, of Dobu, and of the Kwakiutl are not merely heterogeneous assortments of acts and beliefs. They have each certain goals toward which their behaviour is directed and which their institutions further. They differ from one another not only because one trait is present here and absent there, and because another trait is found in two regions in two different forms. They differ still more because they are oriented as wholes in different directions. They are travelling along different roads in pursuit of different ends, and these ends and these means in one society cannot be judged in terms of those of another society, because essentially they are incommensurable.
>
> (223)

All cultural relativists emphasize the diversity of cultures and maintain that they must be studied on their own terms, through analyses of their own social structures, norms, and values rather than by imposing the external, supposedly universal standards of Western culture. Cultural relativism in this sense is "the idea that cultures and cultural processes must be understood in their own terms in the first instance, apart from the observer's ethnocentric standards" (Silverman 269). Since the rise to prominence of the Boasians in the 1920s and their (all too often inconsistent) displacement of the original evolutionary paradigm promoted by, among others, E.B. Tyler, Lewis Henry Morgan, and James George Frazer, this has become common sense among cultural anthropologists.[25] Few take issue with this weak version of cultural relativism.[26] But in Benedict's strong version, cultures are seen "as incommensurate, each particular to itself and comprehensible only in terms of itself" (Silverman 269). Thus, when Benedict does compare her three foreign cultures with each other as well as with her own, she is not looking for universal features shared by all. Instead, she conceptualizes them as opposites. The passage quoted above serves as an example of how Benedict's ethnographic style emphasizes the incommensurability of cultures through insistent reiterations of a rhetoric of wholeness ("goals," "intentions," "as wholes") and difference ("differ," "different forms," "differ," "different directions," "different roads," "different," and "incommensurable").

This style of cross-cultural comparison is integral to the structure of *Patterns of Culture*, in which the Zuni of Chapter 4 and the Kwakiutl of Chapter 6 are not only presented as radically distinct but as polar opposites:

> The Dionysian slant of Northwest Coast tribes is as violent in their economic life and their warfare and mourning as it is in their initiations and ceremonial dances. They are at the opposite pole from the Apollonian Pueblos, and in this they resemble most other aborigines of North America.
>
> (181–82)

Importantly, this opposition is not presented as a mere synchronic fact but as the result of a cultural achievement on the part of the Zuni:

> It is not possible to understand Pueblo attitudes toward life without some knowledge of the culture from which they have detached themselves: that of the rest of North America. It is by the force of the contrast that we can calculate the strength of their opposite drive and the resistances that have kept out of the Pueblos the most characteristic traits of the American aborigines. For the American Indians as a whole, and including those of Mexico, were passionately Dionysian.
>
> (80)

Of course, this presentation of two types of culture owes much to Benedict's dichotomous Nietzschean framework, which her ethnographic style again highlights through a prominent rhetoric of wholeness ("the American Indians as a whole") and difference ("detached," "the rest of North America," "contrast" "opposite drive," "kept out"). But it is also fueled by a desire that jars with our cultural relativists' public assertions of the equality of cultures. As is the case with all dichotomies (the poststructuralists have taught us), this one involves a hierarchy in which the Kwakiutl function as the foil against which the Zuni shine all the more brightly. It is to their benefit that the Zuni have detached themselves from other Native American cultures; it is them who manage to steer clear of Dionysian excesses: "The Zuñi are a ceremonious people, a people who value sobriety and inoffensiveness above all other virtues. Their interest is centered upon their rich and complex ceremonial life" (Benedict, *Patterns* 59). On the morning of August 24, 1925, her last day in the Zuni Pueblo, Benedict wrote to Mead: "When I'm God I'm going to build my city there" (Benedict, *Anthropologist* 293). There is, then, a strongly evaluative dimension to her ethnographic style.

Cultures also function as each other's foils when Benedict compares Zuni culture with her own. It is here that she most visibly gives expression to her longing for a simpler, more authentic and, above all, more harmonious and balanced way of life. Benedict's primitivism is all the more striking because she explicitly dissociates herself from it:

> Nor does the reason for using primitive societies for the discussion of social forms have necessary connection with a romantic return to the primitive. It is put forward in no spirit of poeticizing the simpler peoples. There are many ways in which the culture of one or another people appeals to us strongly in this era of heterogeneous standards and confused mechanical bustle. But it is not in a return to ideals preserved for by primitive peoples that our society will heal itself of its maladies. The romantic Utopianism that reaches out toward the simpler primitive, attractive as it sometimes may be, is as often, in ethnological study, a hindrance as a help.
> (*Patterns* 19–20)[27]

Though twenty-first-century readers will immediately notice that Benedict's reference to "simpler" and "primitive peoples" to whom one may or may not wish to "return" falls prey to the very practice she disavows, passages such as this one testify to her awareness of the impasses of primitivist yearning. What clearly comes to the fore here is that *Patterns of Culture* is primarily addressed to a lay audience: Benedict's ethnographic style assumes a distinctly popular and didactic tone as she validates her readers' desire for a simpler life in complex times, acknowledging that her book may well cater to that desire while disassociating herself from it, for two reasons: Because the cure for modern ills cannot be found in a return to the primitive and because primitivist yearning is incompatible with the ethnographer's scientific ethos.[28] Yet even here, Benedict's distancing is qualified. While the stress is on "hindrance" in the final sentence of this passage, she also suggests that, sometimes, primitivism may come to the ethnographer's aid; it is "as often" the one as the other. Thus, it comes as little surprise that Benedict freely indulges in primitivist discourse elsewhere. She does this, for instance, when writing about the Zuni later in *Patterns of Culture*. Here, she emphasizes their "romantic history," nostalgically looking back to "the golden age of the Pueblos" which produced "the greatest Indian cities north of Mexico" whose traces are still visible in "some of the most romantic habitations of mankind" (57–58). What we can see at work here is what George Stocking calls the "romantic primitivist spirit" of "Apollonian ethnographies" ("Ethnographic Sensibility" 336).

Unlike Mead's *Coming of Age in Samoa: A Psychological Study of Primitive Youth for Western Civilisation* (1928), which wears its primitivism and didactic intent on its sleeve (or, rather, in its subtitle), *Patterns of Culture* does not suggest that the Western world of "heterogeneous standards and confused mechanical bustle" seek its remedy in the structures and practices of premodern societies. But like her younger colleague,

Benedict uses her representations of other cultures to throw the dysfunctionality of her own into relief:

> [The Zuni] do not picture the universe, as we do, as a conflict of good and evil. They are not dualistic. . . . It is difficult for us to lay aside our picture of the universe as a struggle between good and evil and see it as the Pueblos see it. They do not see the seasons, nor man's life, as a race run by life and death. Life is always present, death is always present. Death is no denial of life. The seasons unroll themselves before us, and man's life also. Their attitude involves "no resignation, no subordination of desire to a stronger force, but the sense of man's oneness with the universe."
> (*Patterns* 127–28)[29]

Compared to Mead's, Benedict's cultural critique is subdued. Employing one of the two major modes of her ethnographic style, Benedict uses the other culture as a *foil*, inviting her Western readers to denaturalize fundamental traits of their own. The image of Zuni culture that emerges in this passage and throughout *Patterns of Culture* is that of a harmonious, unified community free of the divisive power of dichotomous thinking. Benedict here taps into a well-established discourse on mythical thought to which some of the most prominent voices in the scientific community of the early twentieth century—among them Sigmund Freud, Jean Piaget, and Lucien Lévy-Bruhl—made substantial contributions. Ernst Cassirer sums up one of the central claims made within that discursive field when he writes, in the second volume of *The Philosophy of Symbolic Forms* (1925), that

> a mere glance at the facts of mythical consciousness shows that it knows nothing of certain distinctions which seem absolutely necessary to empirical-scientific thinking. Above all, it lacks any fixed dividing line between mere 'representation' and 'real' perception, between wish and fulfillment, between image and thing.
> (36)

For both Cassirer and Benedict, the absence of dualisms from mythical thought correlates with its immediacy, both of which Cassirer explains as an effect of one of its most fundamental qualities:

> [I]f we examine myth itself, what it is and what it *knows* itself to be, we see that this separation of the ideal from the real, this distinction between a world of immediate reality and a world of mediate signification, this opposition of 'image' and 'object,' is alien to it.
> (38; emphasis in original)

But there is a significant difference. For Cassirer, the 'primitive' mind's negation of the difference between objects and their representation—its conviction that the totem *is* the animal, that the dead ancestor *is* present in ritual—marks mythical thought as deficient compared to the empirical-scientific thinking that predominates in the West. For Benedict, immediacy and non-dualistic thought are what is most sorely missing from her own culture's episteme. In studying Zuni culture, Benedict is looking for what is lacking in her own.

The second style of cross-cultural comparison shapes Benedict's discussion of the Kwakiutl of the Pacific Northwest. Unlike the Zuni, the Kwakiutl are not presented as Western culture's foil but as its aggravated version. In the second major mode of her ethnographic style, the other culture serves not as a foil but as a *cautionary example*. Benedict devotes most attention to Kwakiutl culture's intense competitiveness—which structures all of social life, including religion and the relations between the sexes—and ostentatious displays of wealth, which manifest themselves most prominently in potlatches. Though Benedict does at one point admit that "we can see in Kwakiutl society and in the rugged individualism of American pioneer life" that "the pursuit of victory can give vigor and zest to human existence" (*Patterns* 248), she zooms in on the deleterious effects of ambition:

> The manipulation of wealth on the Northwest Coast is clearly enough in many ways a parody of our own economic arrangements. These tribes did not use wealth to get for themselves an equivalent value in economic goods, but as counters of fixed value in a game they played to win.
>
> (188–89)

Benedict uses 'parody' in the extended sense of 'travesty' here, but later passages make clear that she does not consider Kwakiutl competitiveness and its social and psychological costs (conspicuous waste, self-aggrandizing, and intense distrust of others among them) as aberrations from American normalcy:

> The segment of human behaviour which the Northwest Coast has marked out to institutionalize in its culture is one which is recognized as abnormal in our civilization, and yet it is sufficiently close to the attitudes of our own culture to be intelligible to us and we have a definite vocabulary with which we may discuss it. The megalomaniac paranoid trend is a definite danger in our society. It faces us with a choice of possible attitudes. One is to brand it as abnormal and reprehensible, and it is the attitude we have chosen in our civilization. The other extreme is to make it the essential attribute of ideal man, and this is the solution in the culture of the Northwest Coast.
>
> (222)

At this point in her argument, Benedict suggests that U.S. culture too harbors Dionysian energies but for the greatest part manages to rein them in. It is not 'here' but 'there'—in Kwakiutl practices such as ecstatic ritual dancing, potlatches, and cannibalism—that these energies unfold their most destructive potential. However, when, on the last pages of *Patterns of Culture*, she follows Mead's prior example as she elaborates on the lessons Western readers should draw from her presentation of foreign cultures, there is a marked shift in tone. Much of Benedict's final chapter, "The Individual and Culture," is dedicated to a discussion of those humans who deviate from their culture's norms. Zooming in on U.S. culture, she mentions 'hoboes,' homosexuals, and mystics, calling for tolerance, recognition of their social usefulness, and for a denaturalization of culturally conditioned ideas of normalcy. Next, Benedict turns to further, less widely recognized forms of aberrancy that she considers either pathogenic or outright pathological: the excessive conformity of "Middletown" (originally an alias for the city of Muncie, Indiana in two sociological case studies and subsequently the shorthand of intellectuals of Benedict's time for what they perceived as the narrow-mindedness and shallowness of American small-town life), the inferiority complexes of those who do not manage to live up to societal expectations, and, finally, "the abnormals who represent the extreme development of the local cultural type" (Benedict, *Patterns* 276). It is in her discussion of this last group that Benedict's cultural critique turns sharpest:

> This group is socially in the opposite situation from the group we have discussed, those whose responses are at variance with their cultural standards. Society, instead of exposing the former group at every point, supports them in their furthest aberrations. . . . In our own generation extreme forms of ego-gratification are culturally supported in a similar fashion. Arrogant and unbridled egoists as family men, as officers of the law and in business, have been again and again portrayed by novelists and dramatists, and they are familiar in every community. Like the behaviour of Puritan divines, their courses of action are often more asocial than those of the inmates of penitentiaries. In terms of the suffering and frustration that they spread about them there is probably no comparison. There is very possibly at least as great a degree of mental warping. Yet they are entrusted with positions of great influence and importance and are as a rule fathers of families. Their impress both upon their own children and upon the structure of our society is indelible. They are not described in our manuals of psychiatry because they are supported by every tenet of our civilization.
>
> (276–77)

It is here, in this feminist critique, that Benedict comes closest to what F.H. Matthews describes as the Boasians' use of anthropology as a tool to attack 'Americanism.' This becomes possible through a curious shift of argument: fifty pages earlier, Benedict claimed that her "civilization" branded as "abnormal and reprehensible" types of behavior that she now considers "supported by every tenet of our civilization." In the first instance, the Kwakiutl way of life still functions as a latent threat in Benedict's own culture. By the closing of the book, the Dionysian energies they embody have permeated the American body politic. The cautionary example receives a new interpretation: it is no longer a latent threat but a manifest pathology.[30] Benedict glosses over this inconsistency through a rhetorical sleight of hand: she makes the Kwakiutl disappear in her concluding dissection of social and psychological American pathologies. As foils and cautionary examples, the Zuni and the Kwakiutl serve Benedict as grounds upon which she stages a critique of her own culture. Comparisons in general and these specific uses of foreign cultures in particular are integral to her ethnographic style, which uses a rhetoric of wholeness and difference, evaluates the relative merits of each culture, employs a popular and didactic tone, and uses other cultures as foils or cautionary examples as she puts cross-cultural comparison in the service of cultural critique, following her own advice to the readers of *Patterns of Culture*:

> There is, however, one difficult exercise to which we may accustom ourselves as we become increasingly culture-conscious. We may train ourselves to pass judgment upon the dominant traits of our own civilization. It is difficult enough for anyone brought up under their power to recognize them. It is still more difficult to discount, upon necessity, our predilection for them.
>
> (249)

In her poetry, the self and the other meet in distinctly different ways. Take "Myth" as an example. The poem remained unpublished during Benedict's lifetime but is included in *Ruth Fulton Benedict: A Memorial*, a 1949 volume edited by Alfred Kroeber, and is now most readily accessible in *An Anthropologist at Work* (1959). Mead includes the poem in the section "Selected Poems: 1941," explaining that [t]he selection is one she [Benedict] herself made in 1941, when she wrote these poems out by hand in a little hand-bound book as a present for me, and it expresses the most recent personal choice of which there is any record of what she liked best. (Benedict, *Anthropologist* 563n.1)

> A god with tall crow feathers in his hair,
> Long-limbed and bronzed, from going down of sun,
> Dances all night upon his dancing floor,
> Tight at his breast, our sorrows, one by one.

Relinquished stalks we could not keep till bloom,
And thorns unblossomed but of our own blood,
He gathers where we dropped them, filling full
His arms' wide circuit, briars and sterile shrub.

And all alone he dances, hour on hour,
Till all our dreams have blooming, and our sleep
Is odorous of gardens,—passing sweet
Beyond all, wearily, we till and reap.

In view of the fact that these lines were penned by an anthropologist, a number of questions immediately impose themselves. What desire does the poem express and how does that desire manifest itself in its dichotomy of sterility and vitality? What are the aesthetic, epistemological, and ethical ramifications of Benedict's combination of Western and non-Western cultural elements? And, most importantly for this chapter's concerns, how does the style of her literary evocation of an ethnic other differ from her ethnographic style of presentation? As we ponder this last question, we find that other cultures serve very different purposes in Benedict's two genres.

It is difficult to pin down with precision the cultural provenance of the poem's dancing god. But we can be fairly certain that it is set in a Southwest Native American community, where Benedict did most of her scant fieldwork (Manganaro 152; Young 65).[31] Quite possibly, given Benedict's admiration for 'Apollonian' Pueblo cultures and the poem's promise of fertility (its evocation of "odorous gardens," of blooming, tilling, and reaping), the actions she portrays are part of the Zuni rain dance, which she describes in her unpublished, undated paper "They Dance for Rain in Zuñi" (*Anthropologist* 222–25) as well as in *Patterns of Culture* (92–93). In that case, the dancing god would be a "masked god" or *kachina*, i.e., a spirit being that may represent any number of entities in the cosmos or natural world and is impersonated by masked dancers wearing feathers in a variety of communal rituals, including rain dances (67–71).

What is most remarkable about the poem is that it approaches its anthropological content with images culled from both the portrayed culture and the Judeo-Christian tradition. For Benedict's European and American readers, combining "thorns" and "our own blood" in a single line (and the thorny "briars" in the same stanza) will immediately evoke the crucifixion and Christ's redemption of humanity through his "own blood" (Acts 20:28; Heb. 9:12, 13:12; Rev. 1:5). Thus, while the "sorrows" of the poetic speaker and her community remain unspecified, Benedict's Christian imagery opens the poem up to an interpretation that locates that source at a level deeper and more concrete than a general disaffection with urban, industrial modernity. Such a 'Christian' reading of "Myth" finds further evidence in the poem's evocation of the scent of "gardens"—a cultural space associated with the Christian idea of paradise rather than Native American mythologies or the Southwestern imaginary. The aesthetic promise invoked by this scent is a redemptive return to innocence before the fall, that ultimate source of all "our sorrows." Thus, mythemes from two different cultures are amalgamated in the actions of the dancing god. It is in his arms that the blocked, "unblossomed" energies of the poetic speaker's own culture are released.

In contrast to her ethnographic work, the other culture does not serve Benedict as a foil or cautionary tale here but as an imaginary space in which a redemptive, aesthetic fusion of the self and the other becomes possible, a space where Christian and Indigenous iconographies merge. As two myths become "Myth," Western culture blooms again, is healed. *Patterns of Culture* and "Myth" employ different methods to different ends: in the ethnographic style of *Patterns of Culture*, two modes of cross-cultural comparison (the foil, the cautionary tale) are inscribed by a rhetoric of wholeness and difference that serves cultural critique. In "Myth," cultures are fused rather than compared. In contrast to her ethnographic style, Benedict's poetic style operates with flattened hierarchies and restrained value judgements, considers wholeness less an attribute of individual cultures than a desirable effect of the fusion of cultures, and is characterized by a syncretism that gives expression to a desire for cultural rejuvenation. Benedict's ethnographic and poetic styles employ different forms to perform different functions: *critical* and *therapeutic*.[32]

What Benedict's two styles share though beyond all differences is that they employ the ethnic other in the service of the self. Though Benedict does participate in the discourses of salvage ethnography, seeking to preserve traces of cultures deemed on the verge of extinction,[33] what appears most sorely in need of redemption in both her poetry and ethnographic work is her own culture. She shares this concern with her fellow Boasian Mead, though Benedict's calls for therapy and critique are much less pronounced than her younger and more famous colleague's, who concludes *Coming of Age in Samoa* with the two overtly didactic chapters "Our Educational Problems in the Light of Samoan Contrasts" and "Education for Choice." Benedict's primitivist rhetoric is also more subdued, but when we read about the "[l]ong-limbed and bronzed" god dancing as the sun goes down, we are not mistaken in seeing the same desire at work that fuels both Mead's mourning of the "dancers" that "no longer form a goddess' face/From the maize sheath" in her own poem "The Need That Is Left" (1927) and her evocation of trysting Samoan youths at the beginning of her important yet notoriously controversial first major ethnographic study. In their poetry and ethnographic writings, Benedict and Mead remind us that, for all its genuinely progressive influence on the humanities and social sciences, Boasian cultural relativism remains tied to a primitivist style that exerts epistemological violence, reminding us of the origin of 'style' in the Latin *stilus*: "a stake or pale, pointed instrument for writing, style of speaking or writing" (OED). A concluding look at the etymological source of 'style,' then, not only invites us to recognize the materiality of writing—the fact that 'style' derives from the word for a writing tool made of iron or reed that scribes from classical antiquity to early medieval Europe used to carve signs into wax tablets and, later, the margins of codices (Gumbrecht, "Schwindende Stabilität" 726–41)—but also to consider the extent to which inscription (with the pointed end of the stylus) and deletion (with its flat end, which is used both for smoothing the surface after inscription and for the deletion of earlier inscriptions) mean violence. As the ethnographer-poet readies the other for the use of the self, she not only preserves traces of other cultures but also leaves marks of her own. In this, Benedict combines salvage ethnography's impulse to save remnants of cultures deemed on the verge of extinction and primitivism's fascination with cultures considered aesthetically pleasing.

Notes

1. The publication in 1982 of Cheryl Walker's *The Nightingale's Burden: Women Poets and American Culture Before 1900* marks the beginning of a renewed interest in nineteenth-century poetry, particularly in women's poetry of the period. Other important anthologies covering a similar terrain include John Hollander's *American Poetry: The Nineteenth Century* (1983), Paula Bernat Bennett's *Nineteenth Century American Women Poets: An Anthology* (1998), and Janet Gray's *She Wields a Pen: American Women Poets of the Nineteenth Century* (1997). The resurgence of interest in nineteenth-century verse is also reflected in monographs such as Betsy Erkkila's *The Wicked Sisters: Women Poets, Literary History, and Discord* (1992), Elizabeth Petrino's *Emily Dickinson and Her Contemporaries: Women's Verse in America, 1820–1885* (1998), Bennett's *Poets in the Public Sphere: The Emancipatory Project of American Women's Poetry, 1800–1900* (2003), Eliza Richards's *Gender and the Poetics of Reception in Poe's Circle* (2004), Mary Loeffelholz's *From School to Salon: Reading Nineteenth-Century American Women's Poetry* (2004) and Angela Sorby's *Schoolroom Poets: Childhood and the Place of American Poetry, 1865–1917* (2005). See also my bibliographical essay in the MLA volume *Teaching Nineteenth-Century American Poetry* (2007) edited by Bennett, Karen Kilcup, and myself.
2. While Lowell does not provide us with any examples or names of secessionist poets, it is clear that she refers to poets like Hart Crane, E.E. Cummings or William Carlos Williams, who published their poetry in the experimental *Secession* magazine. *Secession* was founded by Gorham Munson in 1922, the year before Lowell wrote her essay. It was a programmatic journal, committed to promoting the "new rebels ... those writers who are preoccupied with researches for new forms" (Munson, qtd. in Hammer 40). Hart Crane's biographer Philip Horton describes *Secession* and the writers associated with it in similar terms:

   > The contributors to *Secession*...—Josephson, Cowley, Cummings, Burke, Yvor Winters, W.C. Williams—were primarily interested in aesthetic problems, questions of form and craftsmanship, which grew immediately out of creative activity and could be answered by experimentation. And it was

for the express purpose of printing their work as that of a group with common directions that Munson was publishing the magazine.

(134)

3. By 1930, Untermeyer added the following note to Anne Singleton's poems: "Anne Singleton—the pseudonym under which a well-known anthropologist writes her poems—" (518). Being 'outed' thus, Benedict stopped using pen names and published under her real name instead from 1930 onward. Other pen names that Benedict used for her early poetry are 'Alice Singleton,' 'Ellen Benedict,' 'Anne Chase,' and 'Ruth Stanhope.' She also co-wrote the short story "The Bo-Cu Plant" with her husband Stanley Rossiter Benedict and signed it 'Edgar Stanhope' (Reichel, *Writing* 301–2n.30).

4. A. Elisabeth Reichel has assembled a useful set of quotes about the sales numbers, impact, and importance of Benedict's book:

> Benedict's 1934 study *Patterns of Culture* . . . has inspired broad superlatives in historical accounts of U.S.-American anthropology: Benedict's monograph "remains today the single most influential work by a twentieth-century American anthropologist" according to George Stocking ("Benedict" 73). It presents "the image of modern anthropology most recognized by the public," Marc Manganaro claims, noting only Mead's *Coming of Age in Samoa* as a possible exception (*Culture* 152). He cites *Patterns of Culture* as "the best-selling anthropological work of all time," a statistic to which the book's scholarly merits as well as the postwar paperback revolution contributed. In 1946, *Patterns* was republished in a twenty-five cent paperback edition which sold 10,000 copies in its first year (Caffrey 214; Goldfrank, *Notes* 39) and boosted sales to 1.25 million by 1964 (Dempsey 27). Most recently, William Y. Adams declared that the book—again, with the exception of Mead—"has probably sold more copies in more languages than the works of all the other Boasians combined" (266).
>
> (Reichel, *Writing* 185)

To this list, we can add Charles King's assessment from 2019 that Benedict's book is "arguably the most cited and most taught work of anthropological grand theory ever" (267).

5. Reflecting on her poetry, her use of a pseudonym, and her relationship with her long-estranged husband Stanley, Benedict in her autobiographical sketch "The Story of My Life . . ." writes that

> until I was thirty-five I believed that the things that mattered must always hurt other people to know or make them interfere, and the point was to avoid this. My feeling about my verse and my nom de plume, my relations to Stanley, all are unintelligible without the rule of life I discovered in the haymow.
>
> (*Anthropologist* 102)

The "rule of life" Benedict discovered in an epiphanic moment while hiding in the hay at the age of six, and which she cherished for twenty-nine more years of her life, was "that if I didn't talk to anybody about the things that mattered to me no one could ever take them away" (102).

6. We can see the same kind of argument at work in Handler's discussion of Sapir's poetry:

> After 1922 Sapir's literary pieces become more and more incidental, his last literary reviews appearing in 1928. The publication of Sapir's poetry follows the same course. His first published poems, and his only volume

of poetry (*Dreams and Gibes*), appeared in 1917. From 1918 to 1927 he published a substantial number of poems each year; his last four published poems appeared in 1931. From this 'trait analysis' alone, then, we can guess that for Sapir the late teens were a time of shifting interests and even 'profound rethinking,' as Preston has put it . . . . What Sapir rethought were some of the premises of Boasian science and his intellectual commitment to them.

("Dainty" 292–93)

7. For a brief account of this resurgence, see Gabriele Rippl's, Therese Steffen's, and my introduction to *Haunted Narratives: Life Writing in an Age of Trauma* (2013, 5–7).
8. For an assessment of Barthes', Foucault's, and Derrida's claims, see Seán Burke's *The Death and Return of the Author: Criticism and Subjectivity in Barthes, Foucault, and Derrida* (2010). For a representative sampling of philosophical reflections on the question of authorial intention, see Gary Iseminger's *Intention & Interpretation* (2010).
9. Both in Mead's account of Benedict's life in the chapter introductions of *An Anthropologist at Work* and in Benedict's own life-story, "The Story of My Life . . ." (1935), there is much talk of "the separated parts of her life" (Benedict, *Anthropologist* 87) and the "two worlds" (99) she lived in. While these different parts or worlds of Benedict's life cannot be pinpointed with a high degree of precision, they tend to refer to either her various roles as wife, poet, and anthropologist or to a distinction Benedict herself makes between an inner world that belongs solely to herself and is related to secrecy, reclusion, her dead father, death in general, and the figure of Christ, and an outer world, which is related to her unloved mother's weeping spells, her marriage to Stanley Benedict, most interpersonal relations, and the exigencies of day-to-day existence. As we can gather from Benedict's journals, she was determined to keep her inner life, her "real *me*," hidden behind a "mask" of "cheerfulness" and "gaiety." "The mask," she writes at the age of twenty-five, "was tightly adjusted" (*Anthropologist* 119). However we interpret talk about the various aspects of Benedict's existence, Mead asserts that "the stuff of Indian myth and ritual . . . became one of the doorways through which the separated parts of her life began to be united" (87). More specifically, Mead suggests that it was in "her work on Japan" that "all the themes—anthropological 'sense,' delight in the beauty of a pattern, overwhelming pity for human suffering, and a hope that something might be done about it by an increase in scientific knowledge of human behavior—came together" (*Anthropologist* 96).
10. Sapir's ambivalent attitude in these letters toward *Poetry* and its editor Harriet Monroe is instructive. In many of his letters to Benedict, Sapir dismisses Monroe's taste as well as her selections of poems as timid and sentimental. A case in point is a letter dated May 14, 1925, in which Sapir responds to Monroe's rejection of a number of Benedict's poems. Sapir attributes "Harriet's reaction chiefly to her inveterate softness or sentimentality. Difficult or in any way intellectual verse gets past her only with difficulty. She prefers stuff about sweet love and my baby" (Benedict, *Anthropologist* 179). Even if Monroe's own poetry was decidedly less daring and experimental than the poems she published, this seems a peculiar assessment of the poetic tastes of an editor who was publishing T.S. Eliot, Ezra Pound, Carl Sandburg, and Edgar Lee Masters in the year Sapir wrote his letter. Moreover, similar criticisms of *Poetry* magazine occur too frequently in Sapir's correspondence with Benedict and in too many different contexts to be put down solely to one poet's desire to comfort

another poet about negative editorial decisions. In any case, Sapir's charges of sentimentalism in this and a host of similar assessments of Monroe's tastes are in striking contrast to his exasperation at *Poetry*'s penchant for experimental modernist poetry, expressed in a letter dated 29 September, 1927:

> The age and I don't seem to be on very intimate speaking terms. In the last number of "Poetry," for instance, I find almost nothing that even remotely interests me. I think the ideology of a Hupa medicine formula is closer to my heart than all this nervous excitement of Hart Crane's. Can you tell me what he wants? You spoke of Mark Van Doren's excellence. I've not read his recently published book but the citations in the review in "Poetry" were not very alluring. They sounded more like keen celebration in verse form than poetry. And I'm utterly sick of intelligence and its vanity. It's the arch disease of the time and the reason for its choking vulgarity and its flimsiness. So I don't feel I have anything to say that anybody would want to hear, even if I had a sufficiently great gift of words to say it with, and I doubt greatly if I have that gift. The experimental excitements of this great modern time do not rouse me, they chill me to loathing. The freedoms we hear about are pinchbeck whims of the body and it is as much as one's accredited sanity is worth to even whisper the word 'noble.'
> (Benedict, *Anthropologist* 185–86)

Taken together, Sapir's diverging assessments of *Poetry* magazine testify to an awareness on his part—at whatever level of consciousness—that his own poetic tastes, and maybe his own poetry, occupy a middle ground between a more conventional aesthetic poetic tradition rooted in the nineteenth century and an experimental, perhaps more audacious modernist aesthetics of the twentieth century. This is also very much my own assessment of the place of Benedict's poetry and that of her fellow lyri(ci)sts in U.S. literary history.

11. In his two most productive years as a poet, 1925 and 1926, Sapir published no less than twenty-seven poems each. Around a dozen of these 54 poems came out in renowned literary and cultural magazines such as *The Dial*, *Poetry*, and *The Nation*.

12. In a journal entry dated October 1912, Benedict writes, at the age of twenty-five:

> So much of the trouble is because I am a woman. To me it seems a very terrible thing to be a woman. There is one crown which perhaps is worth it all—a great love, a quiet home, and children. We all know that is all that is worth while, and yet we must peg away, showing off our wares on the market if we have money, or manufacturing careers for ourselves if we haven't. We have not the motive to prepare ourselves for a 'life-work' of teaching, of social work—we know that we would lay it down with hallelujah in the height of our success, to make a home for the right man. . . . It is all so cruelly wasteful. There are so few ways in which we can compete with men—surely not in teaching or in social work. If we are not to have the chance to fulfil our one potentiality—the power of loving—why were we not born men? At least we could have had an occupation then.
> (*Anthropologist* 120)

13. The partially self-ironic quality of such gestures comes to the fore more explicitly when Sapir begins another letter to Benedict written later in the same month with this sentence:

> I was delighted to get the three poems, as you may have gathered from 'Signal,' and shall don my professorial robes at once and discuss them as

best I can. It is wonderful to know you are likely to take your poetic gift seriously and get down to serious work.

(Benedict, *Anthropologist* 161–62)

14. Owned by Richard D. Badger, the Gorham Press was a Boston publishing company that "published books at their authors' expense" ("Richard G. Badger Papers").
15. See Charles Haddon Spurgeon's 1888 sermon "The Rent Veil" for an extended reading of the relevant Biblical passages along those lines.
16. Consider also the ending of "Pool" (n.d.), yet another companion piece to "Unshadowed Pool":

> Far down,
> Secretely,
> With an endless caressing,
> You sway, limb to limb,
> With the tall buoyed weeds in your twilight.
> I know this, pool,
> For I also am secret.

17. For this reason too, Benedict's biographer Margaret M. Caffrey's reading of the poem as a "respons[e] to a world grown unsympathetic to women loving women" (195) and an expression of the author's insight that "women's realization of their love for each other leads to estrangement from society" (196) misses the mark. Note that Caffrey does register the poem's ethnographic source but persists in her biographical reading nevertheless.
18. This account relies on Robert D. Craig's *Handbook of Polynesian Mythology* (39–58). For a historical narrative available in Benedict's time, see George Grey's *Polynesian Mythology and Ancient Traditional History of the Maori as Told by Their Priests and Chiefs* (1855).
19. Alexandra Berlina's most recent translation, "Art, as Device" (2015) adopts this rendering into English of *ostranenie*.
20. James Clifford's recourse to Raymond Williams's concept of 'critical nostalgia' in his discussion of Sapir's culture concept is also relevant to Benedict's use of the 'primitive' for cultural critique:

> Williams traces the constant reemergence of a conventionalized pattern of retrospection that laments the loss of a 'good' country, a place where authentic social and natural contacts were once possible. . . . Williams does not dismiss this structure as simply nostalgic, which it manifestly is; but rather follows out a very complex set of temporal, spatial, and moral positions. He notes that pastoral frequently involves a *critical nostalgia*, a way . . . to break with the hegemonic, corrupt present by asserting the reality of a radical alternative. Edward Sapir's "Culture, Genuine and Spurious" (1966) recapitulates these critical pastoral values. And indeed every imagined authenticity presupposes, and is produced by, a present circumstance of felt inauthenticity.
>
> ("On Ethnographic Allegory" 113–14; emphasis in original)

21. Consider also Benedict's poem "Profit of Dreams," which remained unpublished during the author's lifetime but is available in *An Anthropologist at Work*. This poem, which like "Unshadowed Pool" uses pool imagery, contains the lines "We defame / Blindly our surest blessings, to pursue / Idols of stone whose gross feet and hair / We surfeit with caresses, to subdue / That doubt of beauty we misname despair." As in "In Parables," Benedict here equates idolatry with an excess of attachment and passion.

22. In the French original, the statement reads "Le style n'est que l'ordre et le mouvement qu'on met dans ses pensées" (Leclerc 5). Hans Ulrich Gumbrecht argues convincingly that this characterization of style as a cognitive faculty captures much better Buffon's understanding of the notion than the much more frequently quoted "Le style est l'homme même" (Leclerc 13), which is often wrongly interpreted as giving voice to an aesthetics of expression in which style is the expression of personality (Gumbrecht, "Stil" 754–56).
23. Benedict was a "long-time devotee of Nietzsche—she had sent *Thus Spoke Zarathustra* for Margaret to read on the boat from Samoa" (Lapsley 178). Note that Benedict significantly transforms her Nietzschean framework: While Nietzsche considered Apollonian and Dionysian forces to be divergent aspects of a single culture, Benedict uses the binary to distinguish different cultures from one another. See Manganaro's *Culture, 1922: The Emergence of a Concept* (159).
24. Note that Benedict's characterization of the Kwakiutl as highly competitive and status-driven does not sit easily with Nietzsche's description of Dionysian forces, which in his account efface individuality and bring about a carnivalesque leveling of social hierarchies. As I write this, I can hear the drums and pipes of the Basler *Fasnacht*, my hometown's carnival.
25. Note, however, that the Boasian cultural relativists were not immune to taking recourse to evolutionist arguments. Benedict's most infamous example is her comparison of her own research on 'primitives' to Darwin's study of beetles:

> It is one of the philosophical justifications for the study of primitive peoples that the facts of simpler cultures may make clear social facts that are otherwise baffling and not open to demonstration. . . . Cultural configurations are as compelling and as significant in the highest and most complex societies of which we have knowledge. But the material is too intricate and too close to our eyes for us to cope with it successfully.
>
> The understanding we need of our own cultural processes can most economically be arrived at by a detour. When the historical relations of human beings and their immediate forbears in the animal kingdom were too involved to use in establishing the fact of biological evolution, Darwin made use instead of the structure of beetles, and the process, which in the complex physical organization of the human is confused, in the simpler material was transparent in its cogency. It is the same in the study of cultural mechanisms. We need all the enlightenment we can obtain from the study of thought and behaviour as it is organized in the less complicated groups.
>
> (*Patterns* 55–56)

26. Note, though, Walter Benn Michaels's powerful argument in *Our America: Nativism, Modernism, and Pluralism* (1995) that cultural pluralists promoted a differentialist, essentialist understanding of culture that made race/ethnicity a crucial marker of human identity that, upon closer examination, sits quite comfortably alongside nativist racism. Drawing on Michaels and on Zoë Burkholder's *Color in the Classroom: How American Schools Taught Race, 1900–1954* (2011), Reichel stages a forceful critique of the politics of Boasian cultural relativism (*Writing* 189–91).
27. As Riché J. Daniel Barnes reminds us, it is at least partly such persistent and casual talk about 'primitives' that makes the Boasian founders of modern anthropology so dubious for non-white students of anthropology:

> We cannot be afraid to talk about the way anthropology has been complicit in the degradation of cultures and the accompanying oppression of people. We cannot continue to begin with the 'primitive' and the 'savage' and expect students whose ancestors were part of those populations to find merit in the field.
>
> (qtd. in Canada 28)

28. For a splendid discussion of Benedict's and fellow Boasians' popular social science aesthetics, see Susan Hegeman's "American Popular Social Science: The Boasian Legacy" (2018).
29. The quote in the final sentence is from fellow Boasian Ruth Bunzel's "Introduction to Zuni Ceremonialism" (1932, 486).
30. I do not choose my psychoanalytic vocabulary gratuitously. Benedict's references to psychoanalysis are less extensive and less specific than Mead's but consider her recourse to Jung's elaboration of the Nietzschean Apollonian/Dionysian dichotomy, her extensive reflections on what a psychological or psychiatric look at cultures and cultural types might reveal, and her co-development, with Mead, of the culture-as-personality paradigm (Stocking, "Ethnographic Sensibility" 298; Manganaro 152; Handler, "Vigorous" 149–50).
31. Stocking has done the counting: "Hampered by deafness and diffidence, Benedict did not find fieldwork congenial, and the small amount that she did (no more than eight months altogether) fell into a rather conventional early Boasian mold" ("Ethnographic Sensibility" 296).
32. Note, however, that Benedict's early (but undated) ethnographic poem "Parlor Car—Santa Fe" thrives on the differentialist logic that also characterizes her ethnographic writings. In *Writing Anthropologists, Sounding Primitives*, Reichel shows how the poem stages a primitivist desire for a distinctly different ethnic other by contrasting the dullness and overrefinement of Western culture ("You toy awhile in approved modern way / With the newest art, and explode a sophistical / Conceit of so-and-so's philosophy") to the desirable, sensuous rituals of Native American pueblo culture that the Santa Fe railroad promises access to ("And we would dash our pride with naked hands / To bury once a prayer-plume in the moon / And pour in hearing ears our hot desires"). I am not discussing the poem here because I believe Reichel has already written about it what needs to be written (*Writing* 200–7). I should, however, add that I find Hilary Lapsley's biographical interpretation of the poem as giving expression to Benedict's desire for Mead, who was absent from her side as she conducted her postdoctoral research in Samoa, unconvincing. For Lapsley, the poem was "[p]erhaps . . . too revealing" (132) to be included in *An Anthropologist at Work*. For Reichel and myself, this is what I call an 'ethnographic poem' that has precious little to do with lesbian desire. See also Lois W. Banner's *Intertwined Lives: Margaret Mead, Ruth Benedict, and Their Circle* for another biographical reading of the poem, which misidentifies its addressee with Mead (223).
33. Jacob W. Gruber introduced the notion of 'salvage ethnography' into anthropological debates in "Ethnographic Salvage and the Shaping of Anthropology" (1970), where he describes the salvage imperative thus:

    > In the face of the inevitable and necessary changes, in the face of an almost infinite variety of man whose details were essential to a definition of man, the obligation of both scientist and humanist was clear: he must collect and preserve the information and the products of human activity and genius so rapidly being destroyed.
    >
    > (1293)

    For classic critiques of salvage ethnography's epistemological and ideological impasses, see James Clifford's "On Ethnographic Allegory" and Brian Hochman's *Savage Preservation: The Ethnographic Origins of Modern Media Technology*. See also Manganaro's *Culture, 1922: The Emergence of a Concept* for a pithy discussion of Benedict's trope of the 'broken cup' and its relation to both salvage ethnography and T.S. Eliot's modernist discourse of loss in *The Waste Land* (160–61).

2 Margaret Mead
How to Make It New, Differently

Benedict's student, close collaborator, lover, and friend Mead joins her in using other cultures as foils that help her and her readers perceive the shortcomings of her own culture more clearly. More forcefully than in Benedict, this use of foreign cultures characterizes Mead's ethnographic writings: anthropology is put in the service of cultural critique. Some of her poems, including "Monuments Rejected" (1925) and "America" (1924), participate in this endeavor too, performing a critical function rather than syncretistically fusing the culture of the self and the culture of the other, as much of Benedict's verse does. In others, among them "The Need That Is Left" (1927) and "And Your Young Men Shall See Visions" (1929), the salvage imperative that fuels the Boasians' anthropological research is inscribed in a deeply nostalgic look at supposedly vanishing cultural practices of the other.[1] For that reason, too, Mead's poetry engages less than Benedict's in primitivist appropriations of other cultures as sites for Western cultural rejuvenation. Unlike the modernist primitivists (my point of comparison will be T.S. Eliot), Mead also does not mine other cultures for forms in search of literary innovation. Energized by progressivist convictions and not shy of proposing social engineering, what Mead strives to make new is not literary language but, first, her discipline, then the social world. Given that her pioneering forays into visual anthropology are partially driven by a distrust in the epistemic value of words—a distrust she gives particularly poignant expression to in her 1924 poem "Warning"—such orientation to disciplinary and social rather than linguistic change comes as little surprise.

As Mead tells us in her memoir *Blackberry Winter* (1972), she had been writing poetry since the age of nine (80–81). When she entered Barnard College in 1920, Mead became part of an all-female group of students, the Ash Can Cats, that collectively revered writers such as Louise Bogan and Edna St. Vincent Millay (Stocking, "Ethnographic Sensibility" 311), accomplished poets who wrote traditional lyrical verse—as did both Mead and, if we follow Louis Untermeyer's categorization of her as a 'lyricist,' Benedict. Later, Mead and Benedict would exchange their poetry, discuss it, and dedicate poems to one another. As Mead

DOI: 10.4324/9781003266945-3

remembers in *Blackberry Winter*, "We read and re-read each other's work, wrote poems in answer to poems, shared our hopes and worries about Boas, about Sapir, about anthropology, and in later years about the world" (115). Both of them also exchanged poems with fellow Boasian anthropologist Sapir, who wrote over 660 poems, the most extensive body of verse of the three. Mead herself published only twenty-two poems but wrote over 190.[2] And she had mixed feelings about her lyrical work. Already in her early twenties, the superior talent of one of the members of the Ash Can Cats, the future U.S. poet laureate Léonie Adams, convinced her that her real talents lay elsewhere. In Mead's own words, "the most exciting events" at Barnard College

> centered around Léonie's poetry, for while she was still an undergraduate she was already having poems accepted and published. . . . I too had been writing verse and I continued to do so for several years, but it became an avocation—an enjoyable way of translating experiences for myself and of communicating with friends who were poets. But because Léonie was there, it ceased to be a serious ambition.
>
> (107)[3]

She did keep on writing poetry, though, "particularly during the first intensity of her relationship with Ruth Benedict" (Grosskurth 19).

Reinventing the Social World

Of the twenty-two poems Mead published, she was able to place "For a Proud Lady" and "Rose Tree of Assisi" in *The Measure* and, on Benedict's recommendation (Monroe, "Letter to Ruth Fulton Benedict of April 3, 1928"), "Misericordia" in Harriet Monroe's *Poetry* magazine, where the likes of T.S. Eliot, Ezra Pound, H.D., Wallace Stevens, William Carlos Williams, Amy Lowell and Robert Frost published their verse. The two related questions I want to ask in this section are: Why does a cultural anthropologist write poetry, and how does it compare to her modernist contemporaries' verse? What comes into view as we ask these questions are stylistically very different negotiations of Western modernity and its non-Western others that aim at different kinds of renewals. To readers of canonized modernist verse, Mead's poetic diagnosis of Western modernity rings familiar. When she evokes the sounds of tolling church bells being rudely interrupted by "the whistle of a passing train" in her 1924 poem "Good Friday 1923" or when, in her undated poem "Disillusionment," her poetic speaker's reverie allows her only brief respite from a "troubled, crowded town" in which "work-wracked people pushed along/The flat new pavements in hot haste" and "shrieking trains" pierce the soundscape, we are given poetic visions of an urban modernity that is as alienated, spiritless and desiccated as anything we find in the arid landscape of Eliot's *The Waste Land*, where the "chapel" is "empty" (388), where "[t]he nymphs are departed" (175), and where the "human engine" (216) appears less alive than the "throbbing" (217) taxi.[4] In the undated poem "A Paper World," Mead even fantasizes about watching the "[p]aper world and paper people" of her present being obliterated: "One dimensional they stand," but what, she asks, "should happen if the judges/Should try to smash the paper trust."

It is well known that, in their attempts to 'make it new,' the modernists were often drawn to cultures that they perceived as more authentic and more vital than their own. The primitivism of modernists as different in their styles and media practices as Pablo Picasso, Paul Gauguin, Henri Matisse, Emil Nolde, Tristan Tzara, Gertrude Stein, Langston Hughes, and Henry Moore is a well-researched phenomenon.[5] *The Waste Land* is no exception: if there is a glimmer of hope in Eliot's bleak vision, it is most readily found in its evocations of vegetation myths; in the Buddha's fire sermon; in its recourse to the Sanskrit epic *Mahabharata*; to the Hindu scripture *Brihadaranyaka Upanishad* and what the thunder says in it, "Datta. Dayadhvam. Damyata" (432)—'give,' 'compassion,' 'control'—and in the poem's concluding summoning of "The Peace which passeth understanding": "Shantih shantih shantih" (433). It is equally well-known that *The Waste Land* is heavily influenced by the anthropologist James George Frazer's multivolume opus magnum *The Golden Bough* (1906–15) and the medievalist Jessie L. Weston's account of the Grail legend in *From Ritual to Romance* (1920), which builds on Frazer's work.[6] Eliot acknowledges his debts in the brief introduction to his notes to *The Waste Land* that were first included in the Boni and Liveright edition of December 1922, writing that he is "so deeply . . . indebted" to Weston's book that it "will elucidate the difficulties of the poem much better than my notes can do." About *The Golden Bough* he writes that it "has influenced our generation profoundly," adding that "[a]nyone who is acquainted" with *Adonis, Attis, Osiris*—the relevant two volumes in the twelve-volume edition of *The Golden Bough*—"will immediately recognise in the poem certain references to vegetation ceremonies" (*Waste Land* 71). While Eliot later distanced himself from his notes to *The Waste Land* as mere fillers for the poem's first book-length publication and as "bogus scholarship" ("Frontiers" 109), the influence of Frazerian anthropology is clearly visible in the poem itself and is fully in line with Eliot's recourse to anthropological research in other writings of his, including the lesser known 1919 text "War-Paint and Feathers," a review of an anthology of Native American songs and chants that I will return to below. Eliot's search for spiritual rejuvenation, then, takes a detour through anthropological research, and the fragments that his poetic speaker shores against his ruins are of non-Western as well as of Western provenance.

It would, then, come as little surprise if Mead, the anthropologist-turned-poet (or, better, poet-turned-anthropologist since she wrote poetry first), invested other cultures with similar vital energy when her poetry turns to ethnographic subjects. But Mead's recourse to anthropological knowledge takes different forms. Consider the first two stanzas of "The Need that Is Left," a poem Mead wrote in March 1927 and included in *A Song of Five Springs*, a handbound little volume of eleven poems that Mead very probably compiled for Benedict.

> The victors in the chariot race
> No longer win a sacred wreath;
> Nor dancers form a goddess' face
> From the maize sheath.
> The fisher's luck is now of calculation
> Not of prayer,
> And hunters pour no vain oblation
> On the altar stair.
>
> All the altars now are bare
> Of men's offerings for rain;
> Barren women burn no incense there
> To ease their pain,
> The spring's first thunder is no matter
> For the Gods;
> And Aaron can no longer shatter
> The Egyptians' rods.

In profoundly nostalgic tones, the poem mourns the disappearance of mythical beliefs and ritual practices. As in Eliot, the Greek and Judeo-Christian origins of the Western world—the chariot races and Aaron's magic—are no longer able to sustain a vibrant culture. But unlike in Eliot, the practices and beliefs of other cultures—the corn dances, the sacrifices, the spiritual charging of the weather—are likewise in decline. In Mead's poetic universe, the other usually cannot remedy the loss of the self.[7] More often than not in Mead's ethnographic verse, the subjects of other cultures too have "no past for fuel," as we read in "And Your Young Men Shall See Visions," a poem that her fellow Ash Can Cat and poet Edna Lou Walton published in *City Day: An Anthology of Recent American Poetry* (1929):

> "We have no past for fuel." The young men said.
> "We have no long and dry array of husk-like hours,
> To bind in faggots, furbished for a pyre
> Where all our dead days blossom into fire
> Of dreams, renascent in the mighty fire."

> "Cut then your future down!" The old men said.
> "Fell the tall loveliness of unlived days;
> In such a smoke, new fathered of the green,
> Unsullied smoke, in secret perilous ways,
> The unremembering young have visions seen."

What we get in this poem is a remarkable negotiation of Indigenous subjects' relation to the past and the future. While the "young men" complain that the past is no usable resource, the "old men" paradoxically suggest that, in that case, the youths must use their as yet "unlived" future as a resource to enable "visions" (of the future). The paradox involved in the elder's advice is that the future must, figuratively speaking, be burned in order to allow for the creation of a future. That this paradox is not resolved in the course of the poem emphasizes that, for this fictive Indigenous community, neither the past nor the future are readily available resources for the creation of new ways of being in the world.[8]

To account for the significant differences between Mead's and Eliot's poetic negotiations of non-Western cultures, we need to understand that Mead's ethnographic work is in many ways directly opposed to the kind of anthropological research that Eliot draws on. I have already identified Eliot's main anthropological authorities for *The Waste Land*: Jessie L. Weston and George Frazer. In "War-Paint and Feathers"—a remarkable, little-known review of George W. Cronyn's *The Path on the Rainbow: An Anthology of Songs and Chants from the Indians of North America* (1918), published in the October 17, 1919 issue of *The Athenaeum*—Eliot cites further ethnographic sources that fuel his interest in the 'primitive': the 'Cambridge ritualists' Jane Ellen Harrison and Arthur Bernard Cook, who applied Darwin's theories and contemporaneous anthropological research to the study of ancient Greek culture; Walter Baldwin Spencer and Francis James Gillen's research on Australian Aboriginal culture; Robert Henry Codrington's monograph on Melanesia; the work of the Biblical scholar and Orientalist J. Rendel Harris; Émile Durkheim's studies of totemism; and Lucien Lévy-Bruhl's reflections on 'primitive mentality.' While this is a diverse list of scholars from different disciplines, and while Durkheim's and Lévy-Bruhl's structuralist studies certainly move beyond Darwinian biologism (Voget 571–73), several of the scholars Eliot cites (certainly Harrison, Cook, Spencer, and Harris) share a roughly evolutionary perspective on Indigenous cultures.

When Eliot published "War-Paint and Feathers" in 1919, social evolutionism as represented by Frazer and Edward Burnett Tylor was on the decline but still a powerful force in anthropology.[9] While different representatives of evolutionary anthropology presented different accounts of cultural development, they were united in their belief that, in Tylor's words,

> the history of mankind is part and parcel of the history of nature, that our thoughts, wills, and actions accord with laws as definite as those which govern the motion of waves, the combination of acids and bases, and the growth of plants and animals.
>
> (I: 2)

Evolutionists followed Auguste Comte, Herbert Spencer, and Montesquieu in presuming that human cultures developed progressively, in Montesquieu's model from savagery, to barbarism, to civilization.[10] In the words of Lewis H. Morgan, one of the most influential representatives of sociocultural evolutionism in the U.S.,

> As it is undeniable that portions of the human family have existed in a state of savagery, other portions in a state of barbarism, and still others in a state of civilization, it seems equally so that these three distinct conditions are connected with each other in a natural as well as necessary sequence of progress.
>
> (3)

It is precisely this thinking about culture that Eliot taps into when he writes that

> the poet should know everything that has been accomplished in poetry (accomplished, not merely produced) . . . since its beginnings—in order to know what he is doing himself. He should be aware of all the metamorphoses of poetry that illustrate the stratifications of history that cover savagery.
>
> ("War-Paint" 138)

This is the primitivist variety of "Tradition and the Individual Talent": to become truly modern, the poet must work himself through a tradition that includes not only the European heritage that Eliot draws on so conspicuously in *The Waste Land* (from Dante to Shakespeare, to Wagner, to Verlaine) but also the traditions of so-called primitive or savage cultures:[11]

> And as it is certain that some study of primitive man furthers our understanding of civilized man, so it is certain that primitive art and poetry help our understanding of civilized art and poetry. Primitive art and poetry can even, through the studies and experiments of

> the artist or poet, revivify the contemporary activities. The maxim, Return to the sources, is a good one.
>
> (138)[12]

As a student of Boas, Mead was by no means immune to primitivism: her writings give expression to an intense fascination with and desire for cultures deemed less developed yet more vital and authentic than her own. In this sense at least, much of her ethnographic writing seems aligned with modernist primitivism, which "posit[s] the Other not as a threat that must be contained but as the source of new energies" and considers 'the primitive' as "a conduit to understanding 'civilized' man, art, and poetry, not an endpoint in itself" (Gikandi 458). But the Boasians were fiercely opposed to the evolutionary school of anthropology that Eliot draws on so freely. Boas led his first concerted change against evolutionism in a series of letters that critiqued Otis T. Mason's evolutionary taxonomy at the United States National Museum. Their exchange of letters was published in *Science* in 1887.[13] Following their academic teacher, the Boasians fought the evolutionists' biological determinism, their scientific racism, their armchair approach to research, their lumping together of different cultural practices from widely differing cultures, and their impositions of Western norms and values upon non-Western cultures. The Boasians proposed cultural relativism as an alternative to the evolutionist account, arguing for the potential equality of all cultures and insisting that cultures must be studied and judged on the basis of their *own* norms and values rather than from a supposedly universal but actually Western normative perspective (Stocking, "Ethnographic Sensibility"; Stocking, "Thoughts"). Boas and his followers displaced Tylor's singular notion of 'culture,' which equated it with 'civilization,' with a plural notion of cultures whose distinct internal patterns must be studied.[14] While Boasian anthropology retains uncomfortable ties with evolutionist thinking and racial science, Boas and his students made their mark by opposing and at least partially displacing social evolutionism.[15] In Mead's summation of the Boasian stance:

> Historically our contribution has been a recognition of the co-equal value of human cultures seen as wholes. . . . We have stood out against any grading of cultures in hierarchical systems which would place our own culture at the top and place the other cultures of the world in a descending scale according to the extent that they differ from ours. . . . [W]e have stood out for a sort of democracy of cultures, a concept which would naturally take its place beside the other great democratic beliefs in the equal potentiality of all races of men, and in the inherent dignity and right to opportunity of each human being.
>
> ("Role of Small South Sea Cultures" 193)

This helps explain why Mead's poetry rarely treats the cultures that she studies as sources of Western rejuvenation. From a cultural relativist perspective, cultures (in the plural) are distinct from one another and need to be treated as such. In Ruth Benedict's particularly strong version of cultural relativism, different cultures are even "incommensurable" (*Patterns* 223). For this reason, we can expect that a poet like Mead, who holds cultural relativist beliefs, is at least skeptical of any attempt to revitalize one culture through the infusion of another.

A second explanation for Mead's more strongly elegiac poetic treatment of other cultures is the moral imperative that fuels the Boasians' work. Mead gives an early, particularly poignant expression to that imperative in a letter she wrote to her grandmother on March 11, 1923, two years before she journeyed to Samoa,

> I would so like to be an Anthropologist. For contact with modern civilizations is killing off primitive cultures so fast; in a hundred years there will be no primitive people; the work is so urgent, and there are so few people who even understand the importance of the work, let alone being willing to do it.
>
> ("Letter to Martha Ramsey Mead of March 11, 1923")[16]

Mead here gives expression to salvage ethnography's determination to preserve traces of cultures that are envisaged to vanish under the pressures of modernization and Euro-American influence.[17] A critical glance at the salvage imperative reveals troubling ties between the Boasians and the evolutionists they sought to displace, showing that both rely on an understanding of history in which the ultimate disappearance of premodern ways of life is seen as a given.[18] But the salvage imperative was more central to the Boasian project than to the evolutionist school since cultures that are, according to the evolutionists, bound to disappear may be worth tapping into but not worth preserving. This helps explain why Mead's poetry tends to mourn the passing of so-called primitive cultures rather than jubilate about their revitalizing force for Western culture (though there are, as we will see below, exceptions to that rule). And this has consequences for the way Mead writes.

In their desire to 'make it new,' modernist writers and artists drew on primitive cultures first and foremost as reservoirs of supposedly simpler and more authentic cultural and artistic *forms* that Western artists could draw on to revitalize their own artistic practices and invent new artistic forms. Picasso's use of African masks in painting the nudes of *Les demoiselles d'Avignon* is a particularly famous instance of this (see Figure. 2.1).

This early, moderate example of cubist painting reveals that the modernist move toward abstraction did not grow solely out of a self-reflexive interrogation of the nature and the history of Western art. Cubist abstraction, *Les demoiselles d'Avignon* shows, also has an ethnic origin.

Figure 2.1 Pablo Picasso, *Les demoiselles d'Avignon* (1907)
Source: Courtesy of Museum of Modern Art. Acquired through the Lillie P. Bliss bequest. New York/Scala, Florence

The same applies, of course, also to a good number of verbal avantgarde works of art. Extreme examples abound in Dadaist works, for instance in Hugo Ball's famous poem "Gadji beri bimba." Here is the third and final stanza:

    tuffm im zimbrabim negramai bumbalo negramai bumbalo tuffm
      i zim
    gadjama bimbala oo beri gadjama gaga di gadjama affalo pinx
    gaga di bumbalo bumbalo gadjamen
    gaga di bling blong
    gaga blung

Sound poems like Ball's incorporate vaguely African forms of sounding and morphemes alluding to the continent to restage the destruction of meaning that the First World War has already wrought even as they reinvent language beyond reference. In Ball's poem as in Picasso's painting, it is the merging of Western and non-Western linguistic, musical, and sculptural *forms* that allows Western artists to 'make it new.'

Mead's poetry betrays an awareness of her modernist contemporaries' experiments in form. She does this, for instance, when she writes a four-line poem entitled "Caution to Beauty" and labels it "a fragment." In another poem, she engages in a modest typographical experiment: on a typescript sheet entitled "Fragments," we find two lines, followed by eight lines set off by a line break, which are in turn followed by another six lines that are set off by around eight line breaks:

> The hills held the first color of spring
> Woven of a thousand promised leaves.
>
> The spring sun sifted through the boughs
> Of naked trees that only barred his course,
> But caught in every spice-bush flower
> Transmuted gold, the only thing
> In that wood adequate to hold
> The sun's bright glory. Sleeping trees
> Unbending sloughed the sunset light
> From off their trunks.
>
>
> The sun has made his orisons,
> Now lights the sky's bright hue;
> The first sweet scents of morning
> Are upgathered with the dew,
> And standing waist-deep in the corn
> I await the sight of you.

Whether read as one fragmented poem or as a collection of individual pieces, Mead here makes use of a core modernist device: the fragment. Of course, these partially rhymed lines about spring are nowhere near as experimental or playful as, say, E.E. Cummings's spring poem "in Just—" but they do testify to Mead's awareness and moderate use of poetic techniques that major modernists writers also employed. In yet another, undated and unpublished poem entitled "Madonna of the Breakfast Table," Mead ends her encomium on the poetic addressee's beauty with these lines:

> But morning finds, my glance a quarry,
> Turning in a swift despair
> From the lovely incongruity
> Of your beauty sitting there
> With the starlight still upon you
> And the moon caught in your hair,
> Cutting up the breakfast bacon,
> In the this [sic] stilled and mortal air.

With its end rhymes, its use of conventional tropes, and its praise of a woman's beauty, Mead's poem breaks no new literary ground. No linguistic iconoclast is she. In many ways, this text is worlds apart from canonized modernist poems. This is also true for the thematic issues her poems broach: a majority of them revolve around deeply personal themes such as emotional and physical pain (e.g. "The Penciling of Pain," "The Absence of Pain," "A Tale of Pain"); despair (e.g., "No More Need to Smile," "Desolation"); loss (e.g., "Hollow Heart," "After the Anger Was Over"); loneliness (e.g., "In a Charred Place," "Desire Is a Knife," "Guerdon of Solitude"); death (e.g., "The Fourth Companion," "Unmarked Grave"); alienation (e.g., "On Seeing Rodger Bloomer, May 1923"); dreams (e.g., "As a Dream," "The Way of Dreams"); and, above all, love—both fulfilled and unrequited (e.g., "Economy of Love," "Powerless Roots," "Star Bread," "For Complete Possession," "Dreamer's Penance," "Green Sanctuary," "Wounded"). Much of Mead's poetry fits Earl Miner's description of modern lyrical poetry as "a type of poetry which is mechanically representational of a musical architecture and which is thematically representational of the poet's sensibility as evidenced in a fusion of conception and image" (Miner 715). Susan Stewart's discussion of 'the lyric' fits Mead's poetry even better: she defines it as verse that is "associated with the expression of the senses out of first-person experience" (296). Mead's verse certainly does not fit Eliot's impersonal theory of poetic production according to which "[p]oetry is not a turning loose of emotion, but an escape from emotion; it is not the expression of personality, but an escape from personality" ("Tradition" 43). Other poems of hers such as "Lines to Charon" and "Aliter" delve into Greek mythology, while still others, such as "Cottager's Request," "Judas Iscariot," "Rose Tree of Assisi," "Ecstasy Neglected," and "Good Friday 1923" draw on traditional Christian topoi. Yet other poems explore the natural world (e.g., "Kind Timothy Hay," "The Valley's Benison," "Storm Loveliness,"); transience (e.g., "This Breath"); the modern city (e.g., "Disillusionment"); and prostitution (e.g., "The Prostitute's Requiem").

And yet, despite these notable and clear differences between Mead's poetry and canonized modernist verse, the penultimate line of "Madonna of the Breakfast Table" is reminiscent of that famous third line in Eliot's "The Love Song of J. Alfred Prufrock":

> Let us go then, you and I,
> When the evening is spread out against the sky
> Like a patient etherized upon a table;

Both poems set up readers' expectations concerning love poetry only to thwart them. Moreover, both already announce modernist dissonance in their titles: in Mead's seating of the Madonna at a mundane breakfast table; in Eliot's choice to give the singer of the unsung love song the comically stilted name of J. Alfred Prufrock. Mead seems aware of what other contemporary poets are doing and tries to modernize herself too.

The point here is not to argue that Mead is either as iconoclastic or as great a poet as Eliot. While I join the canon revisionists with a healthy dose of skepticism toward the idea of literary greatness, I think it is safe to say that Mead is not as good a poet as Eliot. From this comparison, it is Eliot who emerges as "il miglior fabbro"—the title he bestowed on Pound in the dedication prefacing *The Waste Land*. What John Berryman wrote about that brutal third line of Eliot's "Prufrock" no critic in their right mind would write about Mead's verse: "With this line, modern poetry begins" (270). Likewise, while such breaks with readers' expectations are rare in Mead's poetry, they are a crucial part of Eliot's poetic project. Consider the first two lines of the four poems that make up his "Preludes" (1917), all of which employ bathos and readily conform to the "Prufrock" pattern:

I

The winter evening settles down
With smell of steaks in passageways.

II

The morning comes to consciousness
Of faint stale smells of beer

III

You tossed a blanket from the bed,
You lay upon your back, and waited;

IV

> His soul stretched tight across the skies
> That fade behind a city block,

Here and in the first three lines of "Prufrock," Eliot puts into practice what he calls for in "Tradition and the Individual Talent" (1919): In order to write truly new poetry, the individual talent must first work himself through the tradition.[19] Louis Menand puts it nicely in an essay published in *The New Yorker* in 2011: "What was important for Pound and Eliot was that the bones of the old are legible (or visible or audible) under the contemporary skin. That's what produces the modernist dissonance" (80). So this is how, to quote Pound's characterization of Eliot in a letter to Harriet Monroe, Eliot "modernized himself."[20] Mead's poetic oeuvre shows no such consistent attempt at self-modernization.

So far, I have identified two reasons for Mead's very modest attempts at formal innovation: her privileging of the salvage imperative over primitivist rejuvenation and her more limited craft. There is yet a third reason why Mead is a reticent renewer of the English language: she quite simply does not trust language. Mead makes this explicit in her 1924 poem "Warning":

> Give not thy treasured vision
> To the custody of words,
> As soon lay thy first-born
> On drawn swords.
>
> Words are avid to betray thee,
> Conspiring to the last
> To besmirch this bright adventure
> With things past.
>
> Rudely fingering the uniqueness
> This one hour has for thee,
> Confusing it with others, muddied
> By eternity.
>
> But take instead a palate [*sic*];
> Colors own no guilty past,
> Mixed anew in this thy moment,
> See, they last.
>
> Wouldst thou find another casket
> Than thy all remembering heart,
> Choose colors, but from old words
> Stay apart.

Clearly, "Warning" is an ethnographic poem in which Mead reflects on anthropologists' choices of media for recording other cultures. For her, words are weighed down by their historical and cultural heritage, making them dubious tools for capturing the differentness of another culture. This is why all words are "old words."[21] As she puts it in *Balinese Character: A Photographic Analysis* (1942), an early work in visual anthropology that she co-authored with Gregory Bateson,

> Most serious of all, we know this about the relationship between culture and verbal concepts—that the words which one culture has invested with meaning are by the very accuracy of their cultural fit, singularly inappropriate as vehicles for precise comment upon another culture.
> (Bateson and Mead xi)

Thus, instead of acknowledging, as Eliot did, the weight and value of the tradition that European languages retain, and instead of working through the tradition to reinvent the language, Mead gives preference to another medium. In this poem, that other medium is painting ('palate' is an obvious misspelling of 'palette'). In her ethnographic work, she likewise privileges visual media, particularly photography and film, which Mead fought hard to make respectable tools of anthropology, a discipline she critically labelled 'a discipline of words.' For Mead, images lack the historical and cultural baggage that weigh down words; images are able to give direct, unmediated, and objective access to the real. This is, of course, less than true, but this is how Mead sees it when she writes, again in *Balinese Character*, that "each single photograph" in this multimedia book "may be regarded as almost purely objective," adding that "the objectivity of the photographs themselves justifies some freedom in the writing of the captions" (53) that accompany them on the facing pages of *Balinese Character*. Mead strikes a similar note in her lively and contentious discussion with Bateson in the appropriately titled piece "For God's Sake, Margaret." In her determined response to Bateson voicing exasperation with the constraints that "cameras on tripods" impose on ethnographic filmmakers, and in opposition to his contention that "the photographic record should be an art form" (Brand 39),[22] Mead says,

> I think it's very important, if you're going to be scientific about behavior, to give other people access to the material, as comparable as possible to the access you had. You don't, then, alter the material. There's a bunch of filmmakers now that are saying, "It should be art," and wrecking everything that we're trying to do. Why the hell should it be art?
> (Brand 40)

As Reichel shows, in maintaining a clear distinction between science and art, Mead is less of a forerunner of the *Writing Culture* debate than is often asserted (*Writing* 168–70). It is in her programmatic essay "Visual Anthropology in a Discipline of Words," a foundational text in the history of visual anthropology, that Mead explains why anthropologists need to use recording instruments beyond "a pencil and a notebook" (4). Already in the essay's long first sentence, she reminds her readers of the urgency of the anthropological endeavor:

> Anthropology, as a conglomerate of disciplines—variously named and constituted in different countries as cultural anthropology, social anthropology, ethnology, ethnography, archaeology, linguistics, physical anthropology, folklore, social history, and human geography—has both implicitly and explicitly accepted the responsibility of making and preserving records of the vanishing customs and human beings of this earth, whether these peoples be inbred, preliterate populations isolated in some tropical jungle, or in the depths of a Swiss canton, or in the mountains of an Asian kingdom.
>
> (3)

Writing from the depths of a Swiss canton, I note that Mead here once more gives expression to the salvage imperative that we have already seen at work in "The Need That Is Left." To stay true to the salvage mission, Mead argues, the supposedly more objective media of photography and film are far more suitable tools than pencil and notebook; they are "instrumentation that can provide masses of objective materials" (10). No wonder, then, that Mead's poems do not work very hard at reinventing the language, a medium that she considers deficient and inadequate, as too subjective and too freighted with the anthropologist's culture and its past. Instead, Mead works hard to reinvent her own discipline as a discipline beyond words.

In another respect, though, there is a clear convergence between Mead's and the modernists' projects. Like the modernists, Mead puts her exploration of other cultures in the service of cultural critique. Like them, she ultimately aims at the renewal of her own culture. However, for reasons outlined above, Mead's cultural critique takes very different forms. Mead, the social scientist, aims at social reform and in that project, the foreign cultures that she explores do not serve as sources for the West's linguistic or spiritual rejuvenation. Instead, they function—as do the Zuni in Benedict's *Patterns of Culture*—as foils that help Westerners first observe and then remedy defects of their own culture.

This already becomes clear in *Coming of Age in Samoa* (1928). Subtitled *A Psychological Study of Primitive Youth for Western Civilization*, Mead's equally famous and infamous first book wears its primitivism literally on its sleeve and engages in it very liberally throughout.[23] The book's second chapter "II. A Day in Samoa" (the first, really, since it comes after "I. Introduction") provides an eloquent panoramic overview of Samoan culture that introduces the reader to "lovers slip[ping] home from trysts beneath the palm trees or in the shadow of beached canoes" (12), to "[g]irls" that "stop to giggle over some young ne'er-do-well who escaped during the night from an angry father's pursuit" (12–13), to "[h]alf-clad, unhurried women, with babies at their breasts" (13) and, in the wee hours, "the mellow thunder of the reef and the whisper of lovers, as the village rests until dawn" (15). Rife as the book is with primitivist depictions of Samoan life ("A Day in Samoa" is a textbook example of primitivism in the history of cultural anthropology), and peppered as it is with appreciative assessments of Samoan culture, where "growing up" is "so easy, so simple a matter" (137), Mead stops short of urging her fellow Americans to adopt Samoan social practices or cultural forms. Instead, she uses her book's final two chapters ("XIII. Our Educational Problems in the Light of Samoan Contrasts" and "XIV. Education for Choice"), which she added upon her publisher William Morrow's request, to report on the lessons American readers should draw from her Samoan research. What Mead found in her research is that adolescence is an unproblematic phase in the lives of Samoan youths, a phase unattended by the tantrums and violent mood swings that American observers (and I) readily associate with adolescence. Mead's explanation for the difference is that, compared to the complexity of U.S. American culture, Samoa has a simple culture with strictly defined social roles that does not force adolescents to choose between a multiplicity of options. "[F]or the explanation of the lack of conflict" during Samoan puberty, Mead writes, "we must look principally to the difference between a simple, homogenous primitive civilisation, a civilisation which changes so slowly that to each generation it appears static, and a motley, diverse, heterogeneous modern civilisation" (142).

Mead returns to her dyadic conception of culture in her 1924 sonnet "America":

> She thrusts into her children's hands
> A bunching of rattling keys,
> And bids them use them as they will
> To unlock life's mysteries.
> These slender keys seem crudely made,
> The brittle edges new and thin,
> And drearily they clatter
> With the disonance [sic] of tin.
>
> Far other had each several key,
> Seemed to an anxious questing eye
> When viewed in separateness beneath

> Some sunny foreign sky.
> Then had it seemed a golden key,
> Wrought in grave coherency.

Mead's poetic negotiation of another culture strikes a markedly different tone than "The Need That Is Left": Instead of expressing salvage nostalgia, it taps into the energies of another culture, using it as a foil to stage a critique of the self. The poem's first stanza allegorizes the nation as a mother that gives her children "slender keys" that "seem crudely made" and "clatter/With the disonance [sic] of tin." By way of contrast, the second stanza asserts that "each several key" when "viewed in separateness beneath/Some sunny foreign sky" had "seemed a golden key,/Wrought in grave coherency." I read the keys as figures for education—cultural tools that allow youths to understand the cultures they live in, to "unlock life's mysteries," as Mead puts it in her poem. In the first stanza, the keys are in a jumble, a "bunching of rattling keys"; in the second, each of the keys is viewed separately, i.e., analyzed. Mead leaves it open whether all of her poem's keys are 'American' or whether we are dealing with two types of keys: American and foreign ones. In the first reading, the "brittle" keys "clatter" only within the confines of the United States, when their meaning is obscured in the thicket of a complex culture, but appear in all their clarity and become fully functional when viewed from the analytic distance that exposure to a foreign culture brings. In the second reading, only the keys of the first stanza are American—irredeemably "rattling," "slender," and "brittle" keys compared to the "golden" keys that unlock the mysteries of a simpler, more coherent culture. In both readings, the other culture functions as the foil that lets the poetic speaker see her own culture more clearly. In disciplinary terms: The ethnographic study of another culture feeds back into cultural self-reflection, letting Americans perceive what the penultimate chapter of *Coming of Age in Samoa* announces: "Our Educational Problems in the Light of Samoan Contrasts."

In Mead's account, Western youths' excess of options is a burden on them that creates the psychological and familial strains of Western adolescence. This reasoning leads Mead to her major (and contested) claim: that adolescence is a cultural, not a biological fact.[24] The advice Mead gives to her American readers in the final two chapters of *Coming of Age in Samoa* is not to return to a simpler, more rigidly ordered social organization. Instead, she invites them to consider how healthy the American model of the nuclear family is, to rethink core principles of American education and sexual morality, and to train, as the title of her final chapter has it, American youths for the choices they will have to make in the course of their lives:

> They must be taught that many ways are open to them, no one sanctioned above its alternative, and that upon them and upon them

alone lies the burden of choice. Unhampered by prejudices, unvexed by too early conditioning to any one standard, they must come clear-eyed to the choices which lie before them.

(169)

To alleviate American youths' stress and anxieties in the face of a complex, heterogeneous society criss-crossed by competing behavioral norms and belief systems, "we must turn all our educational efforts to training our children for the choices which will confront them" (169). In Mead's cross-cultural comparison, Samoa serves as the simpler foil to the stress-inducing complexity of American modernity. Against this foil, the defects of U.S. culture come into sharp focus. In Mead's own words,

> Realising that our own ways are not humanly inevitable nor God-ordained, but are the fruit of a long and turbulent history, we may well examine in turn all of our institutions, thrown into strong relief against the history of other civilisations, and weighing them in the balance, be not afraid to find them wanting.
>
> (160)

Mead was a social scientist determined to put empirical research in the service of providing solutions to real-world social problems. Driven by such progressivist convictions—which she inherited from her mother, a sociologist and social reformer, and her father, a political economist with a keen sense of the practical implications of his research—Mead readily embraced the role of public intellectual to address an astonishingly broad range of topics relevant to American society, including the atom bomb, space exploration, the public perception of scientists, generational conflicts, student protests, race relations, women's rights, education, environmental pollution, poverty, sexuality, old age, and child nutrition. And this is also why she gladly took on multiple public roles, from her work for United Nations organizations, to her presidency of the American Anthropological Association, of the American Association for the Advancement of Science, and her multiple appearances before Congress.[25]

During and after World War II, Mead joined other U.S. social scientists in contributing to the war effort. In 1942, she published *And Keep Your Powder Dry: An Anthropologist Looks at America*, a widely read study of American national character.[26] Some of her war-related activities produced peculiar results. As the executive secretary of the National Research Council's Committee on Food Habits, she searched for solutions to nutrition issues in war zones. In this line of work, Mead contributed to the report "Food and Morale" (1942), which contained lists of essential foods for people of various national origins. Here is an excerpt from the "Condiments" list:

Chinese:	soy sauce, bean sprouts, fresh ginger roots
Mexicans:	chili, peppers
Porto [sic] Ricans:	chili peppers, saffron
Scandinavians:	caraway seeds
Jews:	pickles, poppy seeds
Syrians:	grape leaves, olive oil, nutmeg, ginger

(National Research Council Committee)

Around 1940, she and Bateson also developed a board game coming out of their government work. The game, which is designed to teach some of the fundamental contrasts between dictatorships and democracies, contains cards such as the following:

DICTATOR!

CRIPPLED INDUSTRIES

You have put your leading industrialists into concentration camps.

(lose a card in 5)

DEMOCRACY!

CORRUPTION IN INDUSTRIES

Graft and profiteering turn out
badly made products which are
too expensive.

(lose a card in 5)   (Mead and Bateson)

As Mead noted, "Ideally, for propaganda purposes it should be played by the whole family with Papa explaining the points." Mead and Bateson sought to sell the game to Parker Brothers but were unsuccessful.

Mead did not shy away from social engineering either as she sought to remedy gender inequality by "finding a groundplan for building a society that would substitute real differences for arbitrary ones" so as to "permit the development of many contrasting temperamental gifts in each sex"

(*Sex and Temperament* 217). As she writes at the end of her introduction to *Balinese Character*,

> [W]e have to reorient the old values of many contrasting and contradictory cultural systems into a new form which will use but transcend them all, draw on their respective strengths and allow for their respective weaknesses. We have to build a culture richer and more rewarding than any that the world has ever seen. This can only be done through a disciplined science of human relations and such a science is built by drawing out from very detailed, concrete materials, such as these, the relevant abstractions—the vocabulary which will help us to plan an integrated world.
>
> (Bateson and Mead xvi)

Mead wrote these words in 1942, stressing that knowledge of other cultures can help Americans rethink and reshape their culture into what Boasians such as Sapir, Mead, and Benedict valued most: An "integrated world" that is, in Sydel Silverman's apt characterization of Sapir's notion of cultural integration, "harmonious, vital, organic, and attuned to individual creativity" (264). Mead most intensely contributed to domestic debates in the wake of WWII but the progressivist worldview that informs her interventions is already clearly visible in her first book: "If adolescents are only plunged into difficulties and distress because of conditions in their social environment, then by all means let us so modify that environment as to reduce this stress and eliminate this strain and anguish of adjustment" (*Samoa* 161). Both her ethnographic scholarship and her poems testify to this progressivist project, bearing witness to a desire to make it new, differently. For Mead, the 'it' in 'make it new' is neither language nor spirit but U.S. society.

That this combined project of cultural critique and social change enlists another culture should come as no surprise for those who know that Pound's famous phrase "Make It New" itself derives from a historical anecdote dating from the Shang dynasty (1766–1753 BCE) told in the *Da Xue*, a Chinese book of Confucian wisdom that Pound translated. We learn this from Michael North's insightful retelling of the origins of Pound's phrase in *Novelty: A History of the New* (162–71). The point I have tried to make in this section is different from North's, though. For him, the Pound case serves as one of the book's many memorable examples that reveal the historicity of the new. For me, what is most noteworthy about Pound's recourse to Confucianism is not that the most iconic of all modernist calls for novelty retains intimate ties with the old. For me, it is Pound's search for the new in the cultural other that is most striking, linking the spiritus rector of American literary modernism to a minor poet and major anthropologist who strove to reinvent the social world. As Mead puts it near the end of her introduction to her and Bateson's *Balinese Character*, "we are faced with the problem of building a new world" (Bateson and Mead xvi).

Toward an Anthropology of the Senses

The 1924 poem "Warning" is among the earliest texts by Mead that reflects on the epistemological and ethical consequences of media usage, thus foreshadowing her dedication to disciplinary innovation. Mead wrote "Warning" in the year before she journeyed to American Samoa. Soon after she had arrived on the island, she wrote another poem, the unpublished "Monuments Rejected," and a field note that deepened the earlier poem's inquiry into the social effects that media produce and supplemented it with early forays into the anthropology of the senses.

There are five typescript versions of "Monuments Rejected," three of which end with a note on the poem's place and date of composition. Here is the full text of the poem as it is available in folder 10 of box Q15 of the Margaret Mead Papers at the Library of Congress—one of the three neat versions with near-identical wording and no handwritten revisions.

> The race of men who built in stone
> Were blind to all earth's loveliness,
> Their only thought was where to leave
> Stones in the blossoming wilderness.
>
> And while you sojourn in my heart,
> You take no comfort in the flower-starred sod,
> Eyes closed and scheming how you may
> Clear ground for altars to your God.
>
> Mine is no northern landscape, cold,
> Where great fields lie, arid and waste,
> For arrogant travelers to build
> Pretentious temples sculptured to their taste.
>
> My flowers are for no moving scythe;
> They bloom for joyousness alone,
> And lightly shrink from hands that seek
> To smother them with heavy stone.
>
> So kiss the flowers, and cease to weep!
> In southern gardens there's no way
> To crush while loving and so leave
> A temple there to mark your stay.
>
> Pago Pago,
> September 1, 1925.

Mead indicates that she wrote this poem in the territorial capital of American Samoa. She had arrived in Pago Pago only the day before (Bowman-Kruhm 34), choosing the capital as the site where she prepared for the actual fieldwork that she did on the island of Ta'ū. Mead would report on this research in *Coming of Age in Samoa*.

To whom the "race of men who built in stone" refers is not entirely clear but we may hear echoes of Mead's initial sense of disappointment upon arriving, first, in Honolulu, her last stop on the way to American Samoa, then in Pago Pago itself. As her ship approaches Honolulu harbor on August 11, 1925, Mead notes:

> We woke up this morning at five with land in sight and everyone excited except me. I was blue and disgruntled because I was blue. It seemed a poor fashion to be greeting the Paradise of the Pacific.
>
> Eleanor Dillingham and I watched the ship come into harbor, rounding point after point of rugged clay-colored mountains. There was no color in the landscape, occasional patches of green showed as pale gray. The city itself was hardly resting on the sea, and the wandering mists, which seemed extensions of the clouds which covered the tops of the mountains, hid all the signs of industrial civilization. Two huge straight smokestacks became silver towers with white highlights on one side.
>
> (*Letters* 24)

Her first sensory impressions of Pago Pago as she arrives there on August 31, 1925—the day before she wrote "Monuments Rejected"— are rendered in a similar tone:

> We got in early this morning at daybreak, a cloudy daybreak, with the sun appearing sullenly for a moment and the surf showing white along the shores of the steep black cliffs as we entered the 'only land-locked harbor in the South Seas.' The harbor is the one-time crater of a volcano and the sides are almost perpendicular. It is densely wooded down to the sea and ringed with palm trees along the narrow beach. The Navy have really done nobly in preserving the native tone; their houses are low green-roofed affairs which cluster under the trees much as the native houses do; only the radio stations and one smokestack really damage the scene.
>
> The presence of the fleet today skews the whole picture badly. There are numerous battleships in the harbor and on all sides of the island, mostly not in the harbor because they make the water oily and spoil the governor's bathing. Airplanes scream overhead; the band of some ship is constantly playing ragtime. All the natives on the island and many from Manu'a and Apia are here, laden with *kava* bowls, tapa, grass skirts, models of outrigger canoes, bead necklaces and baskets. They are spread out in the *malae*—market

place—with whole families contentedly munching their lunches around them.

(*Letters* 25–26; emphasis in original)

While the first passage records Mead's visual impressions, the second is more densely sensuous as it gives expression to both the sights she sees and the sounds she hears. In both, Mead's recording of her sensory perceptions sets up oppositions between the paradisiacal character of a foreign, potentially pastoral world ("the Paradise of the Pacific", the volcano, the palms, and "whole families contentedly munching their lunches" in the *malae*) and the technological-industrial disruption of paradise. It is not only the unpleasant sights she sees (the smokestack, the radio stations, and the battleships) and the jarring sounds she hears (the screaming airplanes, ragtime) that "ske[w] the whole picture badly." Mead's emotional disposition ("I was blue and disgruntled because I was blue") and the weather conditions (the mists and the clouds) likewise impact the ethnographer's perception of a foreign world. Both passages testify to David Howes's assertion that Mead was "among the first true predecessors of the 'anthropology of the senses,' as this field would come to be known in the 1990s" (*Sensual Relations* 10), not only because she takes great care to document the sensuous qualities of other cultures but also because she highlights the ethnographer's sensory experience of those cultures and invites us to reflect on the factors that affect this experience. Finally, in singling out the governor and the U.S. Navy as causes of the technological-industrial intrusion into paradise, Mead also stresses the colonial nature of that intrusion. When Mead arrived in Pago Pago at the end of August 1925, American Samoa was under administrative control of the U.S. Navy, which it had been since 1899, when Samoa was divided between Germany and the United States, eastern Samoa came under American rule, and U.S. President William McKinley placed the island group under the Navy's authority (Wendt and Foster).

In "Monuments Rejected," Mead combines images from three realms—anthropology, religion, and gender—to stage a critique of various forms of taking possession. As Mead does in many of her ethnographic poems—"The Need That Is Left" (1927), "I Have Prepared a Place for You" (1928), and "Traveler's Faith" (1925) are three examples—she interweaves the public and the private, the cultural and the personal. In her poem's third stanza, she specifies that the first line's "race of men" are "arrogant travelers." Who are these travelers? To American(ist) readers of this American writer's poem, the travelers' blindness to "all earth's loveliness" in the face of a "blossoming wilderness" renders them akin to the first Puritan settlers, who saw but a "hideous and desolate wilderness, full of wild beasts and wild men" (Bradford 62)[27] instead of the marvels and wonders that Columbus described in his first letter to the Spanish court.[28] Their desire "to build/Pretentious temples sculptured to their taste" likewise suggests that we are dealing with religiously minded intruders, though not necessarily the Puritans, who are hardly a temple-building people. The English, American, and French missionaries who successfully Christianized the Pacific Islands since 1797, when the London Missionary Society sent its first party to Tahiti (Wendt and Foster), emerge as more immediate historical reference points for "[t]he race of men who built in stone." In present-day American Samoa, where Mead wrote her poem, the first representatives of the London Missionary Society arrived in the 1830s (Wendt and Foster). These Congregationalist proselytizers were followed by missionaries from other denominations, primarily Methodists and Catholics, who like the Congregationalists, sought access to power by converting Indigenous chiefs (John Williams's conversion of Samoan chief Malietoa Vainu'upo is the most famous example), recruited local missionaries to spread the gospel, and had churches built on the islands (Ernst and Anisi). It may well be those missionaries that Mead's poetic speaker accuses of "scheming how you may/Clear ground for altars to your God." At the same time, the poem's critique is, of course, of a more general nature, censuring the taking of foreign lands more broadly. What is clear is that the poem draws a sharp contrast between two actors: Those who, "blind" to the beauty of the earth, and with their "[e]yes closed," build rigid, lifeless structures that take up space and those who remain aware of the sensuous fullness of the land, of "earth's loveliness," "the blossoming wilderness," and "the flower-starred sod." What is also clear is that the arrogant travelers come from the north—a space that the poem characterizes, in Eliotesque fashion, as "cold," "arid," and "waste"—while the potential victims of northern intrusion live "[i]n southern gardens." Mead opposes a barren northern culture of stones to a lush southern culture of flowers. These geographical specifications clearly situate the encounter between the two actors in a colonial context, and the poem takes the northern intruders to task, talking back to them—a fact that is underscored by an early title that Mead chose for the poem: "South to North."[29]

But who is it that talks back to the north? Who is the poem's persona? Mead's use of sexually charged flower imagery in the final two stanzas embeds itself in a powerful female artistic tradition that associates flowers with women's anatomy and sexuality, from Emily Dickinson's flower and bee poems to Georgia O'Keeffe's flower paintings and beyond. Mead's use of this imagery strongly suggests that the poem's persona is a woman—a woman who, moreover, lays claim to a heightened sensitivity to the sensuous fullness of the south. What this woman renounces from the third stanza onward is attempts to take possession of her body, a threat that the poem expresses through its violent imagery of deflowering: "My flowers are for no moving scythe," the persona declares, adding that she resists any attempt "[t]o crush while loving." What the poem opposes to the threat of sexual domination and violation is the vision of more loving and more sensual forms of bodily encounter, where "flowers . . . bloom for joyousness alone" and the poem's addressee is invited to "kiss the flowers" rather than taking possession of them and "leav[ing]/A temple there to mark your stay." One does not have to share Mead's psychoanalytical inclinations to conclude that the "southern gardens" of the poem's final stanza are both a geographical and a corporeal marker. Ultimately, the analogy that the text sets up is that between colonial and sexual domination, between the taking of land and the taking of the female body. In regendering the first line's supposedly gender-neutral "race of men" the poem takes aim at both.

Significantly, the poem's vision of harmonious 'southern' bodily encounters returns with force in the book that came out of the fieldwork that Mead was about to begin when she wrote "Monuments Rejected." The second chapter of *Coming of Age in Samoa* already sets the tone as it introduces the reader to the sensuous richness of another culture that Mead presents as more simple, more coherent, more harmonious, and more sensual than her own. The opposition that Mead draws in "Monuments Rejected" between an oppressive, cold, and arid north and a harmonious, fertile, and sensual south returns in different guise in the final two chapters of *Coming of Age in Samoa*, in which she uses Samoan culture, where "[s]ex" is, apparently, "a natural, pleasurable thing" (139) and "casual sex relations carry no onus of strong attachment" (145) as a foil, inviting her American readers to reconsider not only sexual morality but also the model of the nuclear family and the education of American youths. What neither Mead's poem nor her ethnographic study explore to any significant extent is what both the *Writing Culture* debate and the current questioning of anthropologists' right to speak for other subjects and cultures have taught anthropologists: that the cultural relativists' fascination with supposedly simpler cultures, which the poem's sensuous richness gives expression to, was itself in danger of doing the work of domination and reification of "arrogant travelers."[30] Thus, for twenty-first-century readers, the northern blindness that the poem takes to task is at least partially also its Boasian author's own. In both the poem and Mead's first ethnographic study, sexually charged evocations of southern sensuousness take discursive possession of Samoan culture, othering and instrumentalizing it for the critique of 'northern' ways.

Let me return to Mead's sense of disappointment as she first encountered the sights and sounds of Honolulu and Pago Pago. As if trying to assuage the initial letdown, Mead supplements her first impressions with an even fuller account of these places' sensuous richness and her experience of that richness:

> If modern wanderers are to repeat the thrills which early travelers experienced, they will have to cultivate the much neglected senses of taste and smell. The movies and the phonograph have effectually eliminated the other two senses and touch doesn't seem to have

much of a role here. But taste and smell are still untampered with by Asia and Pathé News. And here alone I get my real sense of being in a strange land. The morning I landed in Honolulu, I had papaya for breakfast and Honolulu will always taste like papaya with Chinese oranges. Samoa tastes like papaya without Chinese oranges. There is a great difference here. Papaya and coconut oil and taro, that tasteless yet individual carbohydrate, serve for taste and the frangipani blossoms with their heavy oppressive odor for smell, mixed on the warm breeze with the odor of slightly fermented overripe bananas, an odor which is like bee-stung grapes.

(*Letters* 28)

Written in Tutuila on September 27, 1925, twenty-seven days after she had arrived on American Samoa, this is a remarkable passage, for at least two reasons. First, it deftly shifts the focus from sight and hearing to the less studied senses of smell and taste, senses that, together with touch, have traditionally been seen as lower senses that connect us with animals. As Susan Stewart reminds us,

In medieval and Renaissance topoi overall, the domain of smell, touch, and taste is properly a domain of beasts. This rhetoric of the animal and servile senses, aside from its obvious legitimating force for philosophical abstraction, establishes a subjectivity separated from nature, protected by mediation, and propelled by a desire born out of the very estranged relation thus created. . . . Later Elizabethan and Baroque erotic poetry, as we shall see, often plays on Petrarchan idealizations of sight and hearing and at the same time makes witty, satirical uses of the lower senses of taste, smell, and touch.

(19)

Mead deftly disrupts such hierarchies of the senses, which rank the senses "in relation to their degree of immediacy" (21).[31] A second remarkable feature of the Mead quote above is that it is so very open about its own embeddedness in colonial discourse. What sets a text such as this apart from both the accounts of "early travelers" (or, indeed, the "arrogant travelers" of "Monuments Rejected") and our three Boasians' exploration of sense perception in their ethnographic poems is that it contains the seeds of an anthropology of the senses. Thirty-nine years before Marshall McLuhan would define "the 'message' of any medium or technology" as "the change of scale or pace or pattern that it introduces into human affairs" (8), Mead notes that the introduction of new media radically affects the relationships and hierarchies between the senses. Thus, even before she and Bateson started experimenting with photography and film, Mead reflects on the "distribution of the sensible"—the proper domain of aesthetics, according to Jacques Rancière—across different media.[32] As she will state in her introduction to *Balinese Character*

(1942) the ethnographer's intention is to capture the life of a people in all its sensuous richness:

> This is not a book about Balinese custom, but about the Balinese—about the way in which they, as living persons, moving, standing, eating, sleeping, dancing, and going into trance, embody that abstraction which (after we have abstracted it) we technically call culture.
>
> (Bateson and Mead xii)

What Mead first explores in her field note from 1925, she and Rhoda Métraux would, in *The Study of Culture at a Distance* (1953), insist that the anthropologist seek to capture:

> the student must be able to move from one set of clues to another, so that if he has a painting that shows the costumes worn in a period, a list of expenditures for stuffs, a list of the foods that were sold in the shops, a few bars of religious music, he will be able to *see*, *hear*, and *smell* a thronged medieval street down which a Whitsunday procession passed.
>
> (12; emphases in original)

Mead's inquiry into the epistemological value of all the senses (except, in this specific case, touch) in her 1925 field note reminds us just how closely the development of visual anthropology is related to first stirrings in the history of sensory anthropology. It is early observations such as these that prepared the ground for Mead and Métraux's later, more sustained investigation of the senses, which would allow them to develop a tentative sensory anthropology which recognizes that the human use of smell and taste is "equally systematic" as that of sight and hearing and should be studied as such, for instance through analyses of other cultures' popular media.[33] In our three Boasians' oeuvre, it is in the sensuous richness of Mead's field notes; in their reflections on the relations between anthropology, media, and the senses; and in the literary negotiation of sensory experience in aesthetic objects such as Mead's "Monuments Rejected" that we can find first intimations of such an anthropology as aesthetics in the original sense of the word. If Handler is correct in arguing (as I think he is) that "the essential elements of Sapir's culture theory . . . were elaborated in Sapir's literary and poetic practice between 1916 and 1922" ("Sapir's Poetic Experience" 416), we should add that all three Boasians wrote poetry that explored the aesthetic question of the relation between sensing and knowing well before any one of them theorized it in their anthropological work.

The Public and the Private, In and Out of Verse

It is intriguing to see how early on and how confidently Mead comments on the social effects of media. Mead was twenty-three years old when she wrote about the effects of "[t]he movies and the phonograph." Though she would gain a good deal of publicity and notoriety in response to her publication of *Coming of Age in Samoa* three years later, she was still two decades away from becoming the celebrity she became after WWII. But already here, in this early field note, she displays a keen awareness of the power of the mass media—an awareness that she would channel into a multi-pronged, multi-generic, and multimedia effort to make her voice heard, her image seen, and her writing read well beyond the confines of academia.

Arguably, Mead is the best-known anthropologist of the twentieth century, and she took an active part in shaping her public stature. Early on, she decided to intervene in public debates when, upon her publisher's request, she added two concluding chapters to *Coming of Age of Samoa* that harness insights she gained during her Samoan fieldwork to give advice on American child-rearing. As Susan Hegeman notes in "American Popular Social Science: The Boasian Legacy" (2018), Mead thus inscribes herself into a Boasian tradition of popular social science that includes, among other texts, Boas's *The Mind of Primitive Man* (1911) and *Anthropology and Modern Life* (1928); Elsie Clews Parsons's *The Old-Fashioned Woman* (1913), *Fear and Conventionality* (1914), *Social Freedom* (1915), and *Social Rule* (1916); Benedict's *Patterns of Culture* (1934) and *The Chrysanthemum and the Sword* (1946); and Zora Neale Hurston's *Mules and Men* (1935) and *Tell My Horse* (1938). When Mead added those two chapters to *Coming of Age in Samoa*, she was twenty-seven years old, and she would continue to contribute to popular social science with widely-read books such as *Growing up in New Guinea: A Comparative Study of Primitive Education* (1930); *Sex and Temperament in Three Primitive Societies* (1935); and her study of American national character, *And Keep Your Powder Dry: An Anthropologist Looks at America* (1942). Of all the Boasians, it was Mead who most prominently inserted herself into public debates, rendering her the most broadly recognized spokesperson for Boasian cultural relativism and a major force in making 'culture' a household term and a key concept in the humanities and social sciences.[34] Mead fired on all channels, availing herself of a multiplicity of genres and media in her public interventions: from publishing a children's book, *People and Places* (1959); to contributing, together with Métraux, a regular column to the *Redbook* women's magazine (1962–1978);[35] to giving multiple newspaper, radio, and television interviews; to sharing her cultural observations on two record albums, *An Interview With Margaret Mead* (1959) and *But the Women*

Rose, Vol.2: Voices of Women in American History (1971); to repeatedly testifying before Congress; to giving tele-lectures—where she spoke to audiences over the phone while an image of her was projected against a screen (Francis and Wolfskill, "Margaret Mead as a Cultural Commentator"). She had been teaching at Columbia University since 1940 and The New School since 1954. By the early 1960s, she was a prolific public intellectual who was invited to deliver talks at major universities and conferences, wrote articles for the *New York Times Magazine* and *Foreign Affairs*, and gained full recognition by her field as she assumed the presidency of the American Anthropological Association in 1960. Equally importantly, her long-standing work at the American Museum of Natural History in New York, where she served from 1926 to 1969 (first as an assistant curator, since 1942 as an associate curator, and since 1946 as the curator of ethnology) provided a solid financial and institutional platform for her many forages into the public sphere (Thomas 354).[36] As a public intellectual, Mead was also subject to critiques from well outside of academia (where Derek Freeman staged the most fierce, posthumous attack on her).[37] On the occasion of Mead's suggestion to Congress to make marijuana legal at age sixteen, Florida's Governor Claude Kirk called her a "dirty old lady" while an unknown woman scribbled that

Figure 2.2 Margaret Mead with her trademark cape and walking stick
Source: Courtesy of Associated Press, Keystone SDA

she "MUST BE MAD," "CRAZY," a "DOPE FIEND," and a "DIRTY LOUSE" on a newspaper clipping that announced "Margaret Mead's for Legal Pot" (Francis and Wolfskill, "National Character"). By way of contrast, *TIME* magazine in the same year (1969) declared her "mother to the world." Thirty years later, the same publication would pronounce her an "American icon."[38] Mead was, in short, an eminently public figure—one who, moreover, gladly embraced and performed that role, dressed often in her trademark cape and carrying a conspicuous forked walking stick that she began using after her chronically unstable right ankle had broken for the third time (Lutkehaus, "American Icon" 76).

How does Mead's poetry fit into the career of this eminently public figure? The first point to make is that the bulk of her poetic production dates to the 1920s, decades before she became a significant public intellectual.[39] Her first dated poem, "And Your Young Men Shall See Visions," hails from June 26, 1921 (it was published in 1929), and she continued to write poetry throughout the decade. Only two poems for which we know the dates, "After Love" (1931) and "Without Benefit of Memory" (January 7, 1937), were written in the 1930s; a third, "Misericordia," was written on November 3, 1927 and published in *Poetry* in 1930. After a long hiatus, in January 1947, Mead wrote her last poem, a text dedicated to her daughter Mary Catherine Bateson and variously entitled "Resident's Code" or simply "For M.C.B." (M.C. Bateson 113–14). With the exception of this final poem, then, Mead wrote poetry well before she became a national celebrity.[40]

Mead considered neither her own poems nor those of her fellow Boasians Sapir and Benedict commentaries on societal issues. For her, once she had recognized Léonie Adams's superior talent, she began to consider writing poetry as an "avocation" (Mead, *Blackberry* 107). Moreover, in retrospect, Mead and her fellow poets' verse serves a mnemonic function for her. As she writes in her introduction to *An Anthropologist at Work: Writings of Ruth Benedict*, "I have her poems, both published and unpublished, and Sapir's poems, published and unpublished—which he had sent to her—and the poems I wrote within their writing, to serve as a mnemonic for the ways in which we felt" (Benedict, *Anthropologist* xix). Poetry as an expression of experience, a repository of feelings, and a vehicle of communication among a small community of poets: these are characterizations of the function of poetry quite different from the 'cultural work' most Americanists see literary texts perform ever since Jane Tompkins introduced the term into our disciplinary discourse, defining it as "the way that literature has power in the world," how it "connects with the beliefs and attitudes of large masses of readers so as to impress or move them deeply" (xiv). In Tompkins's and many a fellow Americanists' vision, literature is centrally engaged in "providing society with a means of thinking about itself, defining certain aspects of a social reality which the authors and their readers shared, dramatizing its conflicts, and recommending solutions" (200). Mead's reflections on the work her poems perform follow a more traditional, lyrical understanding of poetry as expression and communication of the poet's interiority. This corresponds not only to common perceptions of verse according to which, we read in the online forum *Poems&Quotes*:

> poetry is an outlet to express your ideas or experiences to others as you wished you could express yourself every time you spoke. . . . [A] transfer [of] emotion from poet to paper to reader—no easy task, but rewarding if accomplished.
>
> (Moss)

It also corresponds to a powerful tradition of poetics and poetic practice. When Benedetto Croce—whom Mead's fellow Boasian Sapir admired (Lowie 49)—writes that beauty is "the expressive activity which . . . triumphantly unfolds itself" (Croce 132) and labels aesthetics "the science of expression" (94), he gives voice to an expressive notion of art that has shaped centuries of literary history and criticism, from the romanticism of a Wordsworth, who in the preface to his *Lyrical Ballads* famously defined poems as the "spontaneous overflow of powerful feelings" whose source is "emotion recollected in tranquility" (98) to Black Mountain poet Charles Olson's theory of projective verse, which considers poems expressions of energy and projections of the poet's breath—and beyond. As Olson's own aversion to *"the private-soul-at-any-public-wall"* (15; emphasis in original) schools of poetry (his specific target was confessional poetry) and the primitivist vision of a pre-European American past that he develops in his *Maximus Poems* (1953–1968) show, poetics of interiority and expression do not necessarily equal a retreat into the private and the apolitical. This is not only so because expressive poetics always also figure in the addressee and thus envisage an act of communication that takes us beyond pure interiority. This is also so because, as revisionist scholarship on eighteenth- and nineteenth-century sentimental prose and poetry by Tompkins, Joanne Dobson, Paula Bernat Bennett (*Poets*), Elizabeth Maddock Dillon, and others has shown, feelings can be put in the service of eminently public cultural critique, from Lydia Huntley Sigourney's protest poems against Indian removal to Stowe's abolitionist sentimental novel *Uncle Tom's Cabin*.

Mead's own poems are hardly ever political in any of these senses but they do move beyond the limited functions she ascribes to them as they trouble the private/public divide. This is particularly true of her ethnographic poems, which deal with subject matters that she also explores in her anthropological work. In these poems, Mead often combines reflections on anthropology's epistemological endeavors and its research objects with the lyrical expression of feelings. Let us begin by returning to "The Need That Is Left." As we have seen in my discussion of the poem earlier in this chapter, the first two stanzas of "The Need That Is Left" mourn the decline of traditional Indigenous social practices, giving expression to the troubled and troubling sense of nostalgia that informs the Boasians' salvage imperative. We find ourselves in a realm of public actions here: the "chariot race" of the first line; ritual practices such as dancing, praying, and sacrificing in lines 3–12; and the Biblical narrative of Aaron's staff, which swallows (or, in Mead's variant, shatters) the Egyptian magicians' staffs, in lines 15–16. These actions are public in a twofold sense: First, they are performed under the eyes of the gods and of the community; second, they are part of the cultural memories of the communities that the poem evokes. These public actions and bodies of knowledge are, the poetic persona suggests, in decline: the victors in the chariot races no longer receive their laurel wreaths; the dances have stopped; the fisher now performs his work according to rational principles instead of praying to the gods; sacrificial offerings cease; the gods are not considered the weather's cause anymore; and Aaron's staff no longer puts up the resistance it once did.

In the first two stanzas of "The Need That Is Left," Mead evokes a mythical world guided by gods and goddesses in whose honor humans compete, dance, pray, and sacrifice. The actions that Mead describes here are also public in the sense that, with the possible exception of the fisher's prayer, they take place in public spaces. In the ancient world, chariot races were eminently public spectacles performed in social centers such as Constantinople's Hippodrome, which seated around 100,000 people (Evans 16), or Rome's Circus Maximus, which was used for chariot races until the sixth century CE and pulled in up to 150,000 spectators during Emperor Augustus's reign (27 BCE—14 CE) and up to a quarter million during Pliny the Elder's lifetime (23–79 CE) (Popkin 112). It stands to reason that the poem's dancers performed before a much smaller audience, and it remains unclear whether the sacrificial offerings are made in a public ritual or in a smaller setting of familial or individual actions. Sacrifices are public practices quite independent of the number of participants though, for at least three reasons: first, they take place in spaces to which more than one person has access (Mead stresses this through her use of the plural: "hunters," "men," "women"); second, the material traces or individual offerings remain visible and smellable to successive sacrificers; third, sacrificial acts assume their meaning only within the framework of a communal mythical worldview.

Crucially, the kinds of sites that the poem's first two stanzas explore are also core subjects of anthropological research, which regularly zooms in on cultural practices of foreign communities such as religious dances and sacrificial offerings, which the poem relates to the culturally less determinate practice of the fisher's prayer on the one hand and the ancient cultural technique of the chariot race, which presumably belongs to the past of the persona's own culture, on the other. As subjects of Mead's own research, such cultural practices are, finally, negotiated in a scientific realm that is by definition public given that much of it is publicly funded; is published in articles, monographs, and essay collections; is put up for discussion in talks; and is the subject of debates within the research community. Given Mead's prominent public stature, her own research was and—though to a lesser extent—still is communicated to a particularly broad public. In sum, the poem's first two stanzas evoke a decidedly public realm, one that Mead herself has been instrumental in communicating in decisively public ways.

The setting changes quite radically as we enter the poem's third and final stanza, whose second line provides the title for *Song of Five Springs*, the slim volume in which the poem appears:

> But to what temple can I take
> My praises that five Springs
> Your hand upon my hand could make
> My flesh take wings?
> The gods no longer give us
> Blood for wine;
> But for this holy joyousness
> I need a shrine.

Mead here turns from a public sphere whose decline her persona laments to the smaller, private realm of an intimate relationship. In this sphere, where but an 'I' and a 'you' hold sway, the persona finds remedy for the spiritual emptiness that the decline of cultic and communal practices in the first two stanzas leaves behind. Redemption is sought and found in a spiritually charged relationship with the poem's addressee. The transition from the second to the third stanza, then, marks a transition from public to private space: from practices that at least potentially relate to the community as a whole to practices that are reserved for the privacy and intimacy of two lovers.

Yet the transition is not a complete one: the "shrine" that the persona requests is not a purely private object. Two senses of 'shrine' are significant here: the first is a more private, intimate one: we may imagine the speaker erecting a shrine to venerate and idolize her beloved and their love. The *Oxford English Dictionary* identifies this sense of 'shrine' as a figurative derivation from its more strongly institutionalized (and public) meaning, "A place where worship is offered or devotions are paid to a saint or deity; a temple, church" (OED). The second relevant sense of shrine is "A receptacle containing an object of religious veneration; occasionally a niche for sacred images." In ancient Egypt, images of the gods were kept in shrines; in Judaism, Torah rolls; in Christianity, relics.

In Mead's secular use, the shrine is designed to conserve another valuable object: the "holy joyousness" of the love between the persona and her addressee. With this refunctioning of the shrine, Mead brings the private and the public together and blurs their boundaries, for this poem's shrine belongs both to the third stanza's private, intimate sphere of love and the public cultic practices negotiated in the first two stanzas.

The poem's final word, moreover, also evokes the poetic topos of immortality, suggesting that the poem itself is the shrine that renders the lovers and their love immortal. With this evocation of the immortality topos, the poem again ventures beyond the private, for poems, their authors, and their addressees achieve immortality precisely because poems can be read long after their original senders and receivers have died. Shakespeare gives expression to this insight in the heroic couplet of Sonnet 18:

> So long as men can breathe or eyes can see,
> So long lives this, and this gives life to thee.

Shakespeare here articulates the paradox that both the poem's and the beloved's immortality depend upon the poem's reception by mortal humans. Mary Catherine Bateson ensured precisely the latter—the continuing reception of her mother's poetry—when, between 1981 to 1988, she gifted additions to the Margaret Mead Papers at the Library of Congress that included her mother's published and unpublished poetry (Kirby). Since Mead only published eight of her poems during her lifetime, this gift is of great value. Without it, the greatest part of her poetic production would be lost to posterity. This also goes for *Song of Five Springs*, the slim volume that contains "The Need That Is Left." None one of the eleven poems included therein has been published while Mead was alive.[41] At first sight at least, this seems to correspond to Mead's wishes since she begins the volume with a brief dedication in verse that is addressed, we may assume, to Benedict:

> I crave no other audience,
> My work is published when it
> meets your eyes.

Mead here creates the fiction that this volume has but a single addressee, thus stressing its private nature. This is, however, less than true, since the very fact that I am able to analyze this poem and quote from it qualifies its private character. We can assume that this is in Mead's spirit and does not constitute an intrusion into the privacy of two women—quite independent of the fact that we should guard against confusing poetic personae and addressees with authors and their intended audience(s). Mead, after all, bequeathed her papers to the Library of Congress in her will dated October 17, 1978, and named her daughter and her professional and personal partner Rhoda Métraux her literary executors (Flannery; Kirby). Moreover, to say that Mead wanted to be heard and read is an understatement, so it comes as little surprise that today, no access restrictions are placed on these poems at the Library of Congress. They are not in the public domain but can be accessed with relative ease. These poems exist, in other words, in a semi-public realm.

Thus, a dialectic between the public and the private that ultimately blurs the distinctions between the two plays out not only in Mead's negotiation of public practices and anthropological subject matters in the first two stanzas of "The Need That Is Left" and the (qualified) turn to private intimacy in the third stanza but also in the poem's distribution. Both the text itself and its history of distribution, moreover, belie the strict demarcation Mead herself draws between the public/anthropology and the private/art when she writes about her and her fellow Boasians' scientific and artistic pursuits:

> We needed some sense of whole cultures, of whole ways to bring home to us what anthropology was really about.
>
> Meanwhile we lived, in a sense, lives in which the arts and the sciences fought uneven battles for pre-eminence. Boas would leave his office and his labor over the particularities of some nearly extinct American language to spend the evening improvising at his piano. Sapir would let his Nootka texts half-finished while he wrote [the poem "Distant Strumming of Strings."] Or he would work at a piece of music. . . . And Ruth Benedict firmly continued to keep the parts of her life separate, signing her married name . . . to such papers as "A Matter for the Field Worker in Folklore" in the *American Journal of Folk-Lore*, and not publishing her poems at all.
>
> (Benedict, *Anthropologist* xiii–xix)

Mead writes these words in her introduction to *An Anthropologist at Work* (1959), the volume she edited for her departed colleague and friend. Concerning Benedict's lyrical production, Mead is wrong on at least two counts. Unlike Mead, who managed to publish only eight out of her 195 poems during her lifetime, Benedict was quite successful at placing 61 out of her 157 poems in magazines including *Poetry*, *The Dial*, *The Nation*, *The Measure*, and *The New Republic*. Second, as I argue in my Benedict chapter, Mead's friend did not keep her scientific and literary pursuits as neatly apart as Mead suggests. In fact, as we have seen, she produced quite a number of ethnographic poems that engage with the subjects and issues of her anthropological research. As my preceding discussion has shown, this is also true for Mead's own "The Need That Is Left," which oscillates between the scientific and the artistic, the public and the private in ways that confuse the distinctions between the two. In her poem, then, Mead blurs the very boundaries she draws in her introduction to *An Anthropologist at Work*. There, at least, the public and the private belong to no separate spheres.

Perhaps, it is no coincidence that Mead challenges the boundaries between the private and the public in her poetry. For poetry is a genre that has always been in a tension between the two: between the confessional poetry of a Sylvia Plath and the radically political interventions of an Amiri Baraka; between the topos of the poet as reclusive genius to the eminently public role of the poet laureate; between the expression of feelings and cultural work. Thus, when Mead suspends the division between the private and the public in "The Need That Is Left," she does what poetry has always done.

Notes

1. Among Boasians, it was Alexander Goldenweiser who put the vanishing Indian topos in the starkest terms:

   > Who are the races whose fate it will be to share the world in the future? The North American Indian is out of the running. Fragments of the once virile and poetic stock still linger on in a state of degeneration and dejection. But their days are counted.
   >
   > (462)

2. Of the twenty-two poems she published, two came out in secondary literature and twelve in a small volume entitled *Time and Measure*, published after her death in 1986. The remaining eight poems she published are "The Penciling of Pain" (published in the *Barnard Barnacle*, June 1, 1923), "For a Proud Lady" (*The Measure*, June 1925), "Rose Tree of Assisi" (*The Measure 57*, November 1925), "And Your Young Men Shall See Visions" (*The City Day: An Anthology of Recent American Poetry*, ed. Edna Lou Walton, 1929), "Misericordia" (*Poetry*, February 1930), and "Absolute Benison" (*The New Republic*, October 19, 1932). I am relying on Reichel (*Writing* 302n.33, 327n.23) and Joan Gordon's *Margaret Mead: The Complete Bibliography, 1925–1975*.
3. In her biographer Joan Mark's words, "Mead did not want to be a failed writer" (19). In this context, consider also Mead's statement, in *An Anthropologist at Work*, about Benedict's "slender gift" for poetry compared to Adams's: "The poems of Léonie Adams gave her pure delight and a measure of her own slender gift" (Benedict, *Anthropologist* 90). In my own humble opinion, "slender gift" is more applicable to Mead's poetic aspirations than to Benedict's.
4. For *The Waste Land*, I am referencing line numbers from the 2005 annotated Yale University Press edition edited by Lawrence Rainey.
5. For fine accounts of modernist primitivism and of what Sieglinde Lemke calls 'primitivist modernism,' see Jack D. Flam and Miriam Deutch's edited volume *Primitivism and Twentieth-Century Art: A Documentary History* (2003), Marianne Torgovnick's *Gone Primitive: Savage Intellects, Modern Lives* (1990), Nicola Gess's *Primitives Denken: Wilde, Kinder und Wahnsinnige in der literarischen Moderne (Müller, Musil, Benn, Benjamin)* (2013), and Lemke's *Primitivist Modernism: Black Culture and the Origins of Transatlantic Modernism* (1998).
6. *The Golden Bough* was originally published in two volumes in 1890, bearing the subtitle *A Study in Comparative Religion*. Its second, 1900 edition

contained three volumes and was titled *The Golden Bough: A Study in Magic and Religion*. Its third, twelve-volume edition was published between 1906 and 1915 under the same title.
7. See below for a discussion of the final stanza, where redemption is found in a more private, intimate realm.
8. Mead also uses smoke imagery in "I Have Prepared a Place for You" (1928), where gods appear in the smoke generated by the burning of green boughs: "Those who have seen their gods already shadowed / In phantom forms above a tended fire, / May be two-minded at the real god's coming / To take the place of smoke outlined desire." In this poem, though, the persona disavows the ritual in question: "But I, more earthly tutored, only searched the forest / Heaping my altar high with boughs of oak, / Busy and troubled, I could never linger / To fashion wraith-gods in my green-fed smoke."
9. Consider Sydel Silverman's account of the institutional situation at the turn of the century:

> In the last decade of the nineteenth century the center of gravity of American Anthropology was in Washington. The men of the Bureau of American Ethnology, the Geological Survey, and the National Museum formed the Anthropological Society of Washington in 1879 and instituted the *American Anthropologist* a decade later.... The Washington establishment was dominated by an evolutionary tradition, as were most of the ethnological writings and museum exhibits of the day.
>
> (260)

10. Montesquieu sketches the major distinctions between savages and barbarians thus: "One difference between savage peoples and barbarian peoples is that the former are small scattered nations, which, for certain particular reasons, cannot unite together. The former are usually hunting peoples; the latter, pastoral peoples" (290). In Montesquieu's scheme, civilized peoples distinguish themselves from the people of the two earlier stages first and foremost through their cultivation of land and use of money (292).
11. Eliot also expresses this conviction in other writings, including "The New Sculpture" (1914), "Tarr" (1918), and *The Use of Poetry and the Use of Criticism* (1933). See David Chinitz's "T. S. Eliot and the Cultural Divide" (2003) for a good discussion of Eliot's brand of primitivism (72–80).
12. Note that Eliot's primitivism comes with a significant twist. Here is how his review begins:

> The Ustumsjiji are a vanishing race. The last repositories of the Monophysite heresy, persecuted and massacred for centuries (on religious grounds) by the Armenians, the remnants of a unique civilization have taken refuge in the remote gorges of the Akim-Baba Range.
>
> ("War-Paint" 137)

It does not take long for the reader to recognize that Eliot is poking fun at both Cronyn, the editor of *The Path on the Rainbow*, and Mary Hunter Austin, the writer who penned the introduction to the volume. The Ustumsjiji and the Akim-Baba Range are Eliot's inventions, which he playfully throws together with arcane knowledge about the historical connection between Armenians and Monophysitism that he culled from Edward Gibbon's *The Decline and Fall of the Roman Empire*. The editors of *The Complete Prose of T. S. Eliot: The Critical Edition* explain:

> TSE's parodic introductory paragraph combines anthropological fictions evidently of his own making—the Ustumsjiji and the Akim-Baba Range, which recall similar names in Spencer and Gillen's *Northern Tribes*

of Central Australia . . . such as the Tjingilli tribe and the Ashburton Range—with details of ancient Christian sects about whom he had been reading in Gibbon's *The Decline and Fall of the Roman Empire*.
(Eliot, "War-Paint" 137)

Thus, the alarmist note that Eliot strikes at the beginning of the review is not to be taken at face value and his stance on salvage anthropology's moral imperative is anywhere between ambivalent and dismissive.

Eliot is also underwhelmed by the literary quality of the Native American songs and chants that Cronyn's volume makes available to the delight of the "New York and Chicago intelligentsia" (138). Having quoted the Chippewa "Maple Sugar Song" included in the anthology ("Maple sugar/is the only thing/that satisfies me"), Eliot turns sardonic:

> The Red Man is here: what are we to do with him, except to feed him on maple sugar?" (138). And yet, while Eliot slates *The Path on the Rainbow*, he affirms the uses of the kind of ethnographic material that the volume makes available: "Just as it is necessary to know something about Freud and something about Fabre, so it is necessary to know something about the medicine-man and his works.
> (138)

13. In his first letter, "The Occurrence of Similar Inventions in Areas Widely Apart" (1887), Boas clearly states his objection to the core assumption that informs Mason's taxonomy: that similar inventions in different cultures have the same causes. Against Mason, Boas maintains that "unlike causes produce like effects," a fact that, if properly considered, "overthrows the whole system" (485) of social evolutionism. Boas elaborates on his critique in "The Limitations of the Comparative Method" (1896). Reasoning that evolutionary accounts, which compare widely differing cultures, are based on the flawed assumption that similar cultural phenomena (e.g., totemism) in different cultures have the same psychological or social causes, Boas maintains that

> We must also consider all the ingenious attempts at constructions of a grand system of the evolution of society as of very doubtful value, unless at the same time proof is given that the same phenomena could not develop by any other method. Until this is done, the presumption is always in favor of a variety of courses which historical growth may have taken.
> (905)

Modern anthropologists, Boas adds, must base their "investigations on the historical results of researches which are devoted to laying clear the complex relations of each individual culture" and "renounce the vain endeavor to construct a uniform systematic history of the evolution of culture" (908). Mead's opposition to the racialism of the evolutionary paradigm already shows itself in her first published paper, "The Methodology for Racial Testing: Its Significance for Sociology" (1926), in which she skewers IQ tests that posit a correlation between intelligence and racial identity. Mead's antievolutionism is also apparent in her determination to explain the differences between Samoan and American puberty and adolescence in cultural rather than biological terms. Her use of Malinowskian participant observation, possibly the first of its kind in the history of American ethnography (Silverman 268), equally set her apart from the armchair anthropologists of the evolutionist school.

14. Tylor provided the first, anthropological definition of 'culture' (in the singular), equating it with 'civilization' understood as a higher form of social

organization: "Culture or Civilization, taken in its wide ethnographic sense, is that complex whole which includes knowledge, belief, art, morals, law, custom, and any other capabilities and habits acquired by man as a member of society" (1).

15. In Mead, evolutionist and racialist residues become visible, for instance when she assigns oral cultures to an earlier stage in human evolution or when she repeatedly expresses her belief that the cultures she studies are bound to disappear. Stocking comments on these residues when he writes that "it is worth noting" among 'Apollonian' Boasians such as Benedict, Mead, and Robert Redfield "also the major orienting influence of a more diffuse body of evolutionary assumption that seems in retrospect quite un-Boasian (though in fact expressions of it can also be found in Boas' work)" ("Ethnographic Sensibility" 335). As Tracy Teslow shows in her chapters on Boas, Harry Shapiro, and Benedict in *Constructing Race: The Science of Bodies and Cultures in American Anthropology*, the Boasians retained far more intimate ties to evolutionism and racial science than is commonly assumed. Boas and his students, Teslow notes, did not reject the concept of race but instead proposed "a . . . vision in which race was neither exclusively somatic nor entirely cultural, but rather was an inextricably interwoven—if analytically separable—set of critical factors: history, heredity, culture, and environment" (36). Building on Teslow's work, Reichel (*Writing* 160–63) shows that Mead too remains imbricated in Boasian racialism and evolutionism, for instance in *Balinese Character* (1942)—her and Bateson's early foray into visual anthropology—and in her children's book *People and Places* (1959).

16. See also Mead's account of how she became convinced that the traces of vanishing cultures must be preserved at all cost:

> I had responded also to the sense of urgency that had been conveyed to me by Professor Boas and Ruth Benedict. Even in remote parts of the world ways of life about which nothing was known were vanishing before the onslaught of modern civilization. The work of recording these unknown ways of life had to be done now—*now*—or they would be lost forever. Other things could wait, but not this most urgent task.
>
> (*Blackberry* 137; emphasis in original)

In her preface to the 1973 edition of *Coming of Age in Samoa*, Mead reflects on the salvage imperative that motivated her to become an anthropologist and do fieldwork in Samoa from August 1925 to May 1926, noting, in hindsight, the resilience of Samoan culture:

> I did not know then, could not know then, how extraordinarily persistent Samoan culture would prove, and how fifty years later the grace that I had attempted to record as something that was surely going to vanish would still be there.
>
> (xxxvi)

17. In James Clifford's astute judgement, "the most problematic, and politically charged, aspect of this 'pastoral' encodation" of ethnic others "is its relentless placement of others in a present-becoming-past" ("On Ethnographic Allegory" 115).

18. These troubling ties become particularly manifest in instances where Mead adopts, strategically perhaps, a cultural evolutionary rhetoric when addressing, as she often did, a broad audience. To give but one example, during a discussion with other scientists published in 1968, Mead gives the cultural

relativist answer to the question of whether, "As an anthropologist, do you always evaluate foreign civilization in terms of our own?" Mead responds, "No. Anthropologists are trained not to evaluate other civilizations in terms of our own" ("Talks" 23). But when asked about the impact of "Western culture" on "a primitive culture" (23), she does not challenge the terms of the question but characterizes the former as "higher" and "advanced," the latter as "lower" and "simple":

> You must first consider that we have been having introductions from a high culture to a lower culture, in the sense of technical differences, for thousands and thousands of years. . . . Not until the mid-twentieth century was there a complete clash or a complete meeting of the most advanced technical things that has ever happened in the world, like an airplane, with the simplest people still alive on earth.
> (33)

Of course, Mead's "still" betrays a view of cultural development that the salvage anthropologists and evolutionists shared: the "simplest" people will ultimately disappear. Consider also Stocking's discussion of evolutionist residues in *Coming of Age in Samoa*:

> [M]any of the contrasts that Mead drew were quite conventionally evolutionary: Samoan culture was 'simpler,' lacking in 'individualization' and 'specialized feeling.' What it offered was not so much a general cultural alternative as a point of critical comparison: 'granting the desirability of [the] development of [a] sensitive, discriminating response to personality, as a better basis for dignified human lives than an automatic, undifferentiated response to sex attraction, we may still, in the light of Samoan solutions, count our methods exceedingly expensive.
> (211)

In the end, Mead's purpose was to realize 'the high point' that only 'a heterogeneous culture' could attain [248]" ("Ethnographic Sensibility" 336).

19. In Eliot's own words,

> [W]hat happens when a new work of art is created is something that happens simultaneously to all the works of art which preceded it. The existing monuments form an ideal order among themselves, which is modified by the introduction of the new (the really new) work of art among them. . . . [F]or order to persist after the supervention of novelty, the whole existing order must be, if ever so slightly, altered. . . . Whoever has approved this idea of order, . . . will not find it preposterous that the past should be altered by the present as much as the present is directed by the past. And the poet who is aware of this will be aware of great difficulties and responsibilities. . . . And the poet cannot reach this impersonality without surrendering himself wholly to the work to be done. And he is not likely to know what is to be done unless he lives in what is not merely the present, but the present moment of the past, unless he is conscious, not of what is dead, but of what is already living.
> ("Tradition" 38–39, 44)

20. In his letter to Monroe of September 30, 1914, Pound puts it thus: "He is the only American I know of who has made what I can call adequate preparation for writing. He has actually trained himself *and* modernized himself *on his own*" (80; emphases in original).

21. Reichel already notes the paradox that Mead stages a verbal critique of verbal representation in *Writing Anthropologists, Sounding Primitives*, where she provides a sound close reading of the poem (146–58).
22. In "Visual Anthropology in a Discipline of Words," Mead elaborates on her ambivalent attitude toward convergences between anthropology and art:

> We do not demand that a field ethnologist write with the skill of a novelist or a poet, although we do indeed accord disproportionate attention to those who do. It is equally inappropriate to demand that filmed behavior have the earmarks of a work of art. We can be grateful when it does, and we can cherish those rare combinations of artistic ability and scientific fidelity that have given us great ethnographic films. But I believe that we have absolutely no right to waste our breath and our resources demanding them. That we do is the unfortunate outcome of both the European tradition of the overriding importance of originality in the arts and the way in which the camera has replaced the artist's brush and so developed film as an art form.
>
> Thus the exorbitant demand that ethnographic films be great artistic productions, combined with the complementary damnation of those who make artistic productions and fail in fidelity to some statistically established frequencies of dramatic events, continues to clutter up the film scene, while whole cultures go unrecorded.
>
> (5–6)

23. Stocking notes both the title's and the book's evolutionist slant: "The presentation of cultural relativism in an evolutionary package ('A Study of Primitive Youth for Western Civilisation') made it possible to appeal simultaneously to motives of romantic primitivism and ethnocentric progressivism" ("Ethnographic Sensibility" 317).
24. For Mead, whose research focused on "fifty [Samoan] girls in three small neighbouring villages" (*Samoa* 10), the "main lesson" of her comparison is "that adolescence is not necessarily a time of stress and strain" (161).
25. See Nancy C. Lutkehaus's *Margaret Mead: The Making of an American Icon* (2008) for a good overview of Mead's many contributions to public debates and the public images of her that resulted from that work.
26. Here is how Mead defines the American national character:

> We have a certain kind of character, the American character, which has developed in the New World and taken a shape all its own; a character that is geared to success and to movement, invigorated by obstacles and difficulties, but plunged into guilt and despair by catastrophic failure or a wholesale alteration in the upward and onward pace; a character in which aggressiveness is uncertain and undefined, to which readiness to fight anyone who starts a fight and unreadiness to engage in violence have both been held up as virtues; a character which measures its successes and failures only against near contemporaries and engages in various quantitative devices for reducing every contemporary to its own stature; a character which sees success as the reward of virtue and failure as the stigma for not being good enough; a character which is uninterested in the past, except when ancestry can be used to make points against other people in the success game; a character oriented towards an unknown future, ambivalent towards other cultures, which are regarded with a sense of inferiority as more coherent than our own and with a sense of superiority because newcomers in America display the strongest mark of

other cultural membership in the form of foreignness. What is the possible role for such a character structure—after winning the war—in working towards building the world anew?

(*Powder* 123)

27. Note that, in trying to reach a wide audience, Mead does not shy away from embracing the Puritan foundational myth. One case in point is *And Keep Your Powder Dry: An Anthropologist Looks at America* (1942), where Mead combines wilderness and *domicilium vacuum* discourse in a stunningly careless way as she looks back at the Puritan settlers:

> Once we lose our moral keystone to an orderly world, the whole structure comes crashing down about our heads, leaving us with a type of American who has neither vision nor humility, who lacks the will and the purpose which have helped us shape a great country from an untouched wilderness, who lacks even the constructive fire which might come from bitterness and a genuine hatred of those who have brought him to such a pass.
> (128–29)

28. See Stephen Greenblatt's *Marvelous Possessions: The Wonder of the New World* (1981) for his influential reading of Columbus's colonial/economic language of wonder.
29. An early version of the poem, also available in box Q15, folder 10 of the Margaret Mead Papers, bears the typewritten title "South to North," which Mead's handwriting changes to "Monuments Rejected."
30. The classic text of the *Writing Culture* debate, which initiated a linguistic turn in cultural anthropology and was instrumental in sharpening anthropologists' awareness of the rhetorical construction of ethnographic authority, is, of course, James Clifford and George E. Marcus's *Writing Culture: The Poetics and Politics of Ethnography* (1986).
31. According to Aristotle, the lowest senses are "taste and touch" because they are "in direct contact with the world"; these two senses are

> Followed by smell, which forms a kind of mean distance to sight and hearing, which operate across distances yet can be called to mind without external stimulation. Sight and hearing, because of their link with philosophical contemplation and abstraction, hold the leading place.
> (Stewart 21)

32. In *The Politics of Aesthetics*, Rancière rethinks aesthetics as a site that explores "the system of self-evident facts of sense perception that simultaneously discloses the existence of something in common and the delimitations that define the respective parts and positions within it" (12). Rancière names Kant as a major ally in his endeavor. For reasons outlined above, I contend that Baumgarten would be the more apposite reference point.
33. In truly structuralist fashion, Mead and Métraux add that "the traditional cuisine of a people can be as distinctive and as organized as a language" (16). Howes notes that this linguistic turn makes Mead and Métraux ambivalent early figures in the history of sensory anthropology:

> This methodological pronouncement, with its privileging of linguistics as a model for cultural analysis, contained the seeds of its own destruction. However, the stripping of the senses that the foregrounding of the language metaphor would eventually precipitate [due to the influence of the

> *Writing Culture* paradigm] was held in check, at least for the time being, by the emphasis on developing *all* the senses.
>
> (Sensual Relations 11)

See also Howes's "Boasian Soundings: An Interrupted History of the Senses (and Poetry) in Anthropology" (2018).

34. In terms of impact on academic discussions of 'culture,' pride of place belongs to Alfred L. Kroeber, though, whose 1917 essay "The Superorganic" and several books on culture, including *Configurations of Culture Growth* (1944), *The Nature of Culture* (1952), and *Culture: A Critical Review of Concepts and Definitions* (1952), which he co-authored with Clyde Kluckhohn, were particularly influential. Among the Boasians, Kroeber was the strictest cultural determinist. In "The Superorganic," he went as far as arguing that cultural phenomena are *entirely* independent of biology and the individual. Especially Sapir vehemently disagreed (Silverman 264, 266).

35. For a detailed analysis of Mead and Métraux's contributions to *Redbook*, which upon the editors' insistence appeared only under Mead's name, see Paul Shankman's "The Public Anthropology of Margaret Mead: *Redbook*, Women's Issues, and the 1960s" (2018).

36. The entry for Mead on the website of the Department of Anthropology at Columbia University contains an telling speculation on why she refused the university's repeated offer of a tenured position: "though Dr. Mead was twice offered a full-tenured professorship at Columbia, in 1958 and again in 1963, she refused both offers, presumably to keep the freedom and independence provided by her job at the museum" (Department of Anthropology).

37. Freeman was Mead's fiercest but by no means only critic from within the profession. Mead's biographer Nancy C. Lutkehaus notes that Mead's multiple forages into the public sphere and political interventions earned her quite frequent rebukes from (male) colleagues:

> Members of the 'high' culture—that is, academic anthropologists—ostracized Mead for having abandoned the critical distance that should characterize the anthropological observer. They criticized her for writing 'science fiction' rather than science because she often used a popular vernacular rather than the specialized language of academic anthropology, because she addressed topics that were not always considered to be within the purview of the anthropologist, because she wrote and spoke about these topics without having performed the requisite amount of research or fieldwork that were hallmarks of the anthropologist, and because she wrote or spoke in venues that were not considered sufficiently professional. In other words, activities such as writing in a colloquial vernacular, publishing in mass media, and appearing on radio and television talk shows associated Mead with various aspects of popular culture—especially mass culture. By stepping outside the boundary that divides high culture from low or popular culture, Mead was a transgressive, hence, a liminal, figure. . . . As theorist of contemporary culture Andreas Huyssen has cogently argued, 'The gendering of mass culture as feminine and inferior had its primary historical place in the late nineteenth century, even though the underlying dichotomy did not lose its power until quite recently.' He goes on to say that 'the universalizing ascription of femininity to mass culture always depended on the very real exclusion of women from high culture and its institutions' [Huyssen 205–6].
>
> ("Margaret Mead: Anthropology's Liminal Figure" 197–98)

38. Lutkehaus's biography of Mead, *Margaret Mead: The Making of an American Icon*, takes its title from the latter *TIME* story.
39. I am relying on Reichel's supremely useful appendix "The Complete Poetry of Edward Sapir, Margaret Mead, and Ruth Benedict" in her *Writing Anthropologists, Sounding Primitives: The Poetry and Scholarship of Edward Sapir, Margaret Mead, and Ruth Benedict* (237–98).
40. Citing Mary Catherine Bateson's characterization of her mother as 'half-famous' in 1950, Lutkehaus notes Mead's rise to fame in the fifties:

    > When Mead's daughter, Mary Catherine Bateson, was about twelve, she complained that it was hard to have 'a 'half-famous' mother because when I assume that people know who you are, so often they don't.' She said that in 1950, just before Mead became a frequent presence on television talk shows and in popular magazines such as *Life, Time, Redbook*, and the *New Yorker*, so much that one journalist referred to her as 'a household name.'
    >
    > (American Icon 12–13)

41. Apart from the dedicatory epigraph I cite below, the volume contains ten poems: "Your Gift" (1927), "Drifted Silence" (1923), "The Closed Door" (1924), "A Craven's Technique" (1924), "Traveler's Faith" (1925), "Refutation" (1926), "The Need That Is Left" (1927), "A Rueful Valentine" (1927), "Green Sanctuary" (1927), and "Cradle Song" (1927). "Refutation" is reproduced in Hilary Lapsley's double biography *Margaret Mead and Ruth Benedict: The Kinship of Women* (1999, 169). All the others are available in the Margaret Mead Papers at the Library of Congress.

3 Exerting Poetic License
Edward Sapir's Poetry

As we have seen in the preceding chapter, when it comes to poetry, Mead, the eminently public and widely published intellectual, had a modest publication record, with under 5% of her poems seeing the light of day in magazines and poetry anthologies during her lifetime. That, with Benedict's support, she did manage to place one of her poems, "Misericordia," in *Poetry* magazine constitutes an exception. The case is quite different with her older colleague Edward Sapir, who managed to publish almost half of his poems, a substantial 318 out of 663. Sapir was not only a widely published poet but out of the three Boasian anthropologists discussed in this book, he was also most successful in placing his poems in major publication outlets. Sapir published no less than twenty-three poems in *Poetry*, ten in *The Measure*, and four in *The Dial*. He also published seven poems in *The Nation* and one in *The New Republic*—weekly journals of political and cultural news, analysis, and opinion that gave him a wider potential readership. Other, lesser-known periodicals to which he contributed frequently are the socialist magazine *The Pagan* (nineteen poems), the British poetry magazine *Voices* (sixteen), the Mexican-based *Palms* (six), and the leftist periodical *The Freeman* (three).[1] As Director of the Anthropological Division in the Geological Survey of Canada in Ottawa from 1910 to 1925, Sapir also placed many of his poems in Canadian publications, including thirty-one in *The Canadian Forum*, four in *The Canadian Bookman*, twelve in *Queen's Quarterly*, and one poem in *Contemporary Verse*, the 'Canadian *Poetry*.'[2] Sapir's verse negotiates a wide range of topics. His poems revolve around myths (e.g., "The King of Thule," "The Water Nymph"); war (e.g., "We Others," "Epitaph of a Soldier," "Del Inferno," "War," "To a Returned Soldier"); death (e.g., "Charon," "Acheron," "Three Hags Come Visiting," "Death"); transience (e.g., "The Measurer," "Time's Wing," "Dirge"); religion (e.g., "God," "God Blows a Message," "Delilah," "Miriam Sings Three Hymns," "The New Religion," "The Sermon on the Mount," "Involvement"); music (e.g., "To Debussy: '*La Cathédrale Engloutie*,'" "Music," "Music Brings Grief," "To One Playing a Chopin Prelude," "After Playing Chopin," "Distant Strumming of Strings, Vague

Flutings, Drum," "On Hearing Plaintive Jazz by Radio"); nature (e.g., "An Easter Day," "Summer in the Woods," "Before the Storm," "The Rain," "Rain-Storm," "Blowing Winds," "The Corn-Field," "Maples," "When the Greens of the Field Are Shot with Gold"); the seasons (e.g., "Spring Light," "The Halt of Summer," "Promise of Summer," "The Soul of Summer," "Autumn Raindrops," "Autumn Leaves," "Winter Approaches," "Snowstorm in the Dusk," "The Snow," "The Tawny Hills"); dreams (e.g., "Dreams," "Dream of the Dead," "Dream Journey"); modernity (e.g., "The Preacher," "The Siding"); literature (e.g., "To Joseph Conrad," "Poetry," "To a Realistic Poet," "Poet's Coterie"); memory (e.g., "Memory," "Oh Say You Are not Dead"); women (e.g., "The Moon's not Always Beautiful," "To a Recruiting Girl," "The Old Maid and the Private," "Women Play Mandolines before Night," "I Cannot Say"); mothers (e.g., "The Firmament Advises Man," "Nocturnal Comfort"), desire (e.g. "Signal," "Everlasting Sun," "I Came to Sing over Your Hair"); and, above all, love (e.g., "Lovers' Night," "Love," "Our Love," "This Age," "How You Were more Beautiful than Dusk," "Worms, Wind and Stone," "Revery Interrupts Time," "When Love Came," "A Fear," "The Parting," "A Song for Lovers").

More so than Mead and Benedict, Sapir experimented with a variety of poetic forms including the ballad, the sonnet, the folk song, the quatrain, and the children's poem. Out of the three Boasians at the heart of this book, he was the only one who published a volume of verse, *Dreams and Gibes* (1917). Sapir also had plans to publish a second volume entitled *Stars in the Sea* and collected children's poetry in an unpublished anthology named *The Streets of Fancifullo*. As a starting point for my inquiry into the aesthetics and politics of Sapir's verse, I begin with a consideration of texts that bridge his Canadian interests and his determination to publish in the major little magazines that put modernism on the literary map.

Little Canadian Flowers

When poets and literary scholars think of *Poetry* magazine, they think first and foremost of its pivotal role in the modernist revolution. At Ezra Pound's urging, T.S. Eliot's "The Lovesong of J. Alfred Prufrock" was published there; as were Pound's own "In a Station of the Metro" and many of his cantos. *Poetry* also published a great number of additional poems that have become fixtures in the modernist canon, among them H.D.'s "The Pool," "Hymen," and "Halcyon"; Wallace Stevens's "Anecdote of the Jar" and "Sunday Morning"; William Carlos Williams's "The Shadow"; Amy Lowell's "The Day That Was That Day!"; and Robert Frost's "Snow." Much of this work is iconoclastic in form and some of it daring in content, prompting angry reactions among some of the magazine's readers, to which its editor Harriet Monroe responded with comments that bore titles such as "The Enemies We Have Made" (May 1914) and "A Word to the Carping Critic" (November 1917). Yet browsing the magazine's early-twentieth-century issues, now freely available in its complete online archive (www.poetryfoundation.org/poetrymagazine/archive), one is struck by their inclusion of a wide variety of poetic forms, only some of which can justly be called experimental in a modernist vein. The early issues of *Poetry* magazine hold in store yet another surprise: their generous inclusion of what was variously called 'folk-songs' or 'folk-poetry' then. The two surprises are related as the modernist search for new forms often takes a detour through supposedly simpler modes of expression. In the well-documented phenomenon of modernist primitivism—from Gauguin's Tahiti paintings to T.S. Eliot's "War-Paint and Feathers"—this engagement is driven by a desire to rejuvenate one's own, Western art and culture through an engagement with artifacts and cultural practices that are perceived as fresher, more authentic, and less corrupted by processes of civilization and modernization.

This brings us to what A. Elisabeth Reichel and I call "salvage primitivism": the convergence of modernist primitivism and salvage ethnography's urge to preserve for posterity cultures deemed on the verge of extinction (Reichel and Schweighauser).[3] With its well-known role in the promotion of modernist poetry and its less-explored interest in ethnographic materials, *Poetry* magazine proves a particularly rewarding test case for an exploration of this convergence. In what follows, I zoom in on Sapir's contributions to the magazine in order to provide an assessment of him as a salvage primitivist. *Poetry*'s July 1920 issue begins with a brief introductory poem by Sapir titled "French-Canadian Folk-Songs." The poem is followed by Sapir's translations into English of four of the eponymous songs: "The Prince of Orange," "The King of Spain's Daughter and the Diver," "White as the Snow," and "The Dumb Shepherdess."[4] Immediately following Sapir's translations of Québécois songs, we find another translation, the poet and literary scholar Albert Edmund Trombly's rendition of "Three Children" from "the Old French." Later in the same issue, at the end of its poetry selection, we encounter Sapir's three-page "Note on French-Canadian Folk-Songs." Why this conspicuous presence of 'folk songs' in an issue of one of the little magazines where U.S. modernism began? One might think that its editor's decision to publish Sapir's songs is an oddity in one of the major vehicles for experimental modernist poetry. But this is not so, for at least three reasons.

First, the editorial staff of *Poetry* awarded Sapir an honorable mention for this work ("Announcement of Awards" 109), thus granting his songs a special status as particularly representative of one kind of literature that the magazine seeks to promote. Further, far from being a rare guest of honor, Sapir contributed regularly to *Poetry*. Between 1919 and 1931, he published no less than twenty-three of his own poems in its pages, sometimes single ones, sometimes groups of poems under headings such as "Backwater" (four poems; May 1921), "Foam-Waves" (eight poems;

January 1926), "Feathered Songs" (four poems; July 1927), or simply "Three Poems" (November 1931). These twenty-three poems represent only a small selection of Sapir's literary work: as we have seen, during his lifetime, and in parallel to his prolific career as a major voice in U.S. linguistics and cultural anthropology, he produced a substantial oeuvre of just over 660 published and unpublished poems. I already hinted at the third reason why the inclusion of Sapir's French-Canadian folk songs in the July 1920 issue of *Poetry* is less of an oddity than may appear at first sight. The magazine's early publication history testifies to a sustained interest in spreading the cultural productions of communities then widely referred to as 'folk.' Sapir rightly judged that Monroe had "shown an interest in folk and exotic poetry" ("Letter to Harriet Monroe of July 5, 1919") when he advertised his Canadian folk songs to her in a letter dated July 5, 1919. Most famously (or infamously), the magazine's so-called 'aboriginal issue' of February 1917 contains lyrical imitations of Native American songs and prayers by four North American poets: Frank S. Gordon, Alice Corbin Henderson, Mary Austin, and Constance Lindsay Skinner.[5] In her editorial comment, Harriet Monroe notes that this work is "[v]ivid . . . in its suggestion of racial feeling and rhythm," adding on a more somber note that

> the danger is that the tribes, in the process of so-called civilization, will lose all trace of it; that their beautiful primitive poetry will perish among the ruins of obliterated states. . . . The phonograph is a valuable aid to these modern investigators.
> (Monroe, Sandburg, and Corbin Henderson, "Aboriginal Poetry" 251–53)

In his editorial comment, Carl Sandburg jokingly suggests that "[s]uspicion arises definitely that the Red Man and his children committed direct plagiarism on the modern imagists and vorticists" (255).

Further examples abound. In the November 1918 issue, Alice Corbin Henderson, one of *Poetry*'s two associate editors and a contributor to its 'aboriginal issue,' reviews *The Path on the Rainbow*, the anthology of Native American songs and chants edited by George W. Cronyn that T.S. Eliot also reviewed, for *The Athenaeum*, as discussed in my Mead chapter. Corbin, who would release an anthology of Indigenous New Mexican poetry herself in the following year and publish selections of these in the August 1920 issue of *Poetry*, applauds the volume's preservation of "authentic Indian poems," noting that the study of Native American poetry requires more than the ethnographer's scientific expertise: "it has remained, and still remains, for the artist and poet to interpret adequately many phases of Indian expression" (Corbin, Rev. of *The Path on the Rainbow* 41). Having dismissed talk about "the vanishing race"—the very talk that Monroe engages in in her editorial note on the 'aboriginal issue'—and having expressed her dislike of the "far-distant-sounding word 'aboriginal,'" Corbin turns Sandburg's joking comparison between Native American and modernist poetry into an utterly serious statement: "Stephen Crane would have qualified as an Indian poet, and in the *Mid-American Chants* of Sherwood Anderson," which were also published in *Poetry*, "one finds almost precisely the mood of the songs accompanying the green corn dances of the pueblo Indians" (42). Like Monroe, Corbin is after authenticity too: she notes the songs' "pristine freshness" (45) and judges them to be "the most consummate, primal art" (46).[6]

As another example of *Poetry* editors' predilection for 'folk cultures,' consider the issue immediately following the July 1920 issue that published Sapir's French-Canadian folk songs. Here we find Cowboy songs, dialect poems of the Western U.S., and Corbin's translations of New Mexican folk songs. In her essay on these songs and poems entitled "The Folk Poetry of these States," Corbin distinguishes between two types of folk poetry: first, the "instinctive," "unconscious," "naive," "primitive," and "unsophisticated" productions of the people themselves; second, the reworking of this material by more refined minds, e.g., James Russell Lowell, John Hay, Bret Harte, Joel Chandler Harris, Paul Laurence Dunbar, and Vachel Lindsay. Corbin identifies several types of American folk poetry of mostly non-European stock, among them "the Negro dialect poems of Thomas Nelson Page or Joel Chandler Harris," which refine the songs and spirituals of "the primitive negro poet" (Corbin, "Folk Poetry" 266); the "primitive poetry of the American Indian" (267); and the "Spanish folk-songs of the Southwest" (269) that Corbin herself is particularly interested in.[7]

What unites all of these folklore contributions to *Poetry* magazine is first and foremost a sustained interest in the cultural productions of 'folk' communities that are imagined to be more primal, more pristine, and more authentic than the authors' own. In this sense, Sapir's folk songs do indeed fit very well into one of the flagship magazines of the modernist movement: they tie in perfectly with modernist primitivism in its various guises (from Tristan Tzara's "Negro Songs" to Picasso's tribal masks in *Les demoiselles d'Avignon*). What becomes clearer here than elsewhere is how closely aligned modernist primitivism is with salvage ethnography's desire to preserve the customs and artifacts of communities that are assumed to vanish in the face of inexorable progress.

Moreover, in particular Corbin's contributions highlight the extent to which salvage primitivism is a nationalist project. While *Poetry* did publish a number of folk songs from outside of North America—the "Old Folk Songs of Ukraina" in the April 1919 issue are an example—it focused mainly on native songs, claiming them as part of an American national heritage. In Corbin's words,

> The soil has to be turned over; we have to examine our roots to know what they are. . . . [S]tudents of folk-songs have placed a greater

emphasis on the survivals of traditional English ballads in our remote mountain regions than on the more truly native and indigenous material that is all around us, which has been overlooked simply because of its more obvious familiarity and its lack of literary ancestry.

("Folk Poetry" 269–70)

For students of U.S. cultural history, this patriotic enlistment of domestic ethnic and minority communities rings familiar, from the personification of America as a violated half-naked Native American woman in the famous anti-British cartoon "The able doctor, or, America swallowing the bitter draught" (1774) to the nationalist origins of transnationalism in Randolph Bourne, for whom internal diversity is a sign of external strength, and beyond. Contributors to early-twenty-first-century debates in cultural anthropology urge us to reject such uses of ethnic others in the attempt to "decoloniz[e] anthropology" (Jobson 267).

Sapir's introductory poem in the July 1920 issue of *Poetry* magazine, entitled "French-Canadian Folk-Songs," strikes a very similar tone:

> The folk-songs fluttered down from upper meadows in the past;
> They settled on a little field
> And wove them tiny roots.
> I heard them as I passed along,
> I heard them sing a tiny song:
>
> We are weaving tiny roots
> In the strange today;
> We are little flowers to wait
> By the highway.
>
> We are not kin of the rose,
> The tulip of flame;
> Nearer to violet
> Our little name.
>
> Whoso cares may turn
> From the highway—
> We shall weave him a tiny wreath
> For the strange today.

Sapir notes that the songs he wishes to make heard come from "the past" and calls them "little flowers" that have "tiny roots" and sing a "tiny song," thus indicating their fragility. To the attentive listener, though, these songs offer something precious: "We shall weave him a tiny wreath/For the strange today." The meaning of these two final lines of the poem is ambiguous. In the most straightforward reading, "strange" is the adjectival modifier of "today," suggesting that "today," that is, present, modern life, is "strange." This reading is the most probable one because it easily accords with the first two lines of the poem's second stanza, "We are weaving tiny roots/In the strange today." In another reading of the poem's final line, however, "today" refers to the moment at which the songs impact the listener and "the strange" are the recipients of the songs' gift. A third reading finds that, in singing, the songs weave a "tiny wreath" dedicated to their own strange selves that is then offered to an other. In that case the songs *themselves*, or the community they sing from, are "strange." In all three readings, the poem highlights the distance between the listener and the songs and attributes redemptive power to those songs. Only by turning "[f]rom the highway"—the poem's spatial metaphor for modernity—can the songs be heard. These "tiny song[s]," these "little flowers," then, either promise to redeem the strangeness of the present or they themselves offer the gift of strangeness. Salvage ethnography's moral imperative—pithily summarized by Gruber as "the savage is disappearing; preserve what you can; posterity will hold you accountable" (1295)—once more meets modernist primitivism's desire for enstrangement and rejuvenation.

Interestingly though, Sapir's companion essay "Note on French-Canadian Folk-Songs" strikes a notably different chord. While it does begin with an assertion of the pristine quality of Québécois culture, which is said to preserve pre-modern French culture because it is unaffected by "[t]he great current of modern civilization" (211), there is no alarmist warning against its impending disappearance. Neither does Sapir wax lyrical about its authenticity. Instead, he acknowledges the extensive research on French-Canadian folk culture done by Marius Barbeau, whom he (rightly) calls "incomparably its greatest authority" (211). Sapir also comments on how the original folk songs were recorded by phonograph and writing, where the songs were collected, what types of songs there are, and which of these types his selections for *Poetry* magazine belong to. The essay ends with a brief general discussion of some issues of translation. In this "Note," then, Sapir wears three different masks: first, that of the poet who can appreciate the quality of these folk songs; second, that of the translator who opts for a literal rather than a lyrical rendition of his material; and third, that of the anthropologist who studies a folk community's artifacts and practices. But Sapir's anthropologist and translator personae are clearly foregrounded here.

That this is so becomes even clearer when we compare Sapir's "Note" to his and Barbeau's joint book *Folk Songs of French Canada*, a collection of French-Canadian folk songs that includes the four translations that Sapir published in *Poetry* plus thirty-seven additional ones.[8] The tone of this volume is markedly different from that of Sapir's note in *Poetry* magazine. In their introduction to the volume as a whole and their brief explanatory notes before each song, Barbeau and Sapir tap deep into nostalgic discourses about the impending disappearance of a primal, authentic culture under the pressures of modern civilization. "Folk songs were once part of the everyday life of French America" (Barbeau and Sapir xiii); on this regretful note begins their introduction, and it ends with an assertion of the songs' vibrant pastness:

> [t]he best claim to recognition of the French folk songs of America undoubtedly rests in their comparative antiquity. Sheltered in woodland recesses, far from the political commotions of the Old World, they have preserved much of their sparkling, archaic flavor.
>
> (xxii)

In Barbeau and Sapir's understanding, these songs are understood as an antidote to a modernity that is painted as equally spiritless and desiccated as Eliot's in *The Waste Land*. Here is how this sounds in the introductory note before "The King of Spain's Daughter":

> In the leisurely days of old, folk songs and tales provided a favorite entertainment for all, high or low, on land and on the sea, under the open sky and by the fireside in the long winter evenings. . . . Ever since man was banned from Eden, work has remained a punishment, a dire law to the many. And the penalty for the sin of Adam has not grown lighter with the lapse of millennia. In a past epoch work was only an incident in life and starvation a too-often recurring accident. Work was the mere provider of necessities, by no means banishing enjoyment out of life, yet, slight as it might be, it was made more attractive by a spontaneous concentration, an artistic refinement unfamiliar to the present generation. Work songs of all kinds sustained the rhythm of the hand in toil, while the mind escaped on the wing of fancy to the enchanted realm of wonderland. Now that labor is sullen under its crushing, mechanical burden, now that profit and luxury have become the very essence of human endeavor, an ominous silence has invaded the workshop.
>
> (100)

Passages such as this one abound; they are suffused with a profound sense of nostalgia that is spatial as well as temporal and in this instance even assumes Biblical proportions, taking, in the final sentences quoted here, the form of a jeremiad or, indeed, that of a Marxist account of alienation.

In marked contrast, in his "Note on French-Canadian Folk-Songs" in the July 1920 issue of *Poetry*, Sapir projects the persona of the distanced, objective observer. Why does this poet-anthropologist adopt this particular stance in an essay for one of his era's major poetry magazines? The answer, I believe, is this: there is no need for Sapir to extol the beauty and authenticity of folk songs here because, for early-twentieth-century readers of *Poetry* magazine, this goes without saying. Others' interpretations and translations of folk songs, others' essays on folk songs, and others' reviews of collections of folk songs provide the framework within which the cultural value of this material is self-evident. Thus, Sapir can adopt the stance of scientific observer to confirm the authenticity of these songs without having to indulge in the same pathos. Sapir's contributions to the July 1920 issue of *Poetry* magazine are thus firmly embedded in the nexus between salvage ethnography and modernist primitivism without wearing that affiliation on their sleeves.

Poetry Magazine

Sapir's contributions to *Poetry* deserve further scrutiny given that, apart from *The Canadian Forum*, where he published thirty-one poems, it is the magazine in which he placed the largest number of poems, twenty-three. While two of those texts, "She Sits Vacant-Eyed" (1921) and "Zuni" (1926), are ethnographic poems in the sense I am using the term in this book, the first question Sapir's notable presence in *Poetry* raises is not epistemological but formal and literary-historical. What were the conditions that allowed a poet who mostly wrote fairly traditional verse with an often decidedly nineteenth-century ring publish a good number of his poems in modernism's flagship little magazine? I have already provided a preliminary answer to this question in exploring his translations of Québécois folk songs: Sapir's concern with 'folk' communities and their cultural practices fits well into a magazine whose early-twentieth-century issues betray a sustained, often primitivist interest in 'folk' materials. In probing this question further, beyond Sapir's French-Canadian folk songs, I shed light not only on his poetic practice and self-understanding as a poet but also provide a new glimpse into one of the major institutions of anglophone modernism. There are a good number of sources that we can draw on to tackle this question: Sapir's own literary-critical essays "The Twilight of Rhyme" (1917), "Realism in Prose Fiction" (1917), "The Heuristic Value of Rhyme" (1920), and "The Musical Foundations of Verse" (1921); his reviews of books by (proto-)modernist writers, most notably of Emily Dickinson, H.D.'s *Collected Poems*, and Edwin Arlington Robinson's work; His remarks on imagism in letters to Amy Lowell; his correspondence about his poetry with *Poetry*'s editor Harriet Monroe and with his fellow Boasian anthropologists Benedict, Alfred L. Kroeber (Sapir, *Sapir-Kroeber Correspondence* 147–248, 281–82, 289–90, 294, 296, 322–25, 354), and Robert H. Lowie (Lowie 13–14, 18, 20, 24, 28, 31–33, 36–37); his comments about Monroe in his letters to Benedict; poems by other writers included in the *Poetry* issues that featured Sapir's verse; and his own, modest attempts to write poems such as "Blue Flame and Yellow" (1919), which in some ways resemble imagist verse.

Unlike most of the material discussed in this book, Sapir's relation to modernism in general and to *Poetry* and *The Dial* in particular has received quite a bit of critical attention. In two important essays—"Vigorous Male and Aspiring Female: Poetry, Personality, and Culture in Edward Sapir and Ruth Benedict" (1986) and "The Dainty and the Hungry Man: Literature and Anthropology in the Work of Edward Sapir" (2007)—as well as in the short piece "Sapir's Poetic Experience" (1984), which summarizes the major arguments of "The Dainty and the Hungry Man," and in his substantial introduction to sections IV ("Reflections on Contemporary Civilization") and V ("Aesthetics") of the *Culture* volume in *The Collected Works of Edward Sapir*, Richard Handler probes the relations between Sapir's poetry and literary and musical criticism on the one hand and his anthropological work on the other. Rather than focusing on either Sapir's poetic treatment of ethnographic subject matters or on his poetry's biographical origins, Handler probes Sapir's engagement with contemporaneous modernist writers and editors ("Vigorous") and explores how his poetry and especially his literary and cultural criticism adumbrate ethnographic theories and concepts that he develops more fully in his scientific studies ("Dainty"). In "Vigorous Male and Aspiring Female," Handler notes that even as he defended the softness and sentimentality of some of his poetry in letters to *Poetry*'s editor (142) and even as he complained about Monroe's literary tastes in letters to Benedict,[9] Sapir strove for an "aesthetic of hardness" (Handler, "Vigorous" 131 et passim) and sincerity of poetic expression akin to what modernist iconoclasts such as Ezra Pound—whose poetry he judged to be "unexpectedly fine-grained and attractive" ("Letter to Harriet Monroe of October 23, 1918") in one letter to Harriet Monroe and as "elaborate fooling" that leaves him "out in the cold" ("Letter to Harriet Monroe of April 5, 1919") in another—and T.E. Hulme were promoting in their imagist manifestoes. In "The Dainty and the Hungry Man," Handler shows that Sapir first explored the concept of culture—most notably the relation between individual creativity and given cultural forms, between subjective experience and objective social structures, between the elements and subjects out of which cultures consist and cultural wholes—in his poetry and literary and musical criticism before he developed it into a fully-fledged theory of culture in anthropological publications such as "Culture, Genuine and Spurious" (1924), "Cultural Anthropology and Psychiatry" (1932), and "Why Cultural Anthropology Needs the Psychiatrist" (1938). In his wide-ranging introductions to Sections IV and V of *The Collected Works*, Handler stresses once more the central insight that connects his two essays and relates Sapir to his modernist contemporaries: his focus, in his writing on poetry, on "the interaction of creativity and tradition, genius and technique" (737) and his conviction—which he shares with the T.S. Eliot of "Tradition and the Individual Talent"

(1919)—that "genuine artists begin with the techniques provided by their culture, but transcend those techniques in the creation of new culture" (Handler, "Introduction" 738).

In *Patterns for America: Modernism and the Concept of Culture* (1999), Susan Hegeman notes the extent to which both Sapir's and Van Wyck Brooks's reflections on 'culture' were attempts to find a place for individual agency in an alienated modern mass society. In Sapir's antimodern critique, contemporary American society is a 'spurious' social ensemble that, unlike 'genuine' cultures such as those of Native American tribes, does not allow for creative individuals' full expressions of their selves. In *Culture, 1922: The Emergence of a Concept* (2002), Marc Manganaro compares Sapir's "Culture, Genuine and Spurious" to *The Waste Land* as two "postwar works that, premised upon the notion of cultural ruin, construct taxonomies of cultural authenticity and a new civilizational order out of the 'fragments' or 'bits' of 'culture' " (10). One major result of that inquiry and of Manganaro's book as a whole is that Boasian holism and the New Critical organic unity doctrine are even more intricately intertwined than a cursory comparison warrants. While this comes out most clearly in Manganaro's chapter on Benedict (151–74),[10] Sapir's reflections on 'genuine culture' are frequently adduced as further support for the comparison,[11] even in that chapter. "A major argument of this volume," Manganaro announces in his introduction, "is that the integrative wholeness that came to characterize, indeed qualify something as, a work of art in modernist criticism does not merely resemble the holism of the culture concept but in fact is a version of it" (29). In *Composing Cultures: Modernism, American Literary Studies, and the Problem of Culture* (2013), Eric Aronoff places Sapir squarely in the midst of a diverse network of ethnographers, literary critics, and writers including Van Wyck Brooks, Willa Cather, Mary Austin, Lewis Mumford, John Crowe Ransom, and others, who conceptualized languages, literary texts, cultures, and selves as integrated, coherent, and self-contained meaningful wholes that serve as foils to an American culture perceived as fragmented, divided, and, to use Sapir's own term, 'spurious.' In Sapir, these positive foils are regional Native American cultures that are said to be more integrated than modern American national culture. Such conceptualizations of culture served, Aronoff shows, both reactionary and progressive ends, contributing both to imperialist appropriations and isolations of minority subjects and groups *and* to liberal critiques of the modern, industrialized nation state.

More recently, James Dowthwaite has shown the extent to which Sapir read fellow contemporary poets—in particular H.D. (whom he recuperates as a distinctly American poet) and Amy Lowell (with whose characterization, in "Rhythms of Free Verse," of free verse as structured by units of time instead of feet Sapir agrees) but also Ezra Pound, Robert Frost, E.A. Robinson, Richard Aldington, and Edgar Lee Masters—through the lens of his linguistic theories. Like Handler, Hegeman, Manganaro, and

Aronoff, Dowthwaite stresses Sapir's emphasis on the role of individual creativity in relation to cultural constraints. But unlike them, Dowthwaite recognizes that both Sapir's conceptualization of individual creativity and his poetic practice put him at odds, not only with the impersonal theory of poetry propounded by modernists like Eliot but also with the linguistic determinism of the Sapir-Whorf hypothesis (Dowthwaite 270–75). A. Elisabeth Reichel significantly expands on Sapir's engagement with modernist writers' reflection on free verse in his essay "The Musical Foundations of Verse," adding that he challenges Amy Lowell's categorical distinction between free and 'unfree' (metrical) verse by making it dependent—in a quintessentially Boasian move—on readers' differing apperceptions of poems (*Writing* 111–17). Reichel adds that Sapir's insistence on the musical foundations of poetry has strong affinities with the imagist mantra "to compose in sequence of the musical phrase, not in sequence of a metronome" (F.S. Flint, qtd. in Reichel, *Writing* 118). Equally importantly, Reichel adds, Sapir's penchant for scientific reflections on poetry put him in touch with modernist writers like Lowell, Eliot, Pound, and Yeats, who had similar aspirations (122–23). Joining Aronoff and Manganaro, Reichel further notes that Boasian holism, including Sapir's preference for integrated, harmonious 'genuine' cultures such as those of Native American tribes, is closely affiliated with the New Critical appraisal of literary texts as autonomous organic wholes, which is why it is fitting that "Civilization and Culture" (1919)—an early version of part of Sapir's influential essay "Culture, Genuine and Spurious" (1924)—was published in *The Dial*, the little magazine that also published *The Waste Land* (Reichel, *Writing* 129–31).

The value of Handler's pioneering work on Sapir's poetry and literary and cultural criticism and that of subsequent engagements with the same by Hegeman, Manganaro, Aronoff, Dowthwaite, and Reichel cannot be overestimated. They urge us to take seriously writings by Sapir that were at best relegated to the margins by anthropologists and, in the case of his poetry, at worst reduced to their biographical origins,[12] thus paving the ground for further treatments of these texts. Taken together, these critics firmly place Sapir in a network of social scientists, literary critics, and writers that made substantial contributions to the conceptualization of 'culture' which remain deeply relevant for twenty-first-century observers. What comes into particularly sharp focus in these contributions are four groups of texts by Sapir that indeed deserve further scrutiny: (1) his literary reviews of books by writers as diverse as Emily Dickinson and Edgar Lee Masters; (2) his literary-critical essays, in particular "The Twilight of Rhyme" (1917), "Realism in Prose Fiction" (1917), "The Heuristic Value of Rhyme" (1920), and "The Musical Foundations of Verse" (1921); (3) his contributions to the conceptualization of culture, first and foremost his influential essay "Culture, Genuine and Spurious" (1924); and (4) his over 660 published and unpublished poems.

Yet extant scholarship on Sapir's poetry and criticism also has three major limitations. First, with the notable exceptions of Reichel (who provides the first book-length literary-critical study of Sapir's, Benedict's, and Mead's poetry), and Dowthwaite (who discusses Sapir's poems "The Soul of Summer" [1917] and "He Implores His Beloved" [1927] at some length), none of these critics provides close readings of any of Sapir's poems, with the effect that what seems to count is the very fact of Sapir's poetic production and his success in placing them in some of the major little magazines rather than the poems themselves. The second limitation of previous treatments of Sapir's poetry and criticism is closely related to the first: in arguing for a close connection between Boasian holism and the New Critical organic unity doctrine, they tend to take for granted New Critical pronouncements concerning the self-contained unity of literary texts without considering whether the organic unity doctrine actually provides a fitting description for either Sapir's or contemporaneous modernist writers' poems. The third major limitation concerns specifically Handler's otherwise seminal work on Sapir, which misreads imagist pronouncements as poetics of expression (about which more below).

Before I embark on close readings of a number of Sapir's poems and situate them in their literary-historical contexts, a good look at some of his literary-critical essays is in order. The earliest of these essays, "The Twilight of Rhyme," was also published in a major little magazine: the August 1917 issue of *The Dial*. The essay begins with an anecdote. At a meeting of an Ottawa debating club, a fierce old Englishman rails against the "pusillanimity" (98) of U.S. President Wilson's peace note of December 18, 1916 to the nations at war in WWI. The unnamed speaker quotes the first three lines of Walter Scott's poem "Breathes there a Man with Soul so Dead":

> Breathes there the man with soul so dead,
> Who never to himself hath said,
> "This is my own, my native land!"
> (98)

Sapir is taken aback and impressed by the old man's forceful intervention, though not quite as much as the other listeners. What mars the experience for him is the speaker's recourse to "rhymed poetry" (98) that Sapir considers outdated, "bungling" (99), "inane jingles" (99). For Sapir, rhyme does have its place in poetry, but a much diminished one: in his day and age, it is fit for but "lighter forms of poetry, the fluffy ruffles of literary art" (99). Yet Sapir's main target in the essay is not the enraged Englishman at the debating club. His main target is Max Eastman, who one year earlier staged an attack on free verse in "Lazy Verse," a short, polemic piece published in *The New Republic* on September 8, 2016. Sapir responds with a properly literary-historical argument as he faults Eastman for believing that there are immutably true ways of creating art:

> Perfection of form is always essential, but the definition of what constitutes such perfection cannot, must not, be fixed once for all. The age, the individual artist, must solve the problem ever anew, must impose self-created conditions, perhaps only dimly realized, of the battle to be fought in attaining self-expression. It would be no paradox to say that it is the blind acceptance of a form imposed from without that is, in the deepest sense, 'lazy,' for such acceptance dodges the true formal problem of the artist, the arrival, in travail and groping, at that mode of expression that is best suited to the unique conception of the artist.
>
> ("The Twilight of Rhyme" 100)

Literary forms change and what was once an excellent vehicle for artistic expression may no longer serve today. What Sapir proposes here is not the kind of purely systemic understanding of literary history that the Russian Formalists were developing as he wrote those words. Artistic self-expression and individual creativity are still at the heart of Sapir's understanding of the work that poetry does. In staging his argument, Sapir also draws on his ethnographic research, stating that it is an illusion to believe that "primitive," "lower" levels of culture (100) were defined by greater freedom and less restraint. Quite the contrary is the case: such cultures set "purely formal limitations . . . on the artist's activity" that "would seem to us almost to preclude the possibility of individual expression at all" while in "higher levels the number of things one may do is vastly greater, the number of things one must do relatively less" (100). Cultural progress, then, comes with an extension of artistic freedom. Restraints imposed on artists' creativity such as Eastman's insistence that poetry must rhyme, are, by way of contrast, remnants of the past that must be overcome:

> Briefly, then, aesthetic progress cannot mean that we hold on to such a feature as rhyme because it is a valuable conquest, a complexity that we have achieved in passing from a less to a more subtle grasp of form (this was true in its day), but that we leave it behind as already belonging to a more primitive stage of artistic consciousness. Once a resplendent jewel, it is now a pretty bauble. In time it will have become an ugly bauble.
>
> (100)

Originally published in the *Queen's Quarterly* in 1920, "The Heuristic Value of Rhyme" is another short essay at the beginning of which Sapir sounds like Shklovsky: "all art is largely technique" (922).

More surprisingly, he sounds not unlike the foil of his earlier essay. Like Eastman, he now praises the disciplining force of rhyme: "Indeed it is more than probable that the very feeling of compulsion often serves as a valuable stimulant in the shaping of [the poet's] thought and imagination" (922). While the discussion that follows this statement gives examples of weak and infelicitous rhymes produced by such compulsion (his cautionary example is the poetry of John Masefield, who went on to become the United Kingdom's poet laureate from 1930 to 1967), the essay as a whole stresses what its title announces: the "heuristic value of rhyme," which Sapir glosses as "the stimulating, or even directly creative, effect that the necessity of finding a rhyming word may exercise on the fancy of the poet" (923). Sapir insists that "many a gorgeous bit of imagery" would have "forever remained undiscovered if not whipped into being by the rhyming slave-driver" (923), and his felicitous examples are lines by Robert Frost, Edwin Arlington Robinson, and John Davidson—writers of very diverse kinds of verse that were, however, united in their use of traditional poetic forms (a blending of traditional meters and colloquialisms in the case of Frost; the sonnet, the quatrain, and the eight-line stanza for Robinson; the ballad for Davidson) that put them at a distance from modernist iconoclasts or, better, morphoclasts. What further unites Sapir's positive examples is that they all wrote what he all but consigned to the past in "The Twilight of Rhyme": rhymed poetry.[13] Then, on the heels of his discussion of Robinson and Davidson, whom he considers "distinguished by a rare combination of intellect and passion" (924), Sapir writes two sentences that Handler, one of his poetry's major interpreters, considers key to his verse: "Perhaps," Sapir speculates,

> it is precisely the passionate temperament cutting into itself with the cold steel of the intellect that is best adapted to the heuristic employment of rhyme. The temperament and the triumphant harnessing of form belong, both of them, to the psychology of sublimation following inhibition.
>
> (924)

Handler cites Sapir's speculation in his two pioneering essays "Vigorous Male and Aspiring Female" and "The Dainty and the Hungry Man" and also devotes attention to it in his introduction to sections IV and V of the third volume (*Culture*) of *The Collected Works of Edward Sapir*. In his first and most extensive discussion of the passage in "Vigorous Male and Aspiring Female," Handler aptly characterizes Sapir's observation as giving expression to an aesthetic of hardness that he finds realized in Sapir's own poem "Blue Flame and Yellow," which he wrote on March 15, 1919:

> I strove for a blue flame
> That would rise like a point of steel,

> Cleaving the vast night
> Up to the starry wheel.
>
> I burned with a yellow flame,
> I was edged with a curl of smoke,
> I went out under the stars,
> Leaves of the world oak.
> (Handler, "Vigorous" 131)

I am in agreement with Handler up to this point but part ways with his literary-historical framing of Sapir's "aesthetic of hardness." Handler likens Sapir's aesthetics to imagism, noting rightly that the imagists strove for hardness, precision, and immediacy. Yet while "Blue Flame and Yellow" may give expression to a yearning to write 'hard' poetry, the poem itself is, in its subject-centeredness (notice its first word and the anaphora in the second quatrain), no imagist poem. In fact, one could argue that the poem thrives on the very romantic, subjectivist poetics of expression from which the imagists sought to dissociate themselves. Moreover, even if Pound admired and supported Frost, the poets that Sapir singles out for praise in "The Heuristic Value of Rhyme"—Frost, Robinson, and Davidson—are no imagists. They are writers much more like Sapir himself, more cautious innovators who kept at least one foot firmly planted in nineteenth-century aesthetics. Equally importantly, while Handler well captures Sapir's own understanding of poetry as self-expression, the Sapir-imagism nexus he postulates leads him to impose a romantic poetics of expression on a group of modernist writers who felt contempt for romanticism and by and large subscribed to Eliot's impersonal theory of poetry instead: "Poetry is not a turning loose of emotion, but an escape from emotion; it is not the expression of personality, but an escape from personality" ("Tradition" 43). This is where the slippage occurs in Handler's argument:

> Pound's equation of the real with the artistically valid is characteristic, and he came to formulate that equation in the aesthetic of what he called hardness, an aesthetic that tempted both Sapir and Benedict. . . . The crucial notion was that sincere self-expression—considered the essence of Art—depended (in poetry) upon an absolutely original use of language, because the individual's unique experience could not be conveyed through conventional language, encumbered as it is with dead metaphors and cliché. . . . [T]he "thing" is any experience the poet has, and his task is to translate that unique experience 'directly,' via an absolutely original use of language.
> ("Vigorous" 129)

In fact, none of the quotations by Pound and T.E. Hulme that Handler adduces support the idea that the imagists considered poetry to be a form of self-expression. These quotations much rather testify to the fact that, for the imagists (and for the modernists more generally), poetry is work on language:

> Direct treatment of the "thing" whether subjective of objective.
> (Pound, qtd. in Handler, "Vigorous" 129)

> each man sees a little differently, and to get out clearly and exactly what he does see, he must have a terrific struggle with language.
> (Hulme, qtd. in Handler, "Vigorous" 129)

> technique [is] the test of a man's sincerity.
> (Pound, qtd. in Handler, "Vigorous" 130)

Handler's slippage testifies to the limitations of discussing Sapir's and Benedict's poetry within a modernist framework. For them, poetry may very well be a form of self-expression, but this is precisely what puts them at odds with writers like Pound, Hulme, and Eliot, who conceived of poetry first and foremost as craftsmanship. After all, in dedicating *The Waste Land* to Pound, whose editorial advice on the poem was crucial, Eliot did not call him a great 'personality' (a keyword for the Boasians) but "il miglior fabbro" (*The Waste Land* 27)—the better craftsman. Thus, when, in his 1925 review of *The Complete Poems of Emily Dickinson*, Sapir chides contemporaneous poets for giving us "everything but the ecstasy of intuitive living" and "curiously little spiritual life" because they do not seem "willing, or able, to take their true selves seriously" ("Emily Dickinson, a Primitive" 1002), he seeks in modernist poets things—the expression of a genuine personality—that many of them have no interest in providing.

Given this, how should we interpret Sapir's own shift from consigning rhymed poetry to the past in "The Twilight of Rhyme" to celebrating its disciplining/hardening function three years later in "The Heuristic Value of Rhyme"? Handler is entirely right in attributing "a bit of self-analysis" to Sapir's pronouncement:

> If we remember that Sapir had previously championed the cause of unrhymed verse, and that he had since begun to use rhyme, it is difficult not to imagine these lines as a bit of self-analysis. They give us a picture of Sapir working out a theory of art, and of culture, as he tried to understand, through introspective analysis, his own artistic praxis.
> ("Vigorous" 303)

Dowthwaite corroborates this assessment as he traces Sapir's early embrace of modernist poetry (which is most pronounced in his praise of imagism in his letters to Amy Lowell) and his later distancing from it (which comes out clearly in his correspondence with Benedict). I would, however, put the emphasis somewhat differently, attributing Sapir's divergent opinions on the value of rhyme less to changes in his personal poetic practice and/or theory of culture than to shifting assessments of his place and position in a literary milieu that produced much more than experimental modernist poetry.

Consider the August 1919 issue of *Poetry*, which contains Sapir's first two contributions to the magazine, "The Soul of Summer" and "Mary, Mary, My Love." While the former "seems to be caught," as Dowthwaite has shown, "between poetic traditions" (261)—between the imagist concision of lines such as "the fine dust drifts in the torpid air" or "a faint blue shadow veil hung before green" and the mixed, clichéd image of the final line, "I know the summer whose laughter pierced my heart"—the latter is a simple love poem resembling a song whose title reverberates as a refrain in every stanza's second line. Here are the first two stanzas:

> Why are you trembling so,
> Mary, Mary, my love?
> Why are your hands so cold,
> Your hands that burn my lips?
>
> And the night is throbbing with us,
> Mary, Mary, my love;
> But your little hands are cold,
> Your hands that have set me aflame.

Lest one think of such simple lines—which Sapir, oddly, characterizes as "a dangerous experiment" ("Letter to Harriet Monroe of October 28, 1918") in a letter to Monroe—as an oddity in *Poetry*, consider the verse that precedes and follows Sapir's two poems. Immediately before "The Soul of Summer," we find Chicago Renaissance poet Eunice Tietjens's "The Tepid Hour," a poem that follows a straightforward ABABA rhyme pattern and which repeats each stanza's first line in its last:

> In such a tepid night as this
> Strange formless sorrowings lie hid,
> Like melancholy in a kiss,
> Like what we dreamed in what we did—
> In such a tepid night as this.

Similarly, the poem that follows Sapir's two contributions—Charles L. O'Donnell's "On Indian Lake"—follows the simple rhyme scheme ABAB and deals in only mildly estranged pastoral imagery:[14]

> Apple trees on a low hill
> And the dead sun behind;
> The water red and still;
> No sound, no wind.

Consider also the January 1926 issue of *Poetry*, which begins with "Foam-Waves," a group of eight poems by Sapir. "Foam-Waves" is followed by "December," a sequence of seven traditional Petrarchan sonnets by Florence Kiper Frank (a frequent contributor to the magazine), all of which strictly follow the form's combination of an octave and a sestet as well as a Petrarchan rhyme scheme (ABBAABBA for the octave; CDCDEE for the sestet).

I am not cherry-picking my examples: In none of the *Poetry* issues that feature poems by Sapir is a poem or group of poems of his preceded or followed by a daring, iconoclastic experiment in verse. Far from being exceptions to the rule, Sapir's poems do in fact fit quite neatly into the magazine that has come to be known as one of the most important catalysts of the modernist movement. This is also true for "She Sits Vacant-Eyed" (1921), one of the two ethnographic poems Sapir published in *Poetry*:

> Surely, surely, there is something for me,
> There is something to fill my spirit's measure.
> Winds tell, rains tell—
> Somewhere, somewhere is my treasure.
>
> They promised it me when a raven spoke
> Back in the reaches of maidenhood.
> He spoke for God, he spoke well—
> I am groping for what I then understood.
>
> Ten thousand pathways ran to treasure—
> The raven spoke, I saw the vision.
> Suns burn, moons burn—
> God, God! I am sitting in prison!
>
> Surely, surely, there is something for me—
> There is something to fill my spirit whole.
> Sun, burn! sun, burn!
> Pity me, make a blaze of my soul!

Composed of four quatrains whose second and fourth lines rhyme, the poem is further integrated by the last quatrain's repetition of the poem's initial line ("Surely, surely, there is something for me") and by the rhyming third lines of the first and the second quatrains (tell—well) as well as of the third and fourth quatrains (burn—burn). With its slightly irregular rhyme scheme (ABCB DECE BFGF AHGH) and irregular meter, "She Sits Vacant-Eyed" does not fit neatly any traditional lyrical form but equally certainly does not constitute experimental modernist poetry either.

In its inclusion of a spiritual quest, a speaking animal, a vision, and of animate natural elements, the poem builds on much the same ethnographic work as Sapir's 'Nootka' essays ("Tom" and "Sayach'apis, a Nootka Trader") and poem ("The Blind, Old Indian Tells His Names"), which I will discuss in detail in the next section. In the mythology of the coastal Indigenous communities of British Columbia, Sapir notes in "The Indians of the Province [of British Columbia]" (1912),

> the mythological Raven is believed to be responsible for daylight and other important facts of existence. Curiously enough, Raven, while spoken of as a powerful transformer and benefactor of mankind, is in other myths, and indeed often in the very same myth, put in the most ridiculous roles.
>
> (345)

Among these communities, there are also several Raven clans or phratries, for instance among the Tlingit Indians, whose "leading crest or emblem" and "most important mythological being" ("Social Organization" 440) is the raven. Sapir elaborates on this in "Indian Tribes of the Coast" (1914):

> The raven is the culture hero and trickster of the [Pacific Northwest Coast tribes] Tlingit, Haida, and Tsimshian. Some of his exploits, as his liberation, for the benefit of future generations, of daylight, which had been kept enclosed in a box by a greedy individual, almost entitle him to be considered a kind of god; yet almost in the same breath incidents are related of him that would put him on the level of a Reynard the Fox or Till Eulenspiegel.
>
> (394)

Finally, in puberty, the boys of the Plateau Indians in British Columbia go on a vision quest to obtain the protection of an animal guardian spirit ("Indians of the Province" 344) such as the Raven. As Sapir's ethnographic work reveals, Raven is as much a culture hero and a guardian spirit as he is a "greedy trickster or buffoon" ("[Religion of the] Vancouver Island Indians" 513). In the poem, Raven/raven plays the former role: he is the culture hero, a creator who brings daylight to humankind ("Suns burn"; "Sun, burn! sun, burn!") and also the guardian spirit whose protection the poem's persona seeks in her vision ("The raven spoke, I saw the vision").[15] Notably, Sapir supplants his ethnographic studies' inquiry into male rites of passage during puberty with a female vision quest. In the poem, it is a woman who sits, as the title of the poem suggests, "vacant-eyed" as she anticipates spiritual insights ("something to fill my spirit's measure"; "something to fill my spirit whole") similar to those she reached in a vision during a liminal phase of her life ("the reaches of maidenhood"), when she heard Raven/raven speaking "for God." The poem's persona is distraught since she remains unable to return to her earlier state of spiritual enlightenment. For this reason, her vacant eyes are coded ambiguously: They are vacant both in anticipation of spiritual insight and in her inability to repeat a past epiphany. The persona, the final line of the third quatrain suggests, remains imprisoned in the present as she yearns for a return to the spiritual fullness of maidenhood but is, within the space of the poem, unable to do so.

The poem's gender politics are ambivalent. On the one hand, Sapir recodes an Indigenous male rite of passage as female, thus providing his persona with an aptitude for spiritual experience beyond the ethnographic source's reach. On the other hand, he locates the possibility for female spiritual experience in the purity of maidenhood, suggesting that the kind of heightened experience available to virgins is out of reach for an adult woman. Read this way, the poem's formal conservatism goes hand in hand with the kind of social conservatism Sapir displays in his infamous 1928 essay "Observations on the Sex Problem in America," in which he posits that sexual liberation is the epitome of a spurious culture of self-realization.[16] As does the sonnet "Zuni," the other ethnographic poem that Sapir managed to place in *Poetry* (and which I will also discuss below), "She Sits Vacant-Eyed" both engages with issues he encountered in his ethnographic work and is written in fairly conventional poetic form. As it turns out, both qualities of these poems—their ethnographic subject matters and their traditional forms—make them excellent candidates for inclusion in a poetry magazine whose early-twentieth-century publication record testifies to a sustained interest in 'folk' and Indigenous materials and to an appreciation of poetic forms much less experimental than those of the modernists the magazine also championed. My inquiry into a major Boasian anthropologist's interaction with one of the major little magazines that shaped the modernist revolution in poetry sheds new light, then, not only on one leading Boasian poet's lyrical production but also on the surprisingly wide-ranging and inclusive publication practices of one of modernism's main literary institutions.

Playing Seriously With Genres

Like Sapir's translations of Québécois folk songs, his most striking use of anthropological materials for poetic purposes is also based on his Canadian researches. Published not in *Poetry* but in the much lesser-known *The Canadian Bookman* in 1921, Sapir's poem "The Blind, Old Indian Tells His Names" grows out of the most sustained research effort in his career. From September to December 1910, in 1913–14, and then again in 1934, Sapir did fieldwork among the Nuu-chah-nulth, a group of fifteen related Indigenous communities of Vancouver Island whom anthropologists of Sapir's time called 'Nootka' (Sapir, "The Indians of the Province"

335; Darnell and Irvine, "Introduction to Section III" 255–57). During his long and distinguished career, Sapir published no less than two book-length collections of Nuu-chah-nulth texts with extensive editorial notes and commentary,[17] two substantial memoirs for the Canadian Geological Survey,[18] fourteen scientific articles, and a set of three texts that focus on Sapir's Nuu-chah-nulth informant Tom Sayach'apis (see Figure. 3.1): the

Tom Sayach'apis: The Nootka Indian who boasted that he could sing without stopping for twenty-four hours, and never the same twice.

Figure 3.1 Photograph of Tom Sayach'apis in Edward Sapir, "The Social Organization of the West Coast Tribes" (1915)
Source: Courtesy of Walter de Gruyter and Company

impressionistic sketch "Tom" (1918), "The Blind, Old Indian Tells His Names" (1921), and a compressed survey of Nuu-chah-nulth culture by way of an account of Tom's biography, "The Life of a Nootka Indian" (1921), an essay that was republished in a slightly revised version under a different title, "Sayach'apis, a Nootka Trader" (1922) in the following year.[19] His first publication on the Nuu-chah-nulth was the article "Some Aspects of Nootka Language and Culture" (1911), his last the posthumously published book *Native Accounts of Nootka Ethnography* (1955), which he co-wrote with his fellow American linguist Morris Swadesh. Sapir's research on the Nuu-chah-nulth constitutes his "most intensive ethnographic effort" (Darnell and Irvine, "Introduction" 26n. 1).

In what follows, I zoom in on the three texts revolving around Tom Sayach'apis to inquire into the ethical and epistemological ramifications of a Boasian anthropologist's transgressions of generic boundaries. While this section probes the intersections of literature, literary studies, and cultural anthropology, the principal addressee of its call for modesty is practitioners within my own discipline, literary studies. More specifically, what I hope comes into view as the argument develops are less auspicious uses of literary forms (here, poetry) and literary-critical concepts (especially poetic license) by a cultural anthropologist than those many a literary scholar and many an ethnographer has become accustomed to since the *Writing Culture* debate of the 1980s and 1990s.

Published in the *Canadian Courier* on December 7, 1918, Sapir's six-page sketch "Tom" begins with an impressionistic account of the foul weather bugging Sapir as he approaches the Nuu-chah-nulth reserve near Alberni on the west coast of Vancouver Island. Partly adopting the perspective of his Indigenous subjects, Sapir describes himself as "the rubber-booted rain-coated individual who had come to get his field data for another of the series of scientific monographs with which ethnology is just now deluging the country" (451). His interpreter's welcome and advice is equally underwhelming:

> At last my half-breed interpreter arrived, smiling blandly. He was just three-quarters of an hour late, for he had been 'very busy.' He had just decided the best thing I could do was to get my information from Tom. Tom did not know a word of English, but we could get along with Chinook, the lingua franca of the Pacific Coast natives, aided by the interpreter's well-paid intermediation.
>
> (451–52)

The sketch continues in the same vein once Sapir has been introduced to blind old Tom and welcomed into his grandson's cabin, which Sapir describes as tasteless, sordid, smelly, and unbearably noisy. It takes a while until Sapir notices that the "young wife of the houseowner . . . was not without a certain oily unkempt charm" (452). Tom has squandered his wealth in potlatches and now appears before Sapir as a dirty, shabby old man who "had had his days of prestige and now rested content in their memory" (453). With financial agreements made, Sapir, Tom, and the interpreter set to work on the next day, "recording the ethnological information that was stored up in Tom's encyclopaedic mind" (453). Tom has to be taught to speak more slowly but soon "acquire[s] an intelligent and repetitive docility worthy of any dictaphone or college professor" (454). Sapir's mildly self-ironic account of his Nuu-chah-nulth informant remains condescending when he characterizes the little jokes Tom makes when welcoming Sapir in the mornings as a "quaint conceit" (454) that amuses no one but Tom himself. But then, at the onset of the penultimate paragraph of this brief sketch, Sapir's tone changes. Here are the essay's two final paragraphs:

> Tom was master of endless chains of song—songs that would make the harpooned whale head for the shore instead of plunging on madly out to sea, lullabys, songs of mourning, gambling songs, marriage songs, sacred songs dealing with the fabulous thunder-bird or the eerie wolf of ritual. He boasted that he could sing uninterruptedly for twenty-four hours without repeating himself. I believe him.
> But Tom was no mere mystery-monger or sentimental ritualist. He had led an extremely active life—traded up and down the coast with canoes, driven hard bargains with the whites at Victoria in the early days, built houses, dabbled with Indian doctoring, sealed and fished and hunted like the rest, given many feasts to his own tribesmen and to alien tribes whom he made his guests, and left his descendants an honored name. And that is how I came to feel that the shabby old man was one of the victorious ones of the earth. Pity of him was an impertinence, for he had tasted of all the fruits that grew on the stem of his tribal life. And when I shook hands with him at the end of my season's work, I took leave not of my 'informant,' but of a genuine man.
> (454)

Sapir is no longer the distanced and bemused observer but himself becomes the subject of a learning process. Of course, the hierarchy remains firmly in place: it is the ethnographer who reserves himself the right to judge that Tom is, after all, "a genuine man." Sapir arrogates all the definitional power to himself: When he takes leave of Tom, his erstwhile informant now is "a genuine man" because Sapir considers him so. But in ending this sketch, which begins on a consistently condescending note, with a paean to the fullness of this First Nations subject's life, to his mastery of songs, his dignity and his legacy, is to admit to the hastiness and wrongness of the ethnographer's initial judgement. In putting 'informant' in scare quotes in the final sentence of this sketch, Sapir—who was, after all, a linguist as well as an ethnographer—also engages in an act of discursive self-reflection as he questions the accuracy of the terms anthropologists use to refer to the subjects of their research.[20] This concern with the power of naming and misnaming, labeling and mislabeling is visible throughout Sapir's oeuvre.

In his poetic work, this is most clearly apparent in "The Mislabeled Menagerie," the opening piece of his poetry collection *Dreams and Gibes* (1917), a book that he published a year before "Tom." There, the persona visits the animals in the menagerie to find out that the cages are misnamed: in the cage labeled "Ursus," a monkey lives, the camel is found in what appears to be the ostrich cage, and so on. The keeper explains, "Oh, well . . . we only moved the animals/This morning, and we've not got round as yet/To move the labels. We'll attend to that." "Discomfited" by this explanation at first, the persona experiences an epiphany when he realizes that human beings too are frequently assigned false epithets:

> Why, yes, mislabeled all!
> Mislabeled all! The grocer was he not
> A sturdy disputant in politics?
> His label should have "statesman" been, no less.
> The mayor hard to say, but I've no doubt
> That "grocer" would have served. Of clergymen
> I know, two should have "broker" called themselves
> And one just "simpleton."

If the menagerie is, as the persona asserts in the first half of the poem, "Topsyturvydom," he sets things right in the second half, where he enters the realm of culture. There, he enacts the fantasy of stripping humans of their false labels, deflating the pretensions of the high and elevating the low to their deserved place. Sapir's persona paradoxically imagines a carnivalesque reversal of hierarchies that restores a topsy-turvy world to order. Appropriately, the linguist's proposed remedy is acts of renaming. Naming is also crucial for a group of poems in which Sapir explores human types.[21] These poems include "The Man of Letters," "The Professor," "The Metaphysician," "Epitaph of a Philosopher," "The Clergyman," "The Stenographer," "The Lexicographer," "The Dainty and the Hungry Man," "The Oil-Merchant," and "The Learned Jew." In the last of these, Sapir engages in a bit of self-analysis as he creates a persona not unlike himself: a scholarly Jew whose "learning was a many-chambered treasure house," a man who knew "the Sabbath and the week-day rituals" and "the Pentateuch by heart," and would "pounce upon" any who would "slur a vowel or misplace a prefixed article" (20). In this ethnographic poem, Sapir occupies himself with a form of participant observation in which he explores his own, Lower East Side Yiddish culture and his own professional role as a linguist. Thus, he does in poetry what the fellow Boasians Zora Neale Hurston and Ella Cara Delorie did in their ethnographies: probe their own culture. Playing the role of both participant and observer, Sapir ends the poem with these two lines: "What was his outward shell? What met the Gentile's eye?/Why, merely this: he kept a peanut stand on Hester Street" (20). As in "The Mislabeled Menagerie," Sapir ruminates on (mis)perception and (mis)labeling, processes in which only insiders—Jews—recognize the true nature of the peanut vendor.

Names and naming likewise play a crucial role in Sapir's three texts about Tom Sayach'apis.[22] In "Tom," we learn that this old man "left his descendants an honored name" (454). In Sapir's poem about the same man, "The Blind, Old Indian Tells His Names," naming is the leitmotif. "Sayach'apis, a Nootka Trader" begins on a note very different from "Tom." While pointing out his subject's poverty, he introduces him as a dignified man of solid reputation:

> Tom is now old and poverty-stricken, but the memory of his former wealth is with his people. The many feasts he has given and the many ceremonial dances and displays he has had performed have all had their desired effect—they have shed luster on his sons and daughters and grandchildren, they have 'put his family high' among the Ts'isha'ath tribe, and they have even carried his name to other, distant Nootka tribes, and to tribes on the east coast of the island that are of alien speech. Nowadays he spends much of his time by the fireside, tapping his staff in accompaniment to old ritual tunes that he is never tired of humming.
>
> ("Sayach'apis" 481)

Tom, we learn, has made his name known beyond the boundaries of his community and ensured his offspring a high standing among his own. To speak of Tom's "name" is misleading, though, for during his lifetime, he had no less than six names. His present name, "Sayach'apis," is "an old man's name of eight generations' standing, that hails from the Hisawist'ath, a now extinct Nootka tribe" and means "Stands-up-high-over-all" ("Sayach'apis" 481). As Sapir explains, names are privileges ('topati' in transliterated Nuu-chah-nulth) that are passed down the generations in Nuu-chah-nulth culture, not unlike songs, legends, and ceremonies. In this specific case, the original bearer of the name received it as a gift from "Sky Chief" in a dream; Tom assumed it at a potlatch he organized in honor of his oldest daughter when he was about fifty years old. Before that, Tom bore a young man's name, Nawe'ik, which is said to translate as "Come here!," a demand made by a spirit whale during a dream of its first bearer. Tom's fourth name was another young man's name, "Kunnuh," which means "Wake up!" This name too has its origin in a dream of a spirit whale (482) and was given to Tom at a naming feast when he was around ten. His third name was Ha'wihlkumuktli, a boy's name that signifies "Having chiefs behind" (483). This name derives from Tom's grandmother's father's father, a successful whaler whose wealth and reputation surpassed other chiefs'. Tom also received it at a feast, which was organized by his paternal grandfather. Tom's second name was "Tl'i'nitsawa," which translates as "Getting-whale-skin." His father chose it because Tom, like other boys, would come to the beach to get slices of skin from caught whales. He got it at a mourning potlatch for his recently deceased father. Tom does not remember his first name, which was a child's nickname that comes with no privileges (483). Sapir comments on Tom's various names at some length because they illustrate the importance of privileges and of descent and kinship ties, all of which determine social status among the Nuu-chah-nulth. Thus, Tom is assigned the role of a representative of his people, whose social structures and ritual activities (from potlatches to marriage ceremonies) are portrayed via the story of one of its men.

Sapir's poem "The Blind, Old Indian Tells His Names" was originally published in 1921. Based on the story of Tom Sayach'apis as we know it from the essays "Tom" and "Sayach'apis, a Nootka Trader," the poem interweaves two voices. The first is a third-person voice that introduces the poem's eponymous figure at the beginning and watches the "Blind, Old Indian" stumble off as the poem ends. The major part of the poem is taken up by the First Nations figure's first-person account of what names he has worn throughout his life and how he received them. This account is reported as direct speech rendered in quotation marks. Three times, the First Nations voice breaks into song. Another three times, the third-person voice briefly comments on the blind, old Indian's movements and actions.

The poem's politics of representation is ambivalent.[23] On the one hand, the greatest part of the poem is given over to the First Nations voice. Thus, there is an attempt on Sapir's part to stage a First Nations subject's act of self-representation. On the other hand, this first-person voice is framed and contextualized by a third-person, Western voice. Given the obvious and close connections between the two essays and the poem, given Tom Sayach'apis' penchant for song, and given that the poem's focus on naming is drawn directly from "Sayach'apis, a Nootka Trader," we may safely call the source of the poem's First Nations voice 'Tom'—provided that we remain aware of a truth that applies to any poem: that neither its persona nor any of the voices that speak in it are identical with either the poem's empirical author or any other living being.

What is most striking about the story of naming that the figure of Tom tells us in "The Blind, Old Indian Tells His Names" is that it does not match the account we get in "Sayach'apis, a Nootka Trader."

The beginning of the poem sticks fairly closely to the narrative that we get in the essay:

> His staff was stamping like beginning rain,
> He smiled beneath a hat all dust and stain,
> And, looking blind into the beaming sun,
> He told his names. We heard the decades run.
> "I have four names. The first is 'Stand-up-high.' " . . .
> Long years ago there came down from the sky
> The Heaven-Chief and stepped into the dream
> My ancestor was dreaming. "Ho! you seem
> To have no care for riches, you that sleep,
> Yet riches I would give, a name to keep
> While generations come and seep away."
> And 'Stand-up-high' became a name that day
>
> (507)

The poem tells us that Tom's first name is " 'Stand-up high' " and that its first bearer received it from "The Heaven-Chief" in a dream. Up to this point, Sapir's verse account of the origins and meaning of Tom's present name, Sayach'apis, corresponds to what we know from the essay, albeit with minor differences: the essay's "Stands-up-high-over-all" becomes the poem's "Stand-up high," and the essay's "Sky Chief" is transformed into the poem's "Heaven-Chief." What may seem a greater discrepancy between the two accounts also appears to be easily resolvable. In the essay's account, "Stand-up high" (or Sayach'apis, though in the poem, we only get the English translation of the name) is Tom's sixth name, his present one. In the poem, it is referred to as his "first." We are led to assume that this apparent incongruity is simply based on a different kind of framing: while the essay tells the story of Tom's various names in reverse chronological order (from his present to his earliest name), the poem begins with the most important name. "Stand-up" is Tom's "first" name in the sense that it is the most prestigious one, the name that comes with the greatest age and the greatest privileges. At least for now, this explanation makes much sense. On a related note, Sapir's decision to have the First Nations figure of the poem say that he has "four names" (rather than the essay's six) seems readily attributable to the author's poetic license in selecting the number of names that fit the poem's verbal economy and in choosing only the more resounding names.[24] To sum up, while there are differences between the narrative of the beginning of the poem and the corresponding passages in the essay, these differences are relatively small. The first quarter of the poem and the essay are largely in sync. But then, things take a different turn.

At first sight, the "second name" mentioned in the poem is nowhere to be found in the essay. It is "Talking-of-the-day":

> He mused a moment. 'Talking-of-the-day,'
> This was my second name. I threw away
> My first, when seven tribes I called to feast
> And scattered wealth like eagle-down released
> Upon the dancing-floor, and took a name
> From Daylight. . . .
>
> (507–8)

As we read on, the mystery partly clears up. Four lines later in Tom's account of the origin of that second name, we encounter a gnome shouting "Wake up or freeze!" to another of Tom's dreaming ancestors. Here is how the poem continues after "From Daylight":

> Winter dawn was breaking flame
> Across the mountain snow, wherein he cowered,
> Sleeping for vision that he might be powered
> For capturing the whale, sea-otter, seal.
> 'Wake up or freeze!' there stumbled on his heel.
>
> (508)

The poem's second name, then, seems to correspond to the essay's fourth name, given as "Kunnuh" in the essay and translated there as "Wake up!" Oddly, though, Sapir changes the sequence of names in the poem. In the poem's account, Tom bore the name "Stand-up high" *before* he bore the name "Talking-of-the-day" (or "Wake up or freeze!"). This is what the poem suggests: " 'Talking-of-the-day,'/This was my second name. I threw away/My first, when seven tribes I called to feast." My earlier hypothesis—that the names in the poem are ordered in terms of social status instead of the chronological arrangement that we find in the essay—crumbles. In the poem, too, the names are given in chronological sequence, though with a significant twist: Sapir reverses the chronological order. In the essay, "Stands-up-high-over-all" is identified as Tom's present and most recent name while "Wake up!" is an earlier name. The reverse holds true for the poem, where "Stand-up high" is an earlier name that Tom "threw away" when he adopted "Talking-of-the-day" (or "Wake up or freeze!"). Should we still speak of Sapir's poetic license here? Do the epistemological and ethical obligations of anthropologists toward their Indigenous subjects radically change when those subjects are transposed into the realm of poetry? These questions become more pressing as we continue reading the poem.

By the time the poem reveals that Tom's "third" name is "Red-Mounded" (508) we have learned to understand that this is again a more recent name that displaces the second name:

> 'Red-mounded' is another whaling name,
> My third . . . A thick and thundering darkness came
> Upon our village shore and killed the day,
> While maddening rain drummed on our ears away.
>
> (508)

Unlike the two earlier names, "Red-Mounded" cannot be linked to any one of the names mentioned in the essay with any degree of certitude. The poem tells us that this third name is "another whaling name" and takes us into a time in which Tom's people suffered from hunger, zooming in on a particular day on which "[a] thick and thundering darkness came/Upon our village shore and killed the day." During this stormy day, a particularly courageous man—Tom himself—braves the weather and spots a whale carcass illuminated by lightning. As Tom announces in a triumphant song that "silence[s] his foes" (510), this whale's flesh ended his people's hunger period. Clearly, there are parallels between this story and Sapir's essay on Nuu-chah-nulth culture. For one, the Nuu-chah-nulth that we know from the essay are a fishing culture that lives primarily off salmon, salmon trout, herring, halibut, cod, shellfish, "mussels and clams and sea urchins, sea cucumbers, and octopuses" (Sapir, "Sayach'apis" 486). In addition, they hunt a variety of highly prized sea mammals:

> Far more important than these mushy foods, though probably subsidiary, on the whole, to salmon and other fish, was the flesh of sea mammals—the humpbacked whale, the California whale, the sea otter, the sea lion, and, most important of all, the hair seal.
>
> (486)

There are additional overlaps between the essay's and the poem's narratives. For dramatic effect, Sapir works the essay's description of Nuu-chah-nulth explanations of natural phenomena into the poem's "Red-Mounded" section. To give but one example: the essay's account of the Nuu-chah-nulth's personification of lightning as "the scaly, knife-tongued, lightning serpent" (492) returns in the poem when "Thunder first/Went flapping through and dropped the lightning snake/Sheer from his middle to the rocks and flake/On flake glowed on the serpent's scaly length" (509).

Still, despite these convergences, the third name of the poem, "Red-Mounded," cannot be identified with any one of the six names mentioned in the essay. Most likely, it collapses three of the essay's names into one: Tom's fifth name Nawe'ik, his fourth name Kunnuh (which is, as we have seen, also linked to another name in the poem), and his third name, the boy's name Ha'wihlkumuktli. All of these names, Sapir's essay tells us, originated in an ancestor's dream of a spirit-whale ("Sayach'apis" 482–83). The whale-spotting story that Sapir weaves around "Red-Mounded" likewise has a dream-like quality; it is set at night and in a partly mystical, partly gothic atmosphere. The poem's story is also dream-like in a second, Freudian sense: it constitutes a wish-fulfillment of sorts since, both the essay and the poem tell us, while Tom caught plenty of seals and sea otters in his lifetime, he never caught a whale ("Sayach'apis" 486–87). As we read in the poem, "I have never hurled a whale harpoon" (508). Thus, while the poem's narrative about the nightly sighting of a whale carcass is nowhere to be found in the essay, that story is woven out of several threads strewn throughout it. In this case, then, there are narrative convergences between poem and essay but no exact correspondences.

The poem ends with Tom playfully suggesting that

> Some day I'll tell my fourth name at a feast,
> Throwing away 'Red-mounded,' laughed and ceased.
> He will have little secrets, hocus-pocus,
> Keeping mum a little to provoke us.
> Off he stumbled, quaintly like a toad,
> His staff went stumping down the dusty road.
>
> (510)

If we compare the poem's ending with the essay's ethnographic account, it is indeed possible that this blind old man will acquire yet another name in the course of his life. As we read in the essay, "Tom did not always have the name of Sayach'apis, nor need he keep it to the end of his days" ("Sayach'apis" 482). But as we have already seen, while the essay suggests that this new name would follow Tom's present name Sayach'apis, the poem suggests that Tom threw away Sayach'apis long ago and that "Red-Mounded" is his present name that he might throw away when he acquires his new name at a future feast.

To sum up, while Sapir's account of Tom's names in the poem "The Blind, Old Indian Tells His Names" obviously draws on his essay "Sayach'apis, a Nootka Trader," the poem departs from the essay in at least five significant ways: First, it reduces the number of names from six to four; second, it gives slightly different English translations of Tom's First Nations names; third, it reverses the chronological sequence of some of the names; fourth, it collapses accounts of three of the essay's names into a new name that is unique to the poem; and fifth, in telling the story of Tom's names, the poem freely draws on various narrative threads of the essay that have little or nothing to do with acts of naming. What do we make of the poem's many departures from the two essays' non-fictional accounts? Given Sapir's exploration of the ethics of naming and misnaming in "Tom," "The Mislabeled Menagerie," and "The Learned Jew," these discrepancies between ethnographic and literary representations of a First Nations voice are remarkable. Of course, from the perspective of literary studies, we could simply put these discrepancies down to the writer's creative freedom. In this account, Sapir the poet is much less bound to a truthful rendering of Tom's narrative than is Sapir the ethnographer. He has what we call poetic license. Moreover, when it comes to the question of truth, writers and literary critics alike have made the argument that fictional representations of the (historical) real may in many cases be more truthful than, or at least provide a different yet equally powerful kind of truth as the professional accounts of historiographers, sociologists, or anthropologists. To give a near-random example: about Jewish-American writer Abraham Cahan's novel *The Rise of David Levinsky* (1917), Cushing Strout writes that

> [i]t brings us into intimate knowledge of the inner meaning of the cultural strain implied in the movement of a Russian Jew to America, and it modulates our understanding of that process in a way that dramatization can achieve better than any sociological generalization.
>
> (433)

More pointedly, E.L. Doctorow states that his invention, in his historiographic metafiction *Ragtime*, of an encounter between J.P. Morgan and Henry Ford in which the two men discuss reincarnation is all the more true *because* it is fictional: "I'm satisfied that everything I made up about Morgan and Ford is true, whether it happened or not. Perhaps truer because it didn't happen" (Levine 69). Strout and Doctorow make related but different assertions concerning the truth value of fiction: For Strout, fiction gives privileged access to the truth of collectively shared individual experience; for Doctorow, it reveals historical truth in the sense that its portrayal of two major public figures of early-twentieth-century America captures the spirit of the era. Raymond Williams's notion of 'structures of feeling' allows us to conceptualize such accounts of the truth value of fiction. For Williams, literature gives expression to more diffuse structures of feeling, to "meanings and values as they are actively lived and felt" and "the relations between these and formal or systematic beliefs" (132), before they are theorized by sociologists and political scientists. Williams's most memorable example in the "Structures of Feeling" essay concerns the novels of Charles Dickens and Emily Brontë, which departed from dominant Victorian explanations of poverty and destitution as effects of moral failure by "specif[ying] exposure and isolation as a *general* condition and poverty, debt or illegitimacy as its connecting instances" (134; emphasis in original). In this, they anticipated Marx's "alternative ideology," which "relate[d] such exposure to the nature of the social order" (134).

If Strout's, Doctorow's, and Williams's insights are transferrable from prose narratives to lyrical ones, we can say that, based on what we know from the essays "Tom" and "Sayach'apis, a Nootka Trader," Sapir's poem "The Blind, Old Indian Tells His Names" does capture some form of truth about Tom Sayach'apis and the community he lived in. For instance, we learn about Tom's striving for an elevated social position, about the past greatness of this poor and feeble old man, about his penchant for singing, about the importance of names in his culture, about the social significance of potlatches, about the centrality of fishing and whaling in the Nuu-chah-nulth economy, and about the fact that Tom's people held slaves: "Tribes have feasted and the slaves have wondered" ("Blind, Old Indian" 507). The poem, in other words, imparts a significant amount of verifiable biographical and ethnographic knowledge.

And yet, one cannot shake the feeling that Sapir's exertion of poetic license violates a contract. What, we may be led to wonder, would the real-life Tom Sayach'apis say about Sapir inventing new names for him and rearranging their chronology? One of the important practical insights that the *Writing Culture* debate of the 1980s and 1990s has bequeathed to cultural anthropologists is that the accounts they give of other peoples must hold up to those peoples' self-understanding and self-descriptions.[25] Torben Monberg's "Informants Fire Back: A Micro-Study in Anthropological Methods" (1975) provides early, pre-*Writing Culture* testimony to this awareness. In the essay, Monberg, a Danish cultural anthropologist, reports on the at times harsh feedback his Polynesian informants gave him on his and Samuel H. Elbert's book *From the Two Canoes* (1965), a "volume of oral traditions from the two Polynesian Outlier islands, Rennell (Mugaba) and Bellona (Mungiki)" that "contained 428 pages, including 236 texts in the language of the two islands comprising mythology, quasi-history and history" as well as "brief ethnographic accounts and information concerning methods of collecting, genealogies, and short biographies of the informants" (218). One Bellonese reviewer reported that "some people think that the book is bad in some ways, because there are bad stories about ancestors and of people who are still alive" (220); another "feel[s] sorry because *our* traditional stories are not in the book" (220; emphasis in original), adding that the anthropologists' selection of stories does not give equal weight to the stories of the two communities—the Bellonese and Rennellese—and is therefore "controversial" and "bad" (221). Monberg's essay registers one of the ethical impasses of anthropological work to which the postmodern anthropologist Stephen A. Tyler responds when he calls for a "post-modern ethnography" that "foregrounds dialogue as opposed to monologue, and emphasizes the cooperative and collaborative nature of the ethnographic situation in contrast to the ideology of the transcendental observer" (126). Tyler's essay is his contribution to the key text of the *Writing Culture* debate, James Clifford and George E. Marcus's edited volume *Writing Culture: The Poetics and Politics of Ethnography* (1986), which post-dates Monberg's essay by eleven and Sapir's texts on Tom Sayach'apis by over sixty years. Moreover, in more recent ethnographic accounts, the substantial contributions that non-white 'informants' such as Tom made to white anthropologists' scientific studies is more fully acknowledged (Bruchac; Blackhawk and Wilner).

It is in hindsight then, with knowledge of the *Writing Culture* debate and current debates within anthropology, that we feel that Sapir, the anthropologist-turned-poet, has a different kind of responsibility toward the subjects he writes about than do other poets. In the specific case of "The Blind, Old Indian Tells His Names," this responsibility is especially pronounced since Sapir exerts his poetic license over a particularly sensitive area of Nuu-chah-nulth culture: names. Throughout Sapir's many publications on the Nuu-chah-nulth, we are reminded of the cultural centrality of naming. Writing about several north-west coast tribes from British Columbia including the Nuu-chah-nulth in "Indian Tribes of the Coast [of British Columbia]" (1914), Sapir notes that "the bearer of each grade of nobility" is "distinguished by a hereditary name, which inhered in a definite family, and by a definite seat assigned to him at ceremonial gatherings" (386–87). In "Indian Legends from Vancouver Island" (1925), he identifies "Nootka" names as "privileges . . . which derive," like songs and dances, "from the ancestral experiences" (525). Sapir and Morris Swadesh's joint volume *Native Accounts of Nootka Ethnography* (1955), published after Sapir's death, includes a multitude of Indigenous accounts that highlight the great significance of names. In one account given by Tom Sayach'apis in the 1920s, we find Maknaa'utl, a Ucluelet man, asking his people's chiefs why they "want to be without a name" given that they "have the name of chiefs" (278). In another of Tom's contributions to the volume from the same decade, we learn about a Tsishaa man praying to the supernatural creator Day Chief, "May I be named by all people. May I be as those dwelling alone. May the different tribes hear only of me. May they know my name. May they mention my name to the end of the coast" (53).[26]

Given the pivotal significance of names and naming among the Nuu-chah-nulth, Sapir's creative reworking of Tom Sayach'apis' names and his invention of new names for his informant may strike us as morally suspect. At what point, we may ask, does Sapir the poet's exertion of poetic license clash with Sapir the anthropologist's ethical and epistemological obligations toward his Indigenous subjects? As we have seen, one of the crucial legacies of the *Writing Culture* debate—a legacy that today's anthropologists embrace—is the demand that ethnographic descriptions should accord with Indigenous subjects' self-descriptions (Bruchac;

Blackhawk and Wilner). Given this, Sapir's play with an Indigenous community's key cultural practice strikes this twenty-first-century reader of "The Blind, Old Indian Tells His Name" carefree to say the least.

Of Desert Sirens

If the massive influence exerted by the *Writing Culture* debate over future generations of anthropologists did indeed, as David Howes argues with conviction in "Boasian Soundings: An Interrupted History of the Senses (and Poetry) in Anthropology" (2018), marginalize the sustained interest in the senses that still characterized the Boasians' work, then a poem that Sapir dedicated to Benedict complicates this account as it provides a fascinating window into two Boasian anthropologists' negotiation of textuality and sensory experience.

At least at first sight, "Zuni," which Sapir dedicates "To R.F.B." (Ruth Fulton Benedict), adopts a negative stance on sensory experience:

> *To R.F.B.*
>
> I send you this. Through the monotony
> Of mumbling melody, the established fall
> And rise of the slow, dreaming ritual,
> Through the dry glitter of the desert sea
> And sharpness of the mesa, keep the flowing
> Of your spirit, in many branching ways!
> Be running mirrors to the colored maze,
> Not pool enchanted nor a water slowing.
>
> Hear on the wing, see in a flash, retreat!—
> Beauty is brightest when the eye is fleet.
> The priests are singing softly on the sand,
> And the four colored points and zenith stand;
> The desert crawls and leaps, the eagle flies.
> Put wax into your ears and close your eyes.

In *Writing Anthropologists, Sounding Primitives*, Reichel provides a compelling, extensive reading of this poem, arguing that it gives expression to what she terms 'sonophobia'—"the rejection of sound and auditory perception as a threatening Other" (29)—to warn its addressee against losing herself in the seductive acoustic atmosphere of another culture (38–52). Sapir wrote this poem in August 1924, one-and-a-half years before he published it in *Poetry* and just in time to reach Benedict before she embarked on her first field trip to the Southwest Pueblos, where she would study the Zuni in 1924, 1925, and then again in 1927 (Mead,

"Benedict" 459–60)—work that would result in her two-volume *Zuñi Mythology* (1935). Reichel notes the final line's reference to the myth of Odysseus, "one of the earliest literary manifestations of sonophobia" (39), and cites the letter Sapir sent to Benedict alongside the poem on August 26, 1924 to corroborate her reading: "You see I am warning you against the Desert Siren. It would be terrible to have you come back overpunctuated with Oh and Ah like any well-behaved acolyte of the Santa Fé school" (Sapir, "Letter to Ruth Fulton Benedict of August 26, 1924"; qtd. in Reichel, *Writing* 40). The "Santa Fé school" was a motley group of anthropologists, artists, writers, tourists, and others who, urged on by the marketing efforts of the Atchison, Topeka, and Santa Fe Railway Company, flocked to the Southwest from the late nineteenth century to the 1930s to experience 'primitive culture' first hand (Dye).[27] Sapir was deeply distrustful of this craze while Benedict's fashioning of the Zuni as an integrated, sober, and well-balanced 'Apollonian' people in *Patterns of Culture* helped promote the destination: For her as for the "Santa Fé school," "[t]he Pueblo Indians of the Southwest are one of the most widely known primitive peoples in Western civilization" (Benedict, *Patterns* 57) and "[t]he Zuñi" in particular "are a ceremonious people, a people who value sobriety and inoffensiveness above all other virtues. Their interest is centered upon their rich and complex ceremonial life" (59).[28] In line with Handler's convincing claim that, "[f]or Sapir, art became a medium in which to work out an approach to questions of culture" ("Dainty" 289), what Sapir gives Benedict in "Zuni" is professional advice in poetic form: Do not let yourself be seduced by the Southwest's alluring sounds and sights; be "running mirrors" that record the sensible rather than immerse yourself in it; try to keep your scientific distance and objectivity. Yet in choosing the genre of poetry to give his advice, Sapir details the sensuous splendor of the Pueblo Southwest before he reins it in again, most explicitly in the volta that marks the transition from the octave to the sestet and in its final line. This impure Petrarchan sonnet derives its power less from the warning it communicates than from its evocation of the "mumbling melody, the established fall/And rise of the slow, dreaming ritual" and the "priests singing softly on the sand." Thus, the final line's Homeric advice cautions against the very allure that the poem itself creates. "Zuni" may warn against the desert siren but it also *is* the desert siren.[29] Ralf Hertel's study *Making Sense: Sense Perception in the British Novel of the 1980s and 1990s* helps us understand what is going on in "Zuni." Hertel focuses on fictions to explore not only our vicarious experiences as we imagine into being literary characters but also ways in which the sensuousness of the text itself affects readers:

> The novels discussed here seem to do exactly this: not only do they discuss the body as a fundamentally unstable site of representation,

but their very language is also endowed with sensuousness. Thus, they speak about the senses but at the same time quite literally 'make sense': they transmit the sensations from the page to the reader.

(Hertel 31)

While poetry only seldom initiates processes of identification between readers and literary figures, a poem like "Zuni" 'makes sense' in Hertel's understanding of the phrase. And in doing that, Sapir's poem also bears witness to Susan Stewart's conviction that "[p]oetry is encountered with and through our entire sensuous being" (329), that "the entire enduring accomplishment of the history of poetic forms awaits as a vast repertoire for anyone who hopes to enter again into an engagement with the senses" (333).

Still, as Sapir's letter to Benedict attests, "Zuni" was also sent as a piece of professional advice and thus goes beyond Sapir's own conception of "true art as subjective truth externalized in unique form" (Handler, "Dainty" 302). So what is the counsel that the poem gives? Consider again the poem's concluding imperative: "Put wax into your ears and close your eyes." This seems an odd piece of advice; for how could a fieldworker possibly gain knowledge about another culture with her eyes shut and her ears plugged? One explanation readily suggests itself: Sapir the poet exerts his poetic license here, staging a hyperbolic command that exceeds the bounds of professional advice-giving that the poem also performs. Yet there is also a second kind of poetic excess at work in this line. An anthropologist who closes her eyes and seals her ears is not shut off from sensory perception: She is still able to smell, taste, and touch her surroundings. She is not cut off from the possibility of sensory experience, but the experience she remains open to is different from that afforded by scientific uses of sight and hearing, potentially closer to the more visceral types of encounters sought by the Santa Fe school. My point is not that Sapir the poet intends to communicate this; my point is that, as it ends, the poem ironically opens itself up to the kind of somatic sensory experience of the Southwest that it cautions against. Thus, "Zuni" provides a glimpse into a dimension of anthropological work that neither its poetic speaker nor its addressee, neither its empirical author nor dedicatee but their mutual friend and colleague Mead would explore most fully. As she notes in her introduction to her *Letters from the Field, 1925–1975* (1977), anthropologists' awareness of the importance of the senses was raised dramatically when fieldwork and participant observation became professional norms and

> anthropologists went to live in the community and shared, twenty-four hours a day, in the sights and sounds, the tastes and smells, the pace and rhythm of a reality in which every detail was not only different in itself but was differently organized as a perceptual scheme.
>
> (16)

It was in their research manual *The Study of Culture at a Distance* (1953) that Mead and Rhoda Métraux most systematically reflected on the consequences of this fact for ethnographic practice. Calling upon fellow anthropologists to understand that "all cultural behavior is mediated by human beings who not only hear and speak and communicate through words, but also use all their senses, in ways that are equally systematic" (16), they pushed for ethnographers' recognition of the sensory foundations of both the cultures that they study and of the work that they do in them. If the final line of Sapir's "Zuni" evokes a world of experience beyond seeing and hearing, it is neither the empirical author of the poem nor his addressee but their younger Boasian colleague who explores the relevance of the other senses in the work that anthropologists do in the most sustained fashion.

In its sensuous richness, its intense self-reflexivity, and its dedication to a Boasian colleague and friend, Sapir's "Zuni" once more reminds us, first, how intimately the aesthetic and the aisthetic are intertwined in Boasian verse; second, how both their poems and their ethnographic research probe the epistemological and ethical consequences of anthropological work; and third, how closely knit a group Sapir, Benedict, and Mead formed. While their research would eventually take them into different directions—with Sapir analyzing Native American languages, Benedict studying Japan at a distance, and Mead staging multiple public interventions—they remained united in their reworking of the Boasian legacy, their commitment to cultural relativism, their shaping of both academic and broader, public discussions of the concept of 'culture,' and their primitivist and, at times, even evolutionist challenges to social evolutionism and scientific racism. As I have shown in my discussion of their ethnographic poems, much of Sapir's, Benedict's, and Mead's verse negotiates these and related anthropological issues in the different linguistic register of poetry, inviting us to ask, each time, what aesthetic, epistemological, and ethical difference it makes whether one writes about cultural others in ethnographic prose or verse.

Notes

1. I am relying on Reichel's appendix in *Writing Anthropologists, Sounding Primitives: The Poetry and Scholarship of Edward Sapir, Margaret Mead, and Ruth Benedict* (237–76). While *The Nation* (1865–) and *The New Republic* (1914–) gave Sapir access to a large audience, as far as venues for the publication of verse were concerned, *Poetry* (1912–), *The Dial* (1840–1929), and *The Measure* (1921–26) are clearly the major periodicals in which Sapir published. Concerning one of the lesser-known titles in the list, Victoria Kingham characterizes *The Pagan* (1916–22) as a socialist Greenwich Village magazine that competed with *The Masses*, "articulated some conflict between those who lived socialism and those who merely embraced it as a fashionable adjunct to Greenwich Village bohemian life" (1), gave a voice to Yiddish writers, and published the early work of a number of

major writers including "Hart Crane, Malcolm Cowley, the ubiquitous Maxwell Bodenheim, and . . . a very young Louis Zukofsky" as well as that of the "anthropologist and linguist Edward Sapir" (22). *Voices* (1919–21) is another short-lived, British literary magazine which featured many lower-class, immigrant, and Jewish poets (Morrison 507). *Palms* (1923–30) was a Mexican magazine based in Guadalajara whose editor Idella Purnell consciously positioned it outside the major metropolitan sites of modernist activity and managed to attract notable writers including Langston Hughes, Countee Cullen, Vachel Lindsay, Mark Van Doren, Helen Hoyt, and D.H. Lawrence (Thacker, "Poetry in Perspective" 333–46). Peter Marks describes *The Freeman* (1920–24) as a 1920s leftist periodical that addressed "national and international concerns, as well as the state of contemporary arts and letters. Commentating on topics of the day in the first section and cultural matters in the second, *The Freeman* ranged over emerging debates on the status of women and the 'New Negro,' the condition of American literature, and topics of general intellectual interest such as Einstein's relativity theories" (858). Its editors' aesthetic tastes were more traditional than *Poetry*'s or The *Dial*'s: it "encouraged the American tradition" and "[w]hen gazing across the Atlantic, . . . it looked to European realism and naturalism' [James Gilbert]" (863).
2. Based in Toronto, *The Canadian Forum* (1920–2000) and *The Canadian Bookman* (1919–1939) were heavily invested in negotiating post-WWI Canadian cultural nationalism and "inaugurated a modernist culture of letters in Anglophone Canada" (Irvine 608). *Queen's Quarterly* (1893–) is the oldest Canadian scholarly journal. Founded at Queen's University in 1893, it is addressed to general readers and regularly publishes poetry and short fiction in its pages. About *Contemporary Verse* (1941–52) Andrew Thacker, the co-editor (with Peter Brooker) of *The Oxford Critical and Cultural History of Modernist* Magazines, writes,

> In 1941 a new 'little magazine' of poetry, *Contemporary Verse*, was founded in Vancouver, one inspired by the example of Harriet Monroe's classic magazine, *Poetry*, started in Chicago in 1912. Alan Crawley, editor of the Canadian magazine, not only took *Poetry* as a point of reference for the new journal, but encouraged poets to send their best pieces to the American magazine first of all: if rejected there, they were then encouraged to submit their work to *Contemporary Verse*.
>
> ("Canada: Introduction" 599)

3. Jacob W. Gruber, who coined the concept of "salvage ethnography" (1298) in his 1970 essay "Ethnographic Salvage and the Shaping of Anthropology," identifies British anthropologist James Cowles Prichard's alarmist 1839 intervention before the British Association for the Advancement of Science as a foundational moment in this specific branch of ethnographic thought and practice and traces its translation into Boasian anthropology.
4. In his "Note on French-Canadian Folk-Songs," Sapir defers to his collaborator Marius Barbeau's judgment as he classifies these four songs:

> *The Dumb Shepherdess* is a religious *complainte*, and is known in the lower St. Lawrence region, both north and south shores. *The King of Spain's Daughter* is a work ballad, especially used as a paddling song, and is based on versions from Temiscouata and Gaspé counties. *The Prince of Orange* is another paddling song, collected at Tadousac, one of the oldest French settlements in Canada, on the lower St. Lawrence. *White as the Snow* is a

good example of the genuine ballad; it is one of the best known folk-songs of Quebec, having been recorded in no less than twelve versions.

(212–13)

5. I could not find any response by Sapir to that issue (though he does trash Skinner's "lucubrations" in a letter to Monroe ("Letter to Harriet Monroe of June 10, 1920"). But here is what he wrote about a related endeavor, Lew Sarett's "Council Talks," which consists of "interpretations of Chipewa character and life studied at first hand during nine summer seasons of life in and near the reservation":

> As for Lew Sarett's 'Council Talks,' I consider them rubbish. (There *is* a field for Indian subjects, but what I have seen of this class of conk is amateurish from the ethnologist's point of view. Some day I should like to tackle the field myself. I have oceans of first-hand material, but I have never thought of poetic utilization.)
>
> ("Letter to Harriet Monroe of December 6, 1919"; emphasis in original)

6. Concerning Monroe's primitivism, consider also her assertion, in the September 1920 issue of *Poetry*, that

> we Americans, who would travel by the many thousand, if we had the chance, to see a Homeric rite in Attica, or a serpent ceremony in old Egypt, are only beginning to realize that the snakedance at Walpi, or the corndance at Cochiti, are also revelations of primitive art, expressions of that original human impulse toward the creation of beauty.
>
> ("In Texas and New Mexico" 326–27)

7. Corbin's words of praise are especially troublesome in regard to Page, the most prominent representative of the Southern plantation romance.
8. Sapir also managed to publish translations of three Canadian folk songs in the *Queen's Quarterly* (1922).
9. In a letter dated November 26, 1924, Sapir writes to Benedict that Monroe's "taste always leans to the pretty and second best" (Benedict, *Anthropologist* 164). Expressing his hope that Benedict's "Moth Wing" will be accepted by *Poetry*, he tells her, in a letter written on June 14, 1925 that "I hope Harriet will have no qualms about accepting it. She doesn't seem to know her own mind sometimes, though" (Benedict, *Anthropologist* 179).
10. Consider Benedict's explicit comparison of artistic and cultural integration in *Patterns of Culture*:

> Gothic architecture, beginning in what was hardly more than a preference for altitude and light, became, by the operation of some canon of taste that developed within its technique, the unique and homogeneous art of the thirteenth century. It discarded elements that were incongruous, modified others to its purposes, and inverted others that accorded with its taste. . . . What has happened in the great art-styles happens also in cultures as a whole. All the miscellaneous behaviour directed toward getting a living, mating, warring, and worshipping the gods, is made over into consistent patterns in accordance with unconscious canons of choice that develop within the culture. Some cultures, like some periods of art, fail of such integration, and about many others we know too little to understand the motives that actuate them. But cultures at every level of complexity, even the simplest, have achieved it. Such cultures are more or less successful attainments of integrated behaviour, and the marvel is that there can be so many of these possible configurations.
>
> (*Patterns* 47–48)

11. See also Handler, who notes that "it is worth stressing that Sapir's notion of what constituted cultural harmony was elaborated in a rhetoric drawn from his thinking about aesthetics. For him, art was a privileged domain of culture because culture was collective art" ("Introduction" 734).
12. Note, though, that at one point, Sapir himself proposed such an approach to literature: "In the long run only criticism grounded in individual psychological analysis has validity in aesthetic problems" (Sapir, qtd. in Handler, "Introduction" 740).
13. Consider also Sapir's expression of an ambivalent attitude toward the sonnet form in a letter to Harriet Monroe dated December 6, 1919: "I am conservative enough to believe the sonnet holds great possibilities still—provided, of course, one gets away from rigid iambic verse and eschews genteel themes" ("Letter to Harriet Monroe of December 6, 1919").
14. Note that, in a letter to Monroe dated August 1, 1919, Sapir expresses his admiration for both O'Donnell's and Tietjens's verse ("Letter to Harriet Monroe of August 1, 1919").
15. In "A Pair of Tricksters," a poem Sapir published in the October-December 1923 issue of the *Queen's Quarterly*, Sapir returns to the raven, now fashioned unequivocally in his guise as trickster:

> O one is a raven, glossy black
> He struts on the low-tide beach
> And he croaks while the mist drifts over his back,
> While the mist lifts out of reach.
> And one is a crested bluejay, shrill
> And pert in the cedar tree
> While the wind blows warm and the wind blows chill,
> He is screaming ecstatically.
> O one is a mind and one is a heart
> And the two are a trickster pair;
> Croaker and screamer—each has an art
> Of escaping from despair.

Like the raven, the bluejay is a mythological animal figure that features in Sapir's ethnographic work. The bluejay makes a brief appearance in "Notes on the Takelma Indians of Southwestern Oregon" (1906), where we learn that the bird's tail feathers adorn the heads of pubescent Takelma girls performing the menstrual dance, blocking their vision (289–90). In "Some Aspects of Nootka Language and Culture" (1911), the Bluejays are one of the Nuu-chah-nulth's two female clubs (333). The animal makes yet another appearance in "Song Recitative in Paiute Mythology" (1910), where the bluejay is the subject of the "Myth Recitative of Mountain-Bluejays," a non-ceremonial song of the southern Paiutes, a Native community of southwestern Utah, that narrates a myth, here the attack of the Badger people and the Mountain-Bluejays in their war on Wolf and Coyote (548–49). We get closer to the ethnographic source of the bluejay in "A Pair of Tricksters" though when we learn, still in "Song Recitative in Paiute Mythology," that the bluejay resembles the raven of British Columbia in being "generally a humorous character" (557). Similarly, Sapir asserts in his "Preliminary Report on the Language and Mythology of the Upper Chinook" (1907), that "Bluejay" figures "prominently as buffoon among the coast tribes" (294) of the state of Washington. While it is difficult to assign the bluejay of "A Pair of Tricksters" to any one of the indigenous communities Sapir studied in his ethnographic work, it seems safe to say that in his poem, he fashions both him and raven as tricksters and possibly also as buffoons. As my discussion of "The

Blind, Old Indian Tells His Names" (1921) will show, Sapir's poetry often takes loose recourse to his anthropological endeavors, the difference being that "A Pair of Tricksters" is even more loosely related to his anthropological work than his earlier poem, so much so that it is rendered largely immune to the charge of cultural appropriation I will level at "The Blind, Old Indian Tells His Names" in the following section. In anthropomorphizing the two birds as a lowly croaking mind and a shrilly, ecstatically screaming heart, respectively, Sapir further removes the two figures from their cultural sources to switch the poem's focus to the existential human condition of despair. And yet, the poem is not completely emptied out of its anthropological content. Consider the final stanza: What allows the raven and the bluejay to escape despair is their "art," a word that in this specific usage denotes "[c]unning; artfulness; trickery, pretence" (OED, sense 11.a.). For tricksters as for humans, escaping despair becomes possible through the kind of rule-bending and rule-breaking that tricksters are famous for. If this reading of the poem makes sense, "art" may additionally be taken to refer to the activity Sapir engages in as he writes his poems: "[a]ny of various pursuits or occupations in which creative or imaginative skill is applied according to aesthetic principles" (OED, sense 7) or "[t]he expression or application of creative skill and imagination, typically in a visual form such as painting, drawing, or sculpture, producing works to be appreciated primarily for their beauty or emotional power" (OED, sense 8.a.). The poem's animals, then, become figures for the creative individual whose societal function Sapir explored in his cultural essays and whose role he assumed in writing verse. In this poem, moreover, art assumes the therapeutic function that has been ascribed to it since Aristotle.

16. See also Handler's discussion of "Observations on the Sex Problem in America" ("Vigorous" 148–49).
17. *Nootka Texts: Tales and Ethnological Narratives with Grammatical Notes and Lexical Materials* (1939) and *Native Accounts of Nootka Ethnography* (1955) are the titles of the two books, both of which Sapir co-wrote with Morris Swadesh.
18. The titles of these memoirs are *Abnormal Types of Speech in Nootka* (1915) and *Time Perspective in Aboriginal American Culture: A Study in Method* (1916).
19. "The Life of a Nootka Indian" appeared in issue 28 (1921) of the *Queens Quarterly*. In the following year, Sapir published a mildly revised version of it under the title "Sayach'apis, a Nootka Trader" in *American Indian Life*, a volume edited by Elsie Clews Parsons. I am citing from the reprint of this second version in volume 4 of *The Collected Works of Edward Sapir*. The footnotes added to the reprint specify the changes that Sapir made.
20. Since the *Writing Culture* debate of the 1980s and 1990s, the term 'informant' has come under scrutiny from cultural anthropologists since it appears to reduce the human beings that anthropologists engage with to mere providers of data. Some of this unease can be felt in Sapir's reflection on the term in "Tom." The Norwegian social anthropologist Olaf H. Smedal offers a more recent, pertinent discussion of 'informant' and possible alternatives to it:

> If adequate sociocultural anthropology is based not on observation alone but also on participation, if by participation we mean interactive engagement in other peoples' lives, and if by such engagement we imply that other peoples' practical and discursively expressed knowledge is not merely relevant but pivotal to our endeavour, then the term 'informant'

seems both inept and unfortunate; conjuring [up] an image of a provider of raw data for advanced processing much as Third World countries deliver raw materials to industrially advanced states. Some anthropologists refer incessantly to what their 'friends' have said or done—while I may well lack these researchers' capacity for making friends I have also learnt much from Ngadha men and women I would not dream of placing in this category. 'Partner in dialogue' is fine but invokes one-to-one conversations rather than the 'multilogues' I suspect characterise much anthropological field research; 'conversational partner' is perhaps better but remains, with 'partners in dialogue', within an implicit framework of spoken words (before one knows it frozen in texts). I alternate in this work between 'Ngadha' or 'Ngadha people,' 'Ngadha men/women,' 'specialist,' 'well informed person' and, sometimes, 'consultant.' The choice of the last after Basso . . . is tentative, for objections can doubtless be raised with respect to this term, too—generating as it perhaps does images in some peoples' minds of Business School graduates or attaché case-equipped sociologists.

(n.p)

21. Note also the importance of naming in current, twenty-first-century debates within cultural anthropology, where the renaming or un-naming of university buildings such as Kroeber Hall at UC Berkeley, which honor anthropologists fallen into disrepute, is at issue (Platt).
22. Note that there are significant differences between "The Mislabeled Menagerie" and "The Blind, Old Indian Tells His Names." While the former belongs to a number of poems by Sapir that stage a critique of the poet's own culture, targeting some of its cultural types and cultural practices, the latter stages an act of cross-cultural presentation that focuses on one individual from another culture. I am indebted to A. Elisabeth Reichel for this insight.
23. Note that Sapir himself was ambivalent about the *quality* of the poem. As he wrote to novelist Madge Macbeth in 1924: "I have not yet the key to the solution of the difficulty inherent in remotely exotic subject matter—probably because my own natural handling of subjects has already something of the remote about it" (qtd. in Darnell, *Edward Sapir* 164–65)
24. Note that the manuscript version of "The Blind, Old Indian Tells His Names" shows that Sapir originally wrote 'six names,' then crossed out 'six' and replaced it with 'four.' Thus, there appears to be an awareness on Sapir's part that writing 'six names' would have been more appropriate.
25. The key text of the *Writing Culture* debate is James Clifford and George E. Marcus's edited volume *Writing Culture: The Poetics and Politics of Ethnography* (1986), which assembles classic essays from some of the main proponents of the self-reflexive, postmodern turn in cultural anthropology, among them the editors, Paul Rabinow, Vincent Crapanzano, and Stephen A. Tyler.
26. The Ucluelet and 'Tsishaa' (now called 'Tseshaht') are two of the fifteen tribes that make up Nuu-chah-nulth culture.
27. Victoria E. Dye notes that

[i]n the early guidebooks published by the AT&SF, the Pueblo people were referred to as 'savage' or 'wild,' and the AT&SF continued to portray Native Americans as 'living relics' of a culture that continued and sometimes struggled to hold on to its ancient religious beliefs and notions of tradition. The railroad used the 'primitive' to sell Santa Fe as a cultural destination.

(97)

28. Benedict's preference for 'Apollonian' cultures (such as the Zuni) over 'Dionysian' cultures (such as the Kwakiutl) is so pronounced that Stocking groups her among "the Apollonians" or "the Apollonian ethnographers" ("Ethnographic Sensibility" 334). On Benedict's romantic Apollonian ethnography, whose unequivocally positive portrayal of pueblo cultures younger Boasians such as Ruth Bunzel and Esther Goldfrank would challenge in the 1930s (Silverman 270), see also Manganaro's *Culture, 1922* (158–61).
29. Consider Toni Flores's interpretation of the poem as a particularly striking example of an anthropologist's reading of Boasian verse that fails to connect it to the author's ethnographic concerns:

> [I]n the wonderful sonnet 'Zuni,' he seeks balance between humanity and nature, ritual and landscape, material and spiritual, stasis and movement, reality and imagination, immersion and distance, connection and transcendence.... Do not be tempted, he seems to say, into a vain attraction to perfect beauty. That way lies only wreckage. Only in the *process* of searching for or making meaning and in the form of the search is there any hope. It is the process and the form, not the thing, which counts.
> (166–67; emphasis in original)

Conclusion

How, then, should we judge Sapir's, Benedict's, and Mead's ethnographic and poetic work from the vantage point of my discipline, literary studies? To answer this question, it makes sense to return to Mead's visual anthropology. The question we asked about Sapir's poem "The Blind, Old Indian Tells His Names" in the preceding chapter—the question concerning an anthropologist's ethical and epistemological responsibilities toward his Indigenous subject—we can also ask about Margaret Mead's offhand remark about the reproduction of a Balinese drawing in her and Gregory Bateson's multimedia book *Balinese Character*.[1] The drawing— one of over 1,200 that Mead and Bateson acquired on Bali (Francis and Wolfskill, "Bali: Personality Formation")—is part of the book's plate thirty-eight ("Autocosmic Symbols: The Baby"), which has the same form as all of the one hundred plates that make up the heart of *Balinese Character*: on one page (here the left page), we see an ensemble of images (in this case, five of Bateson's photographs of Balinese babies and children and two reproductions of related paintings by Balinese artists); on the other page we can read a short introductory text by Mead followed by brief descriptions of each image (see Figure 4.1).[2]

In Mead and Bateson's text-image relations, photographs, paintings, and texts each play a specific role. By combining photographs and paintings, they suggest that everyday Balinese behavior captured in the photographs (images two to six) is expressive of the more general cultural patterns that the paintings (images one and seven) render visible. Some of the captions on the right page perform a purely ekphrastic function, describing the form and content of each image while others combine ekphrasis with interpretation. The introductory text at the top of the right page performs yet another function: it provides the necessary cultural and theoretical contexts for readers far less immersed in Balinese culture than the participant observers Mead and Bateson.

To illustrate, a mother's washing of her baby in the photographic image six (Figure 4.2) is expressive of the more general cultural pattern that can be glimpsed in the painting in the top left corner, where we see a man who at first sight seems to sport a tail (but is in fact wearing a

DOI: 10.4324/9781003266945-5

Conclusion 145

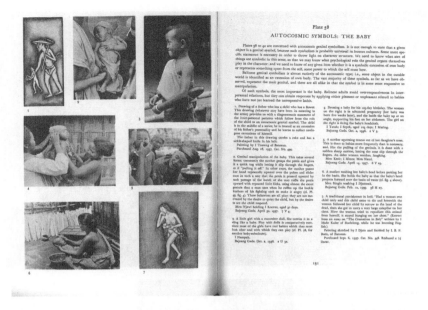

Figure 4.1 Plate thirty-eight in Gregory Bateson and Margaret Mead, *Balinese Character* (1942)
Source: Courtesy of the New York Academy of Sciences

knife in his belt), wears a hat on his head and a rake on his shoulder, and guides, with his right hand, a naked child walking in front of him, holding a flower (Figure. 4.3).

At first sight, the relation between these images is anything but straightforward. But the introductory text at the top of the right page helps us make the connection by giving us the necessary cultural context and theoretical framework. There, we learn that plate thirty-eight as a whole is concerned with 'autocosmic symbolism,' which Mead defines as a type of symbolism in which "some object in the outside world is identified as an extension of [sic] own body" (Bateson and Mead 131). In this specific case, Mead speaks of "autocosmic genital symbolism" (131), where the object in the outside world is identified as an extension of the male genital: "The vast majority of these symbols, so far as we have observed, represent the male genital, and these are all alike in that the symbol is in some sense responsive to manipulation" (131). In Mead's interpretation, the baby is "the most important" autocosmic genital symbol in Balinese culture, which partially explains the various representations of babies and children in the book's images.

Mead's caption for image six is brief and performs solely an ekphrastic function: "A mother washing her baby's head before putting her in the

Figures 4.2 and 4.3 Details of plate thirty-eight in Gregory Bateson and Margaret Mead, *Balinese Character* (1942)

Source: Courtesy of the New York Academy of Sciences

basin. She holds the baby so that the baby's head projects forward over the basin of water" (131). It is in the more extensive caption for image 1 that Mead's theoretical framework and ethnographic knowledge are put to use:

> Drawing of a father who has a child who has a flower. This drawing (whatever may have been its meaning to the artist) provides us with a diagrammatic statement of the inter-personal patterns which follow from the role of the child as an autocosmic genital symbol. The child is on the middle of a series; he is treated as an extension of his father's personality and he learns to collect analogous extensions of himself.
>
> The father in this drawing carries a rake and has a sickle-shaped knife in his belt.
>
> (131)

Mead's interpretation of the painting and, by implication, the photograph becomes clear. In both images, we see the child/baby as an "autocosmic genital symbol," an embodied, symbolic extension of the male genital. While the photograph documents the baby's function as such a symbol in Balinese social life, the painting highlights the general cultural (spiritual, mythical) meaning of Balinese children. In her text, Mead draws on a psychoanalytic framework, as does her teacher and lover Benedict when she makes use of the Nietzschean/Jungian dichotomy of Apollonian and Dionysian cultures to characterize Southwestern Zuni culture and the Kwakiutl culture of the Pacific Northwest, respectively, in *Patterns of Culture* (1934). Rather than elaborating on the Boasians' impositions of Freudian/Jungian analytical frameworks on other cultures (this would require an essay or book of its own), I want to zoom in on Mead's parenthetic comment: "whatever may have been its meaning to the artist."

This offhand remark speaks volumes, especially when read in connection with Sapir's exertion of poetic license in "The Blind, Old Indian Tells His Names" and Benedict's enstranging combination of myths in "In Parables." All three Boasians make moves familiar to literary scholars. In Mead's case, her brushing aside of the artist's intention resonates with any literary scholar who has read William K. Wimsatt and Monroe R. Beardsley's "The Intentional Fallacy" (1946), published four years after *Balinese Character*, or studied equally influential, manifesto-like essays published a quarter century after Mead and Bateson's book such as Roland Barthes's "The Death of the Author" (1967) and Michel Foucault's "What Is an Author?" (1969). Yet what do we, as literary scholars, do when assumptions many of us have learned to take for granted—writers have the right to poetic license; literary language enstranges our perception and experience of the world; the author/creator is either dead or a discursive function; and the intentional fallacy must be avoided—crop up in ethnographic texts and there ring false, smack of ethnocentrism?

148 Conclusion

One of the most important legacies of the *Writing Culture* debate is to raise cultural anthropologists' awareness of the rhetorical construction of ethnographic authority. Major contributions to Clifford and Marcus's trailblazing *Writing Culture* volume draw on concepts from literary studies and its various theoretical frameworks for their critical analyses of ethnographic texts' embeddedness in (post-)colonial power/knowledge nexuses: Vincent Crapanzano discusses George Catlin's, Johann Wolfgang von Goethe's, and Clifford Geertz's hermeneutic strategies of self-authorization in their writing about other cultures; Clifford writes about 'ethnographic allegory'; Paul Rabinow draws on Fredric Jameson's reflections on postmodernism; Michael M. Fischer reads literary texts by African-American, Chicano/a, and First Nations writers as postmodern ethnographic self-descriptions. Thus, the tools of literary studies and the concepts of literary and cultural theory are employed in the service of speaking truth to ethnographic power.

Clearly, the case is different with Sapir, Benedict, and Mead. Their principal aim is not to stage a critique of the ethnographic construction of authority but to describe, represent, and evoke other cultures in poetry, ethnographic prose, and (in Mead's case) images. What connects the early to mid-twentieth-century Boasians and the late-twentieth-century postmodern ethnographers though is their recourse to concepts current in the literary-critical circles of their time. Yet the transfer of literary forms and ideas to cultural anthropology has a very different political valence in these two moments in the history of anthropology. Literary scholars may feel a sense of pride that 'their' terms have been adopted by major cultural anthropologists like Clifford, Marcus, and Rabinow in the service of promoting more self-reflexive and ethically more viable ethnographic writing practices.[3] Yet a close look at Sapir's work on the Nuu-chah-nulth, Benedict's poetic evocation of the Māori foundational myth, and Mead and Bateson's study of the Balinese reveals a different side of such transdisciplinary transfers. In "The Blind, Old Indian Tells His Names," Sapir plays fast and loose with a particularly sensitive area of Nuu-chah-nulth culture: naming. Of course, his exertion of poetic license is perfectly in sync with a modern understanding of artistic autonomy, but it also betrays a carefree, perhaps careless use of ethnographic data that appropriates and reworks biographical and cultural knowledge gained during fieldwork in ways that are difficult to reconcile with and possibly offensive to members of the culture subjected to the anthropologist-poet's gaze. Likewise, while Benedict's recourse to the Māori creation myth enacts a form of enstrangement conceptualized in early-twentieth-century literary theory, it also gives expression to a nostalgic yearning for sensory plenteousness that ties in with the more primitivist moments of her ethnographic work. Finally, while Mead's brushing aside of a Balinese artist's intention easily aligns itself, most probably unintentionally, with formalist (New Critical, structuralist, and post-structuralist) attempts to liberate works of art and their reception from the authoritative force of the artist's intention—attempts that were on their way to becoming literary-critical doxa in the decades after Mead and Bateson published *Balinese Character*—they testify to an anthropologist's disregard for a culture's self-description. In fact, while the Boasians have often been credited with 'writing culture' avant la lettre (Manganaro 157; Fischer 217; Darnell, "Boasian Text Tradition" 45–46; Layton 186), Vincent Crapanzano's acerbic critique of Clifford Geertz in his contribution to the *Writing Culture* volume applies with equal force to Sapir, Benedict, and Mead. In response to Geertz's famous claim in "Deep Play: Notes on the Balinese Cockfight" (1972) that "[t]he culture of a people is an ensemble of texts, themselves ensembles, which the anthropologist strains to read over the shoulders of those to whom they properly belong" (452), Crapanzano writes:

> The image is striking: sharing and not sharing a text. It represents a sort of asymmetrical we-relationship with the anthropologist behind and above the native, hidden but at the top of the hierarchy of understanding. . . . There is never an I-you relationship, a dialogue, two people next to each other reading the same text and discussing it face-to-face, but only an I-they relationship. . . . Despite Geertz's ostensible concern for the understanding of the native's point of view, his essay is less a disquisition on Balinese cockfighting, subjectively or objectively understood, than on interpreting—reading—cultural data. . . . All too often, the ethnographer forgets that the native . . . cannot abide someone reading-over his shoulder. If he does not close his book, he will cast his shadow over it. Of course, the ethnographer will also cast his shadow over it.
>
> (74–76)

One should not overemphasize the similarities between Geertz's method of thick description and Boasian anthropology: for Sapir, Benedict, and Mead, cultures were not texts but more or less successfully integrated wholes (Manganaro 151–57). What unites the two generations of cultural anthropologists though is their recourse to concepts and methods current in the literary-critical circles of their time (in Geertz's case a structuralist understanding of culture as 'text' and a determination to 'read' cultures much like the hermeneutic tradition interprets literary texts). Strikingly, what also unites them is their use of literary-critical doxa in ways that reify the power differential between the anthropologist and the culture that they study. Sapir's poetic appropriation of biographical and ethnographic data collected during fieldwork among the Nuu-chah-nulth, Benedict's integration of Christian and Māori foundational myths, Mead's indifference to a Balinese artist's understanding of his own work, and Geertz's (too) masterful reading of the Balinese cockfight all create "a sort of asymmetrical we-relationship with the anthropologist behind and above the native, hidden but at the top of the hierarchy of understanding." With regard to Sapir, Benedict, and Mead, the point that I wish to make is not that they draw on literary-critical concepts and convictions for nefarious ends. The point I wish to make is that, while many proponents of *Writing Culture* did tap into the critical energies of the "school of suspicion" (Ricoeur 32 et passim) that most literary scholars attend, we should not be overconfident about the emancipatory potential of the literary forms we study and the analytical tools we use. As the examples of Sapir, Benedict, Mead, and Geertz show, the "shadow" that ethnographers cast over other cultures sometimes has a literary hue.

How, then, should we assess the Boasians' politics of representation? In recent contributions to the history of anthropology, Boas and his students have been subjected to a thorough reevaluation. To give an idea of just how divergent assessments of the Boasians can be in this debate, it makes sense to turn our attention to two recent books: Charles King's *Gods of the Upper Air: How a Circle of Renegade Anthropologists Reinvented Race, Sex, and Gender in the Twentieth Century* (2019) and Mark Anderson's *From Boas to Black Power: Racism, Liberalism, and American Anthropology* (2019).

While King does acknowledge that Boas and some of his students at times replaced talk about blacks' racial inferiority with talk about their cultural inferiority (204–5), and while both Boas's and his erstwhile students Sapir's and Alfred Kroeber's problematic roles in the museological and scientific use of Indigenous subjects and their remains are noted (217–23), King portrays the Boasians as key players in the struggle against racism, sexism, and homophobia:

> If it is now unremarkable for a gay couple to kiss goodbye on a train platform, for a college student to read the *Bhagavad Gita* in a Great Books class, for racism to be rejected as both morally bankrupt and self-evidently stupid, and for everyone, regardless of their gender expression, to claim workplaces and boardrooms as fully theirs—if all of these things are not innovations or aspirations but the regular, taken-for-granted way of organizing a society; then we have the ideas championed by the Boas circle to thank for it.
>
> (King 10)

King also makes much of Boas's ardent and highly public opposition to Nazism, which he judged to be a type of *Rassenwahn* (race madness) that was also at work in the United States, where blacks took on the role that Jews did in the so-called Third Reich. Indeed, Boas noted, the Nazis, including Hitler himself, took some of their most loathsome ideas from American books such as Madison Grant's pseudo-scientific *The Passing of the Great Race: Or, The Racial Basis of European History* (1916) and

Henry H. Goddard's eugenicist *The Kalliak Family: A Study in the Heredity of Feeble-Mindedness* (1912) (King 304–11). As King announces in the subtitle of his book, for him, Boas and his followers were 'renegade anthropologists' who bravely took on racism, sexism, and homophobia wherever they reared their ugly heads.

In *From Boas to Black Power*, Mark Anderson arrives at quite different conclusions concerning the Boasians. For him, their treatments of race and racism reveal the limits of anti-racist liberalism—a liberalism that continues to believe in the essential goodness of American ideals, denies the white cosmopolitan anthropologist's ensnarement in both colonialism and systemic racism,[4] negates the all-encompassing force of white supremacy, champions an anti-identitarian diminution of racial consciousness, reifies differences between white and non-white people, and romanticizes or exoticizes racial others understood to be 'primitives.' Anderson does register the Boasians' pronounced anti-racism, acknowledges that they did not entirely displace the discourse of race with that of culture, and admits that they studied what he calls "the social life of race and racism" (16 et al.). But he subjects to critique their "powerful associations with liberalism" and their "deep," exceptionalist and nationalist "commitments to America" (11). In comparison with the post-war black anthropologists William S. Willis and Diane K. Lewis and the radical white ethnographer Charles A. Valentine—all of whom drew energy from the Black Studies and Black Power movements and aimed to decolonize U.S. anthropology—Anderson finds the Boasians wanting, stressing that they "disavowed," in liberal fashion, "the possibility that racism was a constitutive feature of the U.S. social order, and reproduced a foundational presupposition of the republic that equated 'America' with whiteness" (21). To this, Anderson adds that even as they undermined assertions concerning the biological inferiority of blacks and Native Americans, the Boasians continued to rely on a deeply problematic tripartite distinction between Caucasoid (white), Mongolian (Asian), and Negroid (black) races (58–59, 67–69). Boas, moreover, considered miscegenation and the attendant lightening of the African-American population the solution to the 'Negro problem' (70–84). Finally, the Boasians—chief among them Boas and Benedict, the foci of two separate chapters in Anderson's book—tended to engage in false comparisons of the situation of blacks to that of Southern and Easter European immigrants, some of which were not considered white originally but would eventually be assimilated into the American mainstream (59, 103–5, 108–9).

Anderson is seconded by Ryan Cecil Jobson in his polemical essay "The Case for Letting Anthropology Burn: Sociocultural Anthropology in 2019" (2020). In it, the author glosses liberal humanism as "a discourse of moral perfectibility founded in histories of settler colonialism and chattel slavery" (259) that "presupposes an abundance of land and resources primed for colonial appropriation" (263). In the face of climate change, post-truth politics, and global authoritarianism—Donald J. Trump was President when Jobson wrote and published his fiery essay—he calls upon sociocultural anthropology to "abandon its liberal suppositions" (261) and 'let anthropology burn.' In a section of his essay entitled "Against the Boasian Fix: Anthropology in the Wake of the Plantation," Jobson contrasts King's and Anderson's books, siding with the latter while indicting the former for his "tacit assumption of a normative racial and classed subject who is the principal beneficiary of a Boasian relativist tradition" (265). For Jobson, the primary addressee of Boasian cultural relativism and liberal anti-racism is a white, middle to upper class subject who is not at the receiving end of state violence and discriminatory social practices. What is needed instead is a history of U.S. anthropology such as Anderson's which "centers those racialized subjects who failed to benefit from its liberal antiracism" and embraces "more radical projects of reclamation and repair" (265).

What unites King, Anderson, and Jobson despite their widely diverging assessments of the Boasians is their conviction that Boas and his students were liberals. What divides them first and foremost is their different judgments of that politics: for King, the Boasians are liberal heroes who fought courageously against racist, sexist, and homophobic forms of illiberalism; for Anderson and Jobson, it is precisely the Boasians' liberalism that renders them unfit models for twenty-first-century anthropologists. What is the relevance of King's, Anderson's, and Jobson's contrasting appraisals for my own study of Boasian verse?

First and foremost, engaging with these recent contributions to (the history of) cultural anthropology helps me become more keenly aware of the largely implicit liberal trajectory of my own account. For instance, had I adopted the radical position of Anderson or Jobson, I would have judged Benedict's syncretistic fusion of cultures in her poem "Myth" more sternly as an exercise in cultural appropriation. Instead, I compared its politics of representation favorably to the cultural relativist doctrine of the incommensurability of cultures that drives her ethnographic work. Likewise, had I followed Anderson's take on the Boasians, I would have stressed Mead's anti-Americanism less and acknowledged more that, in poems such as "America" and ethnographic works such as *And Keep Your Powder Dry*, she displays a deep and lasting commitment to the American way of life in general and its liberal investments in particular. Finally, had I fully embraced Anderson's or Jobson's critiques of the Boasians, I would have subjected Sapir's publication of translated Québecois folk songs to a more rigorous critique that would have stressed Sapir's exoticism and nostalgia.

Why, then, do I stick, for large parts of this book, to an appreciative reading of the three Boasians and the poetry they wrote? By way of concluding this book, let me propose three answers to this question. First and foremost, one should be careful not to elide the differences between ethnographic and poetic work. While literary critics have become accustomed to judging literary works based on the 'cultural work' (Tompkins) they do, this is by no means the only possible approach to literature. An equally valid method would be to evaluate the aesthetic quality of individual poems. I have taken this approach when comparing Margaret Mead's poem "Madonna of the Breakfast Table" to T.S. Eliot's "The Love Song of J. Alfred Prufrock" and found the former wanting. But judging the quality of poems has not been my main task (for the record, though, I do think that Benedict is the most gifted of the three Boasian poets). A second endeavor more central to my concerns has been to stress the *differentness* of poetic language, which I insisted on most conspicuously when commenting on the 'estranging door' in Benedict's "In Parables." Such an approach to literary texts takes its cue from the Russian Formalists in general and Victor Shklovsky's conviction that poetry is "the language *of impeded, distorted* speech" (13; emphasis in original) in particular. In my book, we should judge the aesthetic, epistemological, and ethical valences of Boasian poems only after we have ascertained their poetic alterity. In relation to the ethnographic poems I am concerned with in this book, the key question we should ask concerns the interplay of poetic and cultural alterity: how does the different language of poetry enable the Boasians to represent cultural others in different ways?

Second, in evaluating the politics of representation of Boasian scientific prose and verse, one should guard against slipping into a presentism that imposes twenty-first-century politics onto early-twentieth-century writing. Concerning our three Boasians' ethnographic texts and public interventions, this means that one should acknowledge the genuinely progressive thrust of their struggle against social evolutionism and scientific racism even as we recognize that they were not immune to evolutionist statements and that their cultural relativism went hand in hand with a primitivism we have learned to reject. Concerning Boasian verse, this means that we recognize both its positive portrayal of cultures that evolutionists considered savage or barbarian and its primitivist slant.

Third and finally, we should ask ourselves whether calling poet-anthropologists 'liberal' necessarily passes a negative judgement on them. Here again, the specter of presentism rears its head. True, for many of today's cultural observers on the left, 'liberalism' is a deeply deficient political ideology. To give a prominent example: in his entry on 'liberalism' in *Keywords for American Cultural Studies*, Nikhil Pal Singh stresses liberalism's equation of human and market freedom, its elitism, its links with exceptionalism, its exclusion or exploitation "of the propertyless, of women, of slaves and aboriginal peoples" (155), and its imbrication with the development of disciplinary techniques among other evils. I do not wish to deny these charges. At the same time, we should not forget the emancipatory force of liberalism, without which neither the American Revolution nor the women's rights movement nor the civil rights movement would have happened (even if in all of these movements, both more conservative and more radical forces than liberalism also played a significant role). More generally, political liberalism aligns itself with democratic institutions, "civil liberties, the rule of law, and the importance of freedom and equality" (A. Anderson 43). With regard to Boasian verse, I take my cue from Amanda Anderson's discussion of what she calls 'bleak liberalism.' For her, "liberalism is best understood as a philosophical and political project conceived in an acute awareness of the challenges and often bleak prospects confronting it" (1). In this account, "liberalism is prompted by enduring challenges, often born of crisis, that exert their pressure on the internal dynamics of liberal thought" (2). Bleak liberalism is, Anderson contends, characterized by "a pessimism or bleakness of attitude that derives from an awareness of all those forces and conditions that threaten the realization of liberal ambitions" (22). Understood thus, liberalism "typically manifests an interplay between hope and skepticism" (24). This, it seems to me, well captures what, in my discussion of Benedict and Mead, I call the therapeutic and critical functions of Boasian verse and ethnography: their use of other cultures as a source of cultural rejuvenation (therapy) and their use of foreign sites as a springboard to censure one's own culture (critique). While both uses of other cultures are in danger of instrumentalizing and othering ethnic others, Mead, Benedict, and Sapir have put their ethnographic and poetic engagements with foreign cultures in the service of a liberal reevaluation of their own culture that is therapeutic, critical, and, above all, necessary.

Notes

1. *Balinese Character* is an early contribution to visual anthropology that includes one hundred double-sided plates, each of which consists of a number of images (photographs and in some plates also reproductions of Balinese drawings) on one page and, on the facing page, a short text by Mead that frames the images, which is followed by descriptions of the images. Next to the plates, the book contains a brief introduction by Mead and Bateson, Mead's fifty-page essay "Balinese Character," Bateson's notes on the photographs and captions, an ethnographic note on Bali, a bibliographic note, and a glossary and index of Indigenous words and personal names.
2. There is some uncertainty concerning the authorship of the captions. In the volume itself, they are credited to Bateson:

    > Gregory Bateson will apply to the behavior depicted in the photographs the same sort of verbal analysis which he applied to his records of Iatmul transvestitism in 'Naven,' and the reader will have the photographic presentation itself to unite and carry further these two partial methods of describing the ethos of the Balinese.
    >
    > (Bateson and Mead xii-xiii)

    Yet earlier on in his "Notes on the Photographs," Bateson writes, "We usually worked together, Margaret Mead keeping verbal notes on the behavior and Gregory Bateson moving around in and out of the scene with the two cameras" (49). It would be odd if these notes by Mead did not lay the basis for the captions. Moreover these captions have a decidedly Meadean ring, particularly when compared to her introductory chapter "Balinese Character" and in their more psychoanalytical moments. Indeed, when ethnomusicologist Caitlin Mullin sat down with Mead's daughter Mary Catherine Bateson, Bateson told her,

> So basically what *Balinese Character* is, as a book, is a book of photographic plates with captions. Gregory had taken all the photographs, Margaret wrote the captions, but each plate would be illustrative of some theme they had observed in the culture.
>
> (Mullin)

In my discussion, I follow this lead and attribute the captions to Mead. There is, however, an argument to be made that they should best be understood as the result of collaborative work, which is what the "Notes on the Captions" at the end of "Balinese Character" suggest in their consistent use of the second-person plural personal pronoun:

> We have assumed that the objectivity of the photographs themselves justifies some freedom in the writing of the captions. We have not hesitated, therefore, to select for emphasis those features of the photograph [sic] which seemed most revealing, and to describe those features which might convey a sense of the emphases in Balinese culture as we understand it.
>
> (Bateson and Mead 53)

3. For a succinct overview of a number of experimental ethnographic writing practices embraced and fostered by proponents of *Writing Culture*, see Marcus's afterword to *Writing Culture*:

   > A sense of experimentation pervades contemporary ethnographic writing even among those who continue to write well within the tradition of realist conventions. [. . .] One trend of experimentation is intensely concerned with getting at the representation of authentic other-cultural experience, with going beyond existing interpretive or symbolic perspectives on cultural meaning toward the most deep-seated and radical level at which difference can be evoked. Some of these experiments, those that fix on differing cultural constructions of the person, remain true to realist conventions. Others shift more radically to modernist concerns with textual form; other cultural experience can only be evoked or represented by a fundamental change in the way we think about the construction of ethnographic texts. Dialogic interchanges between ethnographer and other, the sharing of textual authority with subjects themselves, autobiographical recounting as the only appropriate form for merging other cultural experience with the ethnographer's own—these are all attempts to change radically the way the conventional subject matter of ethnography has been constituted in order to convey authentically other cultural experience.
   >   The other trend of experimentation, and the one to which I limit myself in this paper, is relatively well satisfied with the means interpretive anthropology has developed to represent cultural difference, but instead explores new and more effective ways in which ethnographic texts can take account of the manner in which world-historical political economy constitutes their subjects. These experiments remain well within realist conventions, but they are no less innovative in the kinds of texts they generate.
   >
   > (168n.5)

4. Drawing on the writing of Black Power activists, Anderson provides a noteworthy definition of institutional or systemic racism: "From a Black Power perspective, racism was not a conflict between creed and practice but a systemic feature of U.S. culture and society, saturating its institutions" (171).

Works Cited

Adorno, Theodor W. *Aesthetic Theory*. Trans. and introd. Robert Hullot-Kentor. Eds. Gretel Adorno and Rolf Tiedemann. Minneapolis: U of Minnesota P, 1997. Print.
Anderson, Amanda. *Bleak Liberalism*. Chicago: U of Chicago P, 2016. Print.
Anderson, Mark. *From Boas to Black Power: Racism, Liberalism, and American Anthropology*. Stanford: Stanford UP, 2019. Print.
"Announcement of Awards." *Poetry: A Magazine of Verse* 17.2 (Nov. 1920): 105–14. Print.
Aronoff, Eric. "Anthropologists, Indians, and New Critics: Culture and/as Poetic Form in Regional Modernism." *Modern Fiction Studies* 55.1 (2009): 92–118. Print.
———. *Composing Cultures: Modernism, American Literary Studies, and the Problem of Culture*. Charlottesville: U of Virginia P, 2013. Print.
Baker, Lee D. *From Savage to Negro: Anthropology and the Construction of Race, 1896–1954*. Berkeley: U of California P, 1998. Print.
Ball, Hugo. "Gadji beri bimba." *Gedichte*. Ed. Eckhard Faul. Göttingen: Wallstein, 2007. 67. Print.
Banner, Lois W. *Intertwined Lives: Margaret Mead, Ruth Benedict, and Their Circle*. New York: Knopf, 2003. Print.
Barbeau, Marius, and Edward Sapir. *Folk Songs of French Canada*. New Haven: Yale UP, 1925. Print.
Barthes, Roland. "The Death of the Author." *Image/Music/Text*. Trans. Stephen Heath. New York: Hill and Wang, 1977. 142–47. Print.
Bateson, Gregory, and Margaret Mead. *Balinese Character: A Photographic Analysis*. New York: New York Academy of Sciences, 1942. Print.
Bateson, Mary Catherine. *With a Daughter's Eye: A Memoir of Margaret Mead and Gregory Bateson*. New York: Morrow, 1984. Print.
Baumgarten, Alexander Gottlieb. *Ästhetik [Aesthetica]*. Trans. Dagmar Mirbach. 2 vols. Hildesheim: Felix Meiner, 2007. Print.
———. *Reflections on Poetry/Meditationes philosophicae de nonnullis ad poema pertinentibus*. Trans. Karl Aschenbrenner and William B. Holther. Berkeley: U of California P, 1954. Print.
Bendix, Regina. "Was über das Auge hinausgeht: Zur Rolle der Sinne in der ethnographischen Forschung." *Schweizerisches Archiv für Volkskunde* 102 (2006): 71–84. Print.

Benedict, Ruth Fulton. "Annunciation." *An Anthropologist at Work: Writings of Ruth Benedict*. Ed. Margaret Mead. Westport: Houghton Mifflin, 1959. 475–76. Print.
———. "Another Theseus." *An Anthropologist at Work: Writings of Ruth Benedict*. Ed. Margaret Mead. Westport: Houghton Mifflin, 1959. 478–79. Print.
———. *An Anthropologist at Work: Writings of Ruth Benedict*. Ed. and introd. Margaret Mead. Westport: Houghton Mifflin, 1959. Print.
———. "As a Dream." Typescript. Ruth Fulton Benedict Papers, Vassar College. Folders 47.17. n.d. Print.
———. "At Ending." *An Anthropologist at Work: Writings of Ruth Benedict*. Ed. Margaret Mead. Westport: Houghton Mifflin, 1959. 485. Print.
———. "Brook Turning." Typescript. Ruth Fulton Benedict Papers, Vassar College. Folder 47.20. n.d. Print.
———. "Burial." *An Anthropologist at Work: Writings of Ruth Benedict*. Ed. Margaret Mead. Westport: Houghton Mifflin, 1959. 483–84. Print.
———. "But the Son of Man." *Modern American Poetry: A Critical Anthology*. Ed. Louis Untermeyer. 4th rev. ed. New York: Harcourt Brace, 1930. 518–19. Print.
———. "Countermand." *Poetry: A Magazine of Verse* 35 (1930): 304. Print.
———. "Death Is the Citadel." *The Nation* 128 (Feb. 20, 1929): 231. Print.
———. "Dedication." *An Anthropologist at Work: Writings of Ruth Benedict*. Ed. Margaret Mead. Westport: Houghton Mifflin, 1959. 473. Print.
———. "The Dream." Typescript. Ruth Fulton Benedict Papers, Vassar College. Folder 47.26. n.d. Print.
———. "In Parables." *Palms* 3.6 (1926): 165. Print.
———. "In Praise of Life." Typescript. Ruth Fulton Benedict Papers, Vassar College. Folders 46.24 and 48.3. n.d. Print.
———. "Of Graves." *An Anthropologist at Work: Writings of Ruth Benedict*. Ed. Margaret Mead. Westport: Houghton Mifflin, 1959. 84. Print.
———. "Little Girl-Mother." Typescript. Ruth Fulton Benedict Papers, Vassar College. TS 47.11. n.d. Print.
———. "Lost Leader." *New York Herald Tribune Books* 6.30 (1930): 6. Print.
———."Love That Is Water." *An Anthropologist at Work: Writings of Ruth Benedict*. Ed. Margaret Mead. Westport: Houghton Mifflin, 1959. 474. Print.
———. "Lovers' Wisdom." *An Anthropologist at Work: Writings of Ruth Benedict*. Ed. and introd. Margaret Mead. Westport: Houghton Mifflin, 1959. 161. Print.
———. "Moth Wing." *An Anthropologist at Work: Writings of Ruth Benedict*. Ed. and introd. Margaret Mead. Westport: Houghton Mifflin, 1959. 488. Print.
———. "Myth." *An Anthropologist at Work: Writings of Ruth Benedict*. Ed. and introd. Margaret Mead. Westport: Houghton Mifflin, 1959. 477. Print.
———. "November Burning." *An Anthropologist at Work: Writings of Ruth Benedict*. Ed. Margaret Mead. Westport: Houghton Mifflin, 1959. 484. Print.
———. "Parlor Car—Santa Fe." Typescript. Ruth Fulton Benedict Papers, Vassar College. TS 46.24. n.d. Print.
———. *Patterns of Culture*. Boston: Houghton Mifflin, 1989. Print.
———. "Pool." Typescript. Ruth Fulton Benedict Papers, Vassar College. Folder 48.15. n.d. Print.

———. "Price of Paradise." *An Anthropologist at Work: Writings of Ruth Benedict*. Ed. Margaret Mead. Westport: Houghton Mifflin, 1959. 478. Print.
———. "Profit of Dreams." *An Anthropologist at Work: Writings of Ruth Benedict*. Ed. Margaret Mead. Westport: Houghton Mifflin, 1959. 164–65. Print.
———. "Resurgam." *New York Herald Tribune Books*, Mar. 24, 1929. 6. Print.
———. "Resurrection of the Ghost." *New York Herald Tribune Books*, Aug. 26, 1944. 6. Print.
———. "Rupert Brooke, 1914–1918." *An Anthropologist at Work: Writings of Ruth Benedict*. Ed. Margaret Mead. Westport: Houghton Mifflin, 1959. 5–6. Print.
———. "The Sacrilege." Typescript. Ruth Fulton Benedict Papers, Vassar College. Folder 48.21. n.d. Print.
———. "Sepulchre." Typescript. Ruth Fulton Benedict Papers, Vassar College. Folder 48.22. n.d. Print.
———. "Sirens' Song." Typescript. Ruth Fulton Benedict Papers, Vassar College. Folder 48.23. n.d. Print.
———. "Sleet Storm." *The Measure* 51 (1925): 6. Print.
———. "There Is No Death." *An Anthropologist at Work: Writings of Ruth Benedict*. Ed. Margaret Mead. Westport: Houghton Mifflin, 1959. 484–85. Print.
———. "This Breath." *An Anthropologist at Work: Writings of Ruth Benedict*. Ed. Margaret Mead. Westport: Houghton Mifflin, 1959. 474. Print.
———. "This Is My Body." *An Anthropologist at Work: Writings of Ruth Benedict*. Ed. Margaret Mead. Westport: Houghton Mifflin, 1959. 194–95. Print.
———. "Unshadowed Pool." *Poetry: A Magazine of Verse* 35.6 (March 1930): 304–5. Print.
———. "Verses for One Dancing." Ruth Fulton Benedict Papers, Vassar College. Folder 48.33. n.d. Print.
———. "The Vision in Plains Culture." *American Anthropologist* 24.1 (1922): 1–23. Print.
———. "Withdrawal." *An Anthropologist at Work: Writings of Ruth Benedict*. Ed. Margaret Mead. Westport: Houghton Mifflin, 1959. 482. Print.
———. *Zuñi Mythology*. New York: Columbia UP, 1935. Print.
Bennett, Paula Bernat. *Nineteenth Century American Women Poets: An Anthology*. Maldon: Blackwell, 1998. Print.
———. *Poets in the Public Sphere: The Emancipatory Project of American Women's Poetry, 1800–1900*. Princeton: Princeton UP, 2003. Print.
Bennett, Paula Bernat, Karen Kilcup, and Philipp Schweighauser, eds. *Teaching Nineteenth-Century American Poetry*. New York: MLA, 2007. Print.
Berryman, John. "Prufrock's Dilemma." *The Freedom of the Poet*. New York: Farrar, Straus, 1976. 270–78. Print.
Blackhawk, Ned, and Isaiah Lorado Wilner, eds. *Indigenous Visions: Rediscovering the World of Franz Boas*. New Haven: Yale UP, 2018. Print.
Boas, Franz. "Commencement Address at Atlanta University, May 31, 1906." *Atlanta University Leaflet* 19 (1906). Print.
———. "Introduction." *Patterns of Culture*. Ed. Ruth Fulton Benedict. Boston: Houghton Mifflin, 1989. xix–xxi. Print.
———. "The Limits of the Comparative Method of Anthropology." *Science* 4.103 (1896): 901–8. Print.
———. "The Occurrence of Similar Inventions in Areas Widely Apart." *Science* 9.224 (1887): 485–86. Print.

Böhme, Gernot. *Aisthetik: Vorlesungen über Ästhetik als allgemeine Wahrnehmungslehre*. Munich: Fink, 2001. Print.
———. *Atmosphäre*. Frankfurt a.M.: Suhrkamp, 1995. Print.
Bourne, Randolph S. "Trans-National America." *The Atlantic* (July 1916): 86–97. Print.
Bowman-Kruhm, M. *Margaret Mead: A Biography*. Westport: Greenwood Press, 2003. Print.
Bradford, William. *Of Plymouth Plantation, 1620–1647*. Ed. and introd. Samuel Eliot Morison. New York: Alfred A. Knopf, 2002. Print.
Brand, Stewart. "'For God's Sake, Margaret': Conversation with Gregory Bateson and Margaret Mead." *The CoEvolution Quarterly* 10 (1976): 32–44. Print.
Bruchac, Margaret M. *Savage Kin: Indigenous Informants and American Anthropologists*. Tucson: U of Arizona P, 2018. Print.
Bunzel, Ruth L. "Introduction to Zuni Ceremonialism." *Annual Report of the Bureau of American Ethnology* 47 (1932): 467–544. Print.
Burke, Seán. *The Death and Return of the Author: Criticism and Subjectivity in Barthes, Foucault, and Derrida*. Edinburgh: Edinburgh UP, 2010. Print.
Burkholder, Zoë. *Color in the Classroom: How American Schools Taught Race, 1900–1954*. New York: Oxford UP, 2011. Print.
Caffrey, Margaret M. *Ruth Benedict: Stranger in This Land*. Austin: U of Texas P, 1989. Print.
Canada, Tracie. "Special Focus: Engaging *The Second Generation of African American Pioneers in Athropology*." *History of Anthropology Review* 45 (2021): 1–36. Print.
Cassirer, Ernst. *The Philosophy of Symbolic Forms. Vol. 2: Mythical Thought*. Trans. Ralph Manheim. New Haven: Yale UP, 1955. Print.
Castro, Michael. *Interpreting the Indian: Twentieth-Century Poets and the Native American*. Albuquerque: U of New Mexico P, 1983. Print.
Chakkalakal, Silvy. "Ethnographic Art Worlds: The Creative Figuration of Art and Anthropology." *Boasian Aesthetics: American Poetry, Visual Culture, and Cultural Anthropology*. Eds. Philipp Schweighauser et al. Spec. issue of *Amerikastudien/American Studies* 63.4 (2018): 489–515. Print.
———. "Sensible Ethnographien—Modernistische Empfindsamkeit als Modus einer ethnographischen Ästhetik." *Die Sinnlichkeit des Sozialen: Wahrnehmung und materielle Kultur*. Eds. Hanna Göbel and Sophia Prinz. Bielefeld: Transcript, 2015. 341–61. Print.
Chinitz, David E. *T. S. Eliot and the Cultural Divide*. Chicago: Chicago UP, 2003. Print.
Classen, Constance. "Foundations for an Anthropology of the Senses." *International Social Science Journal* 153 (1997): 401–20. Print.
———. *Worlds of Sense: Exploring the Senses in History and Across Cultures*. London: Routledge, 1993. Print.
Clifford, James. "Histories of the Tribal and the Modern." *The Anthropology of Art: A Reader*. Eds. Howard Morphy and Morgan Perkins. Malden: Blackwell, 2006. 150–66. Print.
———. "On Ethnographic Allegory." *Writing Culture: The Poetics and Politics of Ethnography*. Eds. Clifford and George E. Marcus. Berkeley: U of California P, 2011. 98–121. Print.
Clifford, James, and George E. Marcus, eds. *Writing Culture: The Poetics and Politics of Ethnography*. Berkeley: U of California P, 2011. Print.

Connelly, Frances S. *The Sleep of Reason: Primitivism in Modern European Art and Aesthetics 1725–1907*. University Park: Pennsylvania State UP, 1995. Print.

Corbin Henderson, Alice. "The Folk Poetry of These States." *Poetry: A Magazine of Verse* 16.5 (Aug. 1920): 264–73. Print.

———. "Rev. of *The Path on the Rainbow: An Anthology of Songs and Chants from the Indians of North America*. Ed. George W. Cronyn, with an introd. Mary Austin." *Poetry: A Magazine of Verse* 14.1 (April 1919): 41–47. Print.

Craig, Robert D. *Handbook of Polynesian Mythology*. Santa Barbara: ABC-CLIO, 2004. Print.

Crapanzano, Vincent. "Hermes's Dilemma: The Masking of Subversion in Ethnographic Discourse." *Writing Culture: The Poetics and Politics of Ethnography*. Eds. James Clifford and George E. Marcus. Berkeley: U of California P, 2011. 51–76. Print.

Croce, Benedetto. *The Aesthetic as the Science of Expression and of the Linguistic in General*. Trans. Colin Lyas. Cambridge: Cambridge UP, 1992. Print.

Darnell, Regna. "Benedict, Ruth." *Biographical Dictionary of Social and Cultural Anthropology*. Ed. Vered Amit. New York: Routledge, 2004. 45–47. Print.

———. "The Boasian Text Tradition and the History of Anthropology." *Culture* 12.1 (1992): 39–48. Print.

———. *Edward Sapir: Linguist, Anthropologist, Humanist*. Berkeley: U of California P, 1990. Print.

Darnell, Regna, and Judith T. Irvine. "Introduction." *The Collected Works of Edward Sapir. Vol. 3: Culture*. Eds. Judith T. Irvine Darnell and Richard Handler. Berlin: De Gruyter, 1994. 21–26. Print.

———. "Introduction to Section III: Ethnography of North America." *The Collected Works of Edward Sapir. Vol. 4: Ethnology*. Eds. Darnell and Judith T. Irvine. Berlin: De Gruyter, 1994. 255–66. Print.

Department of Anthropology, Columbia University. "Margaret Mead." Columbia UP, 2019. Web. Jan. 3, 2019.

Dillon, Elizabeth Maddock. "Sentimental Aesthetics." *American Literature* 76.3 (2004): 495–523. Print.

Dobson, Joanne. "Reclaiming Sentimental Literature." *American Literature* 69.2 (1997): 263–88. Print.

Dowthwaite, James. "Edward Sapir and Modernist Poetry: Amy Lowell, H.D., Ezra Pound, and the Development of Sapir's Literary Theory." *Modernist Cultures* 13.2 (2018): 255–77. Print.

Dye, Victoria E. *All Aboard for Santa Fe: Railway Promotion of the Southwest, 1890s to 1930s*. Albuquerque: U of New Mexico P, 2005. Print.

Eliot, T. S. *The Annotated Waste Land with Eliot's Contemporary Prose*. 1922. Ed. with annotations and introd. Lawrence Rainey. New Haven: Yale UP, 2005. Print.

———. "The Frontiers of Criticism." *On Poetry and Poets*. London: Faber, 1957. 103–21. Print.

———. "The Love Song of J. Alfred Prufrock." *Poetry: A Magazine of Verse* 6.3 (June 1915): 130–35. Print.

———. "The New Sculpture." *Egoist* 1 (1914): 67–68. Print.

———. "Preludes." *Prufrock and Other Observations*. New York: A. A. Knopf, 1920. 17–19. Print.

———. "Tarr." *Egoist* 5 (1918): 105–6. Print.

———. "Tradition and the Individual Talent." *Selected Prose of T.S. Eliot*. Ed. Frank Kermode. New York: Farrar, Straus, and Giroux, 1975. 37–44. Print.

———. *The Use of Poetry and the Use of Criticism*. Cambridge: Harvard UP, 1933. Print.

———. "War-Paint and Feathers." *The Complete Prose of T. S. Eliot: The Critical Edition*. Eds. Anthony Cuda and Ronald Schuchard. Baltimore: Johns Hopkins UP and Faber & Faber, 2014. 137–40. Print.

———. *The Waste Land: The Waste Land and Other Poems*. 1922. New York: Harcourt Brace, 1962. 27–54. Print.

Erkilla, Betsy. *The Wicked Sisters: Women Poets, Literary History, and Discord*. New York: Oxford UP, 1992. Print.

Ernst, Manfred, and Anna Anisi. "The Historical Development of Christianity in Oceania." *The Wiley Blackwell Companion to World Christianity*. Eds. Lamin Sanneh and Michael J. McClymond. Vol. 1. Hoboken: John Wiley & Sons, 2016. 588–604. Print.

Evans, James Allan Stewart. *The Emperor Justinian and the Byzantine Empire*. Westport: Greenwood Press, 2005. Print.

Fabian, Johannes. *Time and the Other: How Anthropology Makes Its Object*. New York: Columbia UP, 1983. Print.

Fischer, Michael M. J. "Ethnicity and the Post-Modern Arts of Memory." *Writing Culture: The Poetics and Politics of Ethnography*. Eds. James Clifford and George E. Marcus. Berkeley: U of California P, 2011. 194–233. Print.

Flam, Jack D., and Miriam Deutch, eds. *Primitivism and Twentieth-Century Art: A Documentary History*. Los Angeles: U of California P, 2003. Print.

Flannery, Jeffrey M. "Library Question—Answer [Question #12663903]. Message to the Author." Aug. 9, 2017. E-mail. Print.

Flores, Toni. "The Poetry of Edward Sapir." *Dialectical Anthropology* 11 (1986): 157–68. Print.

Foucault, Michel. "What Is an Author?" *Textual Strategies: Perspectives in Post-Structuralist Criticism*. Ed. Josué V. Harari. Ithaca: Cornell UP, 1979. 141–60. Print.

Francis, Patricia A., and Mary Wolfskill. "Margaret Mead: Human Nature and the Power of Culture: Bali: Personality Formation." Library of Congress 2001. Web. Jan. 4, 2019.

———. "Margaret Mead: Human Nature and the Power of Culture: Margaret Mead as a Cultural Commentator." Library of Congress 2001. Web. Oct. 27, 1969.

———. "Margaret Mead: Human Nature and the Power of Culture: National Character." Library of Congress 2001. Web. Jan. 4, 2019.

Frank, Florence Kiper. "December." *Poetry: A Magazine of Verse* 27.4 (Jan. 1926): 183–87. Print.

Frazer, James George. *The Golden Bough: A Study in Magic and Religion*. 12 vols. London: Macmillan, 1906–1915. Print.

Freeman, Derek. *The Fateful Hoaxing of Margaret Mead: A Historical Analysis of Her Samoan Research*. Boulder: Westview Press, 1999. Print.

———. *Margaret Mead and Samoa: The Making and Unmaking of an Anthropological Myth*. Cambridge: Harvard UP, 1983. Print.

Geertz, Clifford. "Deep Play: Notes on the Balinese Cockfight." *The Interpretation of Cultures: Selected Essays by Clifford Geertz*. New York: Basic Books, 1973. Print.

Gess, Nicola. *Primitives Denken: Wilde, Kinder und Wahnsinnige in der literarischen Moderne (Müller, Musil, Benn, Benjamin)*. Munich: Wilhelm Fink, 2013. Print.

Gikandi, Simon. "Picasso, Africa, and the Schemata of Difference." *Modernism/Modernity* 10.3 (2003): 455–80. Print.

Goldenweiser, Alexander. "Can There Be a 'Human Race'?" *The Nation* 120 (1925): 462–63. Print.

Greenblatt, Stephen. *Marvelous Possessions: The Wonder of the New World*. Oxford: Clarendon P, 1981. Print.

Grey, George. *Polynesian Mythology and Ancient Traditional History of the Maori as Told by Their Priests and Chiefs*. London: A. D. Willis, 1855. Print.

Grimshaw, Anna. *The Ethnographer's Eye: Ways of Seeing in Modern Anthropology*. Cambridge: Cambridge UP, 2001. Print.

Grosskurth, Phyllis. *Margaret Mead: A Life of Controversy*. London: Penguin, 1988. Print.

Gruber, Jacob W. "Ethnographic Salvage and the Shaping of Anthropology." *American Anthropologist* 72.6 (1970): 1289–99. Print.

Gumbrecht, Hans Ulrich. "Schwindende Stabilität der Wirklichkeit: Eine Geschichte des Stilbegriffs." *Stil: Geschichten und Funktionen eines kulturwissenschaftlichen Diskurselements*. Eds. Gumbrecht and Karl Ludwig Pfeiffer. Frankfurt a.M.: Suhrkamp, 1986. 726–88. Print.

———. "Stil." *Reallexikon der deutschen Literaturwissenschaft: Neubearbeitung des Reallexikons der deutschen Literaturgeschichte*. Eds. Georg Braungart et al. 3rd ed. Vol. 3. Berlin: De Gruyter, 2003. 509–13. Print.

Hammer, Langdon. *Hart Crane and Allen Tate: Janus-Faced Modernism*. Princeton: Princeton UP, 1993. Print.

Handler, Richard. "The Aesthetics of Sapir's Language." *New Perspectives in Language, Culture, and Personality: Proceedings of the Edward Sapir Centenary Conference*. Eds. William Cowan, Michael Foster, and E. F. K. Koerner. Amsterdam: John Benjamins, 1986. 433–54. Print.

———. "Anti-Romantic Romanticism: Edward Sapir and the Critique of American Individualism." *Anthropological Quarterly* 62.1 (1989): 1–13. Print.

———. *Critics Against Culture: Anthropological Observers of Mass Society*. Madison: U of Wisconsin P, 2005. Print.

———. "The Dainty and the Hungry Man: Literature and Anthropology in the Work of Edward Sapir." *Edward Sapir: Critical Assessments of Leading Linguists*. Ed. E.F.K. Koerner. New York: Routledge, 2007. 289–311. Print.

———. "Introduction to Sections Four and Five: Edward Sapir's Aesthetic and Cultural Criticism." *The Collected Works of Edward Sapir. Volume 3: Culture*. Eds. Regna Darnell, Judith T. Irvine, and Handler. Berlin: Mouton de Gruyter, 1999. 731–47. Print.

———. "Ruth Benedict and the Modernist Sensibility." *Modernist Anthropology: From Fieldwork to Text*. Ed. Marc Manganaro. Princeton: Princeton UP, 1990. 163–80. Print.

———. "Sapir's Poetic Experience." *American Anthropologist* 86.2 (1984): 416–17. Print.

———. "Vigorous Male and Aspiring Female: Poetry, Personality, and Culture in Edward Sapir and Ruth Benedict." *Malinowski, Rivers, Benedict, and*

Others: Essays on Culture and Personality. Ed. George W. Stocking, Jr. Madison: U of Wisconsin P, 1986. 127–55. Print.

Harris, Marvin. *The Rise of Anthropological Theory: A History of Theories of Culture*. Updated ed. Walnut Creek, CA: AltaMira Press, 2001. Print.

Hegeman, Susan. "American Popular Social Science: The Boasian Legacy." *Boasian Aesthetics: American Poetry, Visual Culture, and Cultural Anthropology*. Eds. Philipp Schweighauser et al. Spec. issue of *Amerikastudien/American Studies* 63.4 (2018): 441–56. Print.

——. *Patterns for America: Modernism and the Concept of Culture*. Princeton: Princeton UP, 1999. Print.

Heider, Karl G. *Ethnographic Film*. 2nd rev. ed. Austin: U of Texas P, 2006. Print.

Hempenstall, Peter. *Truth's Fool: Derek Freeman and the War over Cultural Anthropology*. Madison: U of Wisconsin P, 2017. Print.

Hertel, Ralf. *Making Sense: Sense Perception in the British Novel of the 1980s and 1990s*. Amsterdam: Rodopi, 2005. Print.

Hochman, Brian. *Savage Preservation: The Ethnographic Origins of Modern Media Technology*. Minneapolis: U of Minnesota P, 2014. Print.

Hockings, Paul, ed. *Principles of Visual Anthropology*. 3rd ed. Berlin: Mouton de Gruyter, 2003. Print.

Holl, Ute. *Kino, Trance & Kybernetik*. Berlin: Brinkmann & Bose, 2002. Print.

Hollander, John, ed. *American Poetry: The Nineteenth Century*. 2 vols. New York: Library of America, 1993. Print.

Horton, Philip. *Hart Crane: The Life of an American Poet*. New York: Viking, 1957. Print.

Howard, Jane. *Margaret Mead: A Life*. London: Harvill, 1984. Print.

Howes, David. "Controlling Textuality: A Call for a Return to the Senses." *Anthropologica* 32.1 (1990): 55–73. Print.

——. *Sensual Relations: Engaging the Senses in Culture and Social Theory*. Ann Arbor: U of Michigan P, 2003. Print.

Howes, David, Clifford Geertz, and Roseline Lambert. "Boasian Soundings: An Interrupted History of the Senses (and Poetry) in Anthropology." *Boasian Aesthetics: American Poetry, Visual Culture, and Cultural Anthropology*. Eds. Philipp Schweighauser et al. Spec. issue of *Amerikastudien/American Studies* 63.4 (2018): 473–87. Print.

Huyssen, Andreas. "Mass Culture as Woman: Modernism's Other." *Studies in Entertainment: Critical Approaches to Mass Culture*. Ed. Tania Modleski. Bloomington: Indiana UP, 1986. 188–208. Print.

Irvine, Dean. "'Little Magazines' in English Canada." *The Oxford Critical and Cultural History of Modernist Magazines. Vol. 2: North America 1894–1960*. Eds. Peter Brooker and Andrew Thacker. Oxford: Oxford UP, 2009. 602–28. Print.

Iseminger, Gary, ed. *Intention & Interpretation*. Philadelphia: Temple UP, 2010. Print.

Iser, Wolfgang. "On Translatability." *Surfaces* 4 (1994): 5–13. Print.

Jacknis, Ira. "Margaret Mead and Gregory Bateson in Bali: Their Use of Photography and Film." *Cultural Anthropology* 3.2 (1988): 160–77. Print.

Jobson, Ryan Cecil. "The Case for Letting Anthropology Burn: Sociocultural Anthropology in 2019." *American Anthropologist* 122.2 (2020): 259–71. Print.

King, Charles. *Gods of the Upper Air: How a Circle of Renegade Anthropologists Reinvented Race, Sex, and Gender in the Twentieth Century*. New York: Doubleday, 2019. Print.
Kingham, Victoria. "The Pagan, Joseph Kling, and American Salon Socialism." *Journal of Modern Periodical Studies* 1.1 (2010): 1–37. Print.
Kirby, Bruce. "Library Question—Answer [Question #12381627]. Message to A. Elisabeth Reichel." Mar. 30, 2017. E-mail.
Kohl, Karl-Heinz. *Abwehr und Verlangen: Zur Geschichte der Ethnologie*. Frankfurt a.M.: Edition Qumran, 1987. Print.
Kroeber, Albert L., and Clyde Kluckhohn. *Culture: A Critical Review of Concepts and Definitions*. Cambridge: Harvard UP, 1952. Print.
Kroeber, Alfred L. *Configurations of Culture Growth*. Berkeley: U of California P, 1947. Print.
———. *The Nature of Culture*. Chicago: U of Chicago P, 1952. Print.
———. "The Superorganic." *American Anthropologist* 19.2 (1917): 163–213. Print.
Lapsley, Hilary. *Margaret Mead and Ruth Benedict: The Kinship of Women*. Amherst: U of Massachusetts P, 1999. Print.
Layton, Robert. *An Introduction to Theory in Anthropology*. Cambridge: Cambridge UP, 1997. Print.
Leclerc, Georges-Louis [Comte de Buffon]. *Oeuvres complètes de Buffon, mises en ordre et précédés d'une notice historique*. Ed. M.A. Richard. Paris: Baudouin Frères, 1827. Print.
Lemke, Sieglinde. *Primitivist Modernism: Black Culture and the Origins of Transatlantic Modernism*. Oxford: Oxford UP, 1998. Print.
Levinas, Emmanuel. *Totality and Infinity*. Trans. Alphonso Lingis. Pittsburgh: Duquesne UP, 1969. Print.
Levine, Paul. "The Writer as Independent Witness." Interview by Paul Levine. *E. L. Doctorow: Essays and Conversations*. Ed. Richard Trenner. Princeton, NJ: Ontario Review P, 1983. 57–69. Print.
Loeffelholz, Mary. *From School to Salon: Reading Nineteenth-Century American Women's Poetry*. Princeton: Princeton UP, 2004. Print.
Lowell, Amy. "Two Generations in American Poetry." *Poetry and Poets: Essays*. New York: Biblo and Tannen, 1971. 111–22. Print.
Lowie, Robert H. *Letters from Edward Sapir to Robert H. Lowie*. Berkeley: Privately Printed, 1965. Print.
Lutkehaus, Nancy C. "American Icon." *Natural History* 110.10 (2001): 14–15. Print.
———. "Margaret Mead and the 'Rustling-of-the-Wind-in-the-Palm-Trees School' of Ethnographic Writing." *Women Writing Culture*. Eds. Ruth Behar and Deborah A. Gordon. Berkeley: U of California P, 1995. 186–206. Print.
———. "Margaret Mead: Anthropology's Liminal Figure." *Reading Benedict/Reading Mead: Feminism, Race, and Imperial Visions*. Eds. Dolores Janiewski and Lois W. Banner. Baltimore: Johns Hopkins UP, 2004. 193–204. Print.
———. *Margaret Mead: The Making of an American Icon*. Princeton: Princeton UP, 2008. Print.
MacDougall, David. "The Subjective Voice in Ethnographic Films." *Fields of Vision: Essays in Film Studies, Visual Anthropology, and Photography*. Eds.

Leslie Devereaux and Roger Hillman. Berkeley: U of California P, 1995. 256–91. Print.

Manganaro, Marc. *Culture, 1922: The Emergence of a Concept*. Princeton: Princeton UP, 2002. Print.

Marcus, George E. "Contemporary Problems of Ethnography in the Modern World System." *Writing Culture: The Poetics and Politics of Ethnography*. Eds. James Clifford and George E. Marcus. Berkeley: U of California P, 2011. 165–93. Print.

Mark, Joan. *Margaret Mead: Coming of Age in America*. Oxford: Oxford UP, 1999. Print.

Marks, Peter. "The Left in the 1920s: *Good Morning* (1919–22), the *Freeman* (1920–4); and the *Modern Quarterly* (1923–9)." *The Oxford Critical and Cultural History of Modernist Magazines. Vol. II: North America 1894–1960*. Eds. Peter Brooker and Andrew Thacker. Oxford: Oxford UP, 2009. 857–80. Print.

Matthews, F. H. "The Revolt against Americanism: Cultural Pluralism and Cultural Relativism as an Ideology of Liberation." *Canadian Review of American Studies* 1.1 (1970): 4–31. Print.

McLuhan, Marshall. *Understanding Media: The Extensions of Man*. New York: McGraw Hill, 1964. Print.

Mead, Margaret. "The Absence of Pain." Typescript. The Papers of Margaret Mead, Library of Congress, Manuscript Division. Q15/7. 1924. Print.

———. "Absolute Benison." *The New Republic* 72.933 (1932): 255. Print.

———. "After the Anger Was Over." Typescript. The Papers of Margaret Mead, Library of Congress, Manuscript Division. Q15/15. 1927. Print.

———. "Aliter." Typescript. The Papers of Margaret Mead, Library of Congress, Manuscript Division. Q19/6. n.d. Print.

———. "America." Typescript. The Papers of Margaret Mead, Library of Congress, Manuscript Division. Q15/5. 1924. Print.

———. "And Your Young Men Shall See Visions." *The City Day: An Anthology of Recent American Poetry*. Ed. Edna Lou Walton. New York: Roland Press, 1929. 95. Print.

———. *And Keep Your Powder Dry: An Anthropologist Looks at America*. New York: Berghahn, 2000. Print.

———. "Anthropology and the Camera." *Encyclopedia of Photography*. Ed. Willard D. Morgan. New York: National Educational Alliance, 1963. 266–83. Print.

———. "Art Deserted." Typescript. The Papers of Margaret Mead, Library of Congress, Manuscript Division. Q15/20. 1929. Print.

———. "As a Dream" Typescript. The Papers of Margaret Mead, Library of Congress, Manuscript Division. Q19/6. n.d. Print.

———. *Blackberry Winter: My Earlier Years*. New York: Kodansha, 1995. Print.

———. "Caution to Beauty, a Fragment." Typescript. The Papers of Margaret Mead, Library of Congress, Manuscript Division. Q19/6. n.d. Print.

———. *Coming of Age in Samoa: A Psychological Study of Primitive Youth for Western Civilization*. New York: HarperCollins, 2001. Print.

———. "Cottager's Request." Typescript. The Papers of Margaret Mead, Library of Congress, Manuscript Division. Q15/10. 1925. Print.

———. "Desire Is a Knife." Typescript. The Papers of Margaret Mead, Library of Congress, Manuscript Division. Q15/15. 1927. Print.

———. "Desolation" Manuscript. The Papers of Margaret Mead, Library of Congress, Manuscript Division. Q19/5. n.d. Print.

———. "Disillusionment." Typescript. The Papers of Margaret Mead, Library of Congress, Manuscript Division. Q19/5. n.d. Print.

———. "Dreamer's Penance." Typescript. The Papers of Margaret Mead, Library of Congress, Manuscript Division. Q15/13. 1926. Print.

———. "Economy of Love." Typescript. The Papers of Margaret Mead, Library of Congress, Manuscript Division. Q19/5. 1925. Print.

———. "Ecstasy Neglected." Typescript. The Papers of Margaret Mead, Library of Congress, Manuscript Division. Q15/10. 1925. Print.

———. "The Fourth Companion." Typescript. The Papers of Margaret Mead, Library of Congress, Manuscript Division. Q15/5. 1925. Print.

———. "For Complete Possession." Typescript. The Papers of Margaret Mead, Library of Congress, Manuscript Division. Q15/13. 1926. Print.

———. "For a Proud Lady." *The Measure* 52 (1925): 16. Print.

———. "Fragments." Typescript. The Papers of Margaret Mead, Library of Congress, Manuscript Division. Q19/5. n.d. Print.

———. "Good Friday 1923." Typescript. The Papers of Margaret Mead, Library of Congress, Manuscript Division. Q15/5. 1924. Print.

———. "Green Sanctuary." Typescript. The Papers of Margaret Mead, Library of Congress, Manuscript Division. S9/5. 1927. Print.

———. *Growing up in New Guinea: A Comparative Study of Primitive Education*. New York: William Morrow, 1930. Print.

———. "Guerdon of Solitude." Typescript. The Papers of Margaret Mead, Library of Congress, Manuscript Division. Q15/18. 1928. Print.

———. "Hollow Heart." Typescript. The Papers of Margaret Mead, Library of Congress, Manuscript Division. Q15/10. 1925. Print.

———. "I Have Prepared a Place for You." Typescript. The Papers of Margaret Mead, Library of Congress, Manuscript Division. Q15/18. 1928. Print.

———. "In a Charred Place." Typescript. The Papers of Margaret Mead, Library of Congress, Manuscript Division. Q15/10. 1925. Print.

———. "Judas Iscariot." Typescript. The Papers of Margaret Mead, Library of Congress, Manuscript Division. Q15/10. 1925. Print.

———. "Kind Timothy Hay" Typescript. The Papers of Margaret Mead, Library of Congress, Manuscript Division. Q19/5. 1924. Print.

———. *Letters from the Field, 1925–1975*. New York: Harper & Row, 1977. Print.

———. "Letter to Martha Ramsey Mead of March 11, 1923." Typescript. The Papers of Margaret Mead, Library of Congress, Manuscript Division. Print.

———. "Lines to Charon." Typescript. The Papers of Margaret Mead, Library of Congress, Manuscript Division. Q19/6. n.d. Print.

———. "Madonna of the Breakfast Table." Typescript. The Papers of Margaret Mead, Library of Congress, Manuscript Division. Q19/5. n.d. Print.

———. "The Methodology for Racial Testing: Its Significance for Sociology." *Studying Contemporary Western Society: Method and Theory*. Ed. and introd. William O. Beeman. New York: Berghahn Books, 2004. 77–86. Print.

———. "Misericordia." *Poetry: A Magazine of Verse* 35.5 (1930): 253. Print.

———. "Monuments Rejected." Typescript. The Papers of Margaret Mead, Library of Congress, Manuscript Division. Q15/10. 1925. Print.
———. "The Need That Is Left." Typescript. The Papers of Margaret Mead, Library of Congress, Manuscript Division. S9/5. 1927. Print.
———. "No More Need to Smile." Typescript. The Papers of Margaret Mead, Library of Congress, Manuscript Division. Q15/5. 1923. Print.
———. "On Seeing Rodger Bloomer, May 1923." Typescript. The Papers of Margaret Mead, Library of Congress, Manuscript Division. Q15/5. 1925. Print.
———. "A Paper World." Typescript. The Papers of Margaret Mead, Library of Congress, Manuscript Division. Q19/6. n.d. Print.
———. "The Penciling of Pain." *Barnard Barnacle* 1.1 (1923): 6. Print.
———. *People and Places*. Cleveland: World Publishing Company, 1959. Print.
———. "Powerless Roots." Typescript. The Papers of Margaret Mead, Library of Congress, Manuscript Division. Q15/10. 1925. Print.
———. "Preface." *Patterns of Culture*. Ruth Fulton Benedict. Boston: Houghton Mifflin, 1989. xi–xiv. Print.
———. "The Prostitute's Requiem." Typescript. The Papers of Margaret Mead, Library of Congress, Manuscript Division. Q15/10. 1925. Print.
———. "The Role of Small South Sea Cultures in the Post War World." *American Anthropologist* 45 (1943): 193–96. Print.
———. "Rose Tree of Assisi." *The Measure* 57 (1925). Print.
———. "Ruth Fulton Benedict, 1887–1948." *American Anthropologist* 51.3 (1949): 457–68. Print.
———. *Sex and Temperament in Three Primitive Societies*. New York: William Morrow, 1935. Print.
———. "A Song of Five Springs." Booklet, Typescript. The Papers of Margaret Mead, Library of Congress, Manuscript Division. S9/5. c. 1927. Print.
———. "Star Bread." Typescript. The Papers of Margaret Mead, Library of Congress, Manuscript Division. Q15/10. 1925. Print.
———. "Storm Loveliness." Typescript. The Papers of Margaret Mead, Library of Congress, Manuscript Division. Q15/7. 1924. Print.
———. "A Tale of Pain." Typescript. The Papers of Margaret Mead, Library of Congress, Manuscript Division. Q19/5. 1924. Print.
———. *Talks with Social Scientists: Margaret Mead on What Is a Culture? What Is a Civilization?* New York: Berghahn Books, 2004. 16–27. Print.
———. "This Breath." Typescript. The Papers of Margaret Mead, Library of Congress, Manuscript Division. Q19/6. n.d. Print.
———. "Traveler's Faith." Typescript. The Papers of Margaret Mead, Library of Congress, Manuscript Division. Q15/10. 1925. Print.
———. "Unmarked Grave." Typescript. The Papers of Margaret Mead, Library of Congress, Manuscript Division. Q15/10. 1925. Print.
———. "The Valley's Benison." Typescript. The Papers of Margaret Mead, Library of Congress, Manuscript Division. Q15/7. 1924. Print.
———. "Visual Anthropology in a Discipline of Words." *Principles of Visual Anthropology*. Ed. Paul Hockings. Berlin: Mouton de Gruyter, 2003. 3–10. Print.
———. "Warning." Typescript. The Papers of Margaret Mead, Library of Congress, Manuscript Division. Q15/7. 1924. Print.
———. "The Way of Dreams." Typescript. The Papers of Margaret Mead, Library of Congress, Manuscript Division. Q19/6. 1928. Print.

———. "Wounded." Typescript. The Papers of Margaret Mead, Library of Congress, Manuscript Division. Q19/6. n.d. Print.
Mead, Margaret, and Gregory Bateson. "Disaster for Dictators: Crippled Industries." "Danger for Democracies: Corruption in Industries." Playing Cards for Board Game. Library of Congress, Manuscript Division. 247g-j. c. 1940. Print.
Mead, Margaret, and Frances Cooke Macgregor. *Growth and Culture: A Photographic Study of Balinese Childhood*. New York: Putnam, 1951. Print.
Mead, Margaret, and Rhoda Métraux. *The Study of Culture at a Distance*. New York: Berghahn Books, 2000. Print.
Menand, Louis. "Practical Cat: How Eliot Became Eliot." *The New Yorker*, Sept. 19, 2011. 76–83. Print.
Michaels, Walter Benn. *Our America: Nativism, Modernism, and Pluralism*. Durham: Duke UP, 1995. Print.
Miner, Earl. "Lyric." *The New Princeton Encyclopedia of Poetry and Poetics*. Eds. Alex Preminger and T.V.F. Brogan. Princeton: Princeton UP, 1993. 713–27. Print.
Mitchell, Paul Wolff, ed. "Special Focus: The Morton Cranial Collection and Legacies of Scientific Racism in Museums." Spec. issue of *History of Anthropology Review* 45 (2021).
Modell, Judith. *Ruth Benedict: Patterns of a Life*. London: Hogarth, 1984. Print.
Monberg, Torben. "Informants Fire Back: A Micro-Study in Anthropological Methods." *The Journal of the Polynesian Society* 84.2 (1975): 218–24. Print.
Monroe, Harriet. "In Texas and New Mexico." *Poetry: A Magazine of Verse* 16.6 (Sept. 1920): 324–28. Print.
———. "Letter to Ruth Fulton Benedict of April 3, 1928." Manuscript. The Papers of Margaret Mead, Library of Congress, Manuscript Division. Q90/1. Print.
———. "A Word to the Carping Critic." *Poetry: A Magazine of Verse* 11.2 (Nov. 1917): 89–92. Print.
Monroe, Harriet, Carl Sandburg, and Alice Corbin Henderson. "Aboriginal Poetry." *Poetry: A Magazine of Verse* 9.5 (Feb. 1917): 251–56. Print.
———. "The Enemies We Have Made." *Poetry: A Magazine of Verse* 4.2 (May 1914): 61–64. Print.
Montesquieu, Charles de. *The Spirit of the Laws*. Trans. and ed. Anne M. Cohler, Basia Carolyn Miller, and Harold Samuel Stone. Cambridge: Cambridge UP. Print.
Morgan, Lewis Henry. *Ancient Society or Researches in the Lines of Human Progress from Savagery through Barbarism to Civilization*. Chicago: Charles H. Kerr, 1877. Print.
Morrison, Mark S. "The Cause of Poetry: Thomas Moult and *Voices* (1919–21), Harold Monto and *the Monthly Chapbook* (1919–25)." *The Oxford Critical and Cultural History of Modernist Magazines. Vol. I: Britain and Ireland 1880–1955*. Eds. Peter Brooker and Andrew Thacker. Oxford: Oxford UP, 2009. 405–27. Print.
Moss, David. "What Does Poetry Mean to You?" Poems&Quotes 2007. Web. Jan. 8, 2019.
Mullin, Caitlin. "Mead's Use of Film." Psychoculturalcinema. Nov. 15, 2013. Web. Jan. 28, 2019.

Myers, Fred. "'Primitivism,' Anthropology, and the Category of 'Primitive Art'." *Handbook of Material Culture*. Eds. Christopher Tilley et al. London: Sage, 2006. 267–84. Print.

National Research Council Committee on Food Habits. "Food and Morale, Appendix I." Typescript. Library of Congress, Manuscript Division. 244c. Nov. 19, 1942. Print.

North, Michael. *Novelty: A History of the New*. Chicago: U of Chicago P, 2013. Print.

O'Donnell, Charles L. "On Indian Lake." *Poetry: A Magazine of Verse* 14.5 (Aug. 1919): 249. Print.

OED Online. Oxford UP. March 2018. Web. April 4, 2018.

Olson, Charles. "Projective Verse." *Selected Writings*. New York: New Directions, 1966. 15–30. Print.

Petrino, Elizabeth. *Emily Dickinson and Her Contemporaries: Women's Verse in America, 1820–1885*. Hanover: UP of New England, 1998. Print.

Pink, Sarah. *Doing Sensory Ethnography*. London: Sage, 2009. Print.

———. *Doing Visual Ethnography: Images, Media and Representation in Research*. 2nd ed. London: Sage, 2007. Print.

Platt, Tony. "Kroeber Hall and Berkeley Anthropology: What's in an Un-Naming?" *The Asia-Pacific Journal* 18.16 (2020): 1–6. Print.

Plessner, Helmuth, ed. *Anthropologie der Sinne*. Frankfurt a.M.: Suhrkamp, 1980. Print.

Popkin, Maggie L. *The Architecture of the Roman Triumph: Monuments, Memory, and Identity*. Cambridge: Cambridge UP, 2016. Print.

Pound, Ezra. "Letter to Harriet Monroe of Sept. 30, 1914." *The Letters of Ezra Pound, 1907–1941*. Ed. D.D. Paige. London: Faber and Faber, 1951. 80. Print.

Rancière, Jacques. *The Politics of Aesthetics*. Trans. Gabriel Rockhill. New York: Continuum, 2004. Print.

Reichel, A. Elisabeth. "'For You Have Given Me Speech!'—Gifted Speakers, Inarticulate Others, and Media Epistemologies in the Writing of Margaret Mead." *Postcolonial Interventions* 6.1 (2021): 195–245. Print.

———. "On the Poetry of a Boasian Cultural Anthropologist: Ruth Benedict's Palimpsestuous Writings." *Palimpsests in Ethnic and Postcolonial Literature and Culture: Surfacing Histories*. Eds. Yiorgos D. Kalogeras et al. London: Palgrave Macmillan, 2021. 171–90. Print.

———. "Sonic Others in Early Sound Studies and the Poetry of Edward Sapir: A Salvage Operation." *Soundscapes and Sonic Cultures in America*. Eds. Nassim Balestrini et al. Spec. issue of *Journal of the Austrian Association of American Studies* 1.2 (2020): 303–16. Print.

———. "Sonophilia/Sonophobia: Sonic Others in the Poetry of Edward Sapir." *Literature, Ethics, Morality: American Studies Perspectives*. Eds. Ridvan Askin and Philipp Schweighauser. Tübingen: Gunter Narr, 2015. 215–29. Print.

———. *Writing Anthropologists, Sounding Primitives: The Poetry and Scholarship of Edward Sapir, Margaret Mead, and Ruth Benedict*. Lincoln: U of Nebraska P, 2021. Print.

Reichel, A. Elisabeth, and Philipp Schweighauser. "Folk Communities in Translation: Salvage Primitivism and Edward Sapir's French-Canadian Folk Songs." *American Communities: Between the Popular and the Political*. Eds. Lukas Etter and Julia Straub. Tübingen: Gunter Narr, 2017. 61–83. Print.

Works Cited

"Richard G. Badger Papers: Guide." Houghton Library, Harvard UP 1999. Web. Aug. 29, 2014.

Richards, Eliza. *Gender and the Poetics of Reception in Poe's Circle*. New York: Cambridge UP, 2004. Print.

Ricoeur, Paul. *Freud and Philosophy: An Essay on Interpretation*. Trans. Denis Savage. New Haven: Yale UP, 1979. Print.

Rippl, Gabriele, Philipp Schweighauser, and Therese Steffen. "Introduction: Life Writing in the Age of Trauma." *Haunted Narratives: Life Writing in an Age of Trauma*. Eds. Gabriele Rippl et al. Toronto: U of Toronto P, 2013. 3–18. Print.

Roffman, Karin. "Finding Freedom from Museums and Libraries in Ruth Benedict's Poetry." *From the Modernist Annex: American Women Writers in Museums and Libraries*. Tuscaloosa: U of Alabama P, 2010. 143–81. Print.

Ruby, Jay. "The Professionalization of Visual Anthropology in the United States—1960s and 1970s." *Visual Anthropology Review* 17.2 (2002): 2–12. Print.

Santayana, George. "A Brief History of My Opinions." *The Philosophy of Santayana*. Ed. Irwin Edman. New York: Modern Library, 1936. 1–21. Print.

———. "The Genteel Tradition in American Philosophy." *Winds of Doctrine: Studies in Contemporary Opinion*. London: J.M. Dent, 1940. 186–215. Print.

Sapir, Edward. *Abnormal Types of Speech in Nootka*. Ottawa: Government Printing Bureau, 1915. Print.

———. "Acheron." Typescript. The Papers of Margaret Mead, Library of Congress, Manuscript Division. Q15/8. 1924. Print.

———. "After Playing Chopin." Typescript. William Cowan's Typescript in Edward Sapir Papers, Library, American Philosophical Society, Philadelphia. 1918. 73. Print.

———. "Autumn Leaves." Typescript. William Cowan's typescript in Edward Sapir Papers, Library, American Philosophical Society, Philadelphia. 1924. 174. Print.

———. "Autumn Raindrops." *Poetry* 39.2 (1931): 80. Print.

———. "The Blind, Old Indian Tells His Names." *The Collected Works of Edward Sapir. Vol. 4: Ethnology*. Eds. Regna Darnell and Judith T. Irvine. Berlin: De Gruyter, 1994. 507–10. Print.

———. "Blowing Winds." *Poetry: A Magazine of Verse* 30.4 (1927): 194. Print.

———. "Charon." *Poetry: A Magazine of Verse* 27.4 (1926): 180–81. Print.

———. "The Clergyman." *Dreams and Gibes*. Boston: Gorham Press, 1917. 18–19. Print.

———. "The Corn-Field." *The Canadian Forum* (Sept. 1922): 753. Print.

———. "Cultural Anthropology and Psychiatry." *Selected Writings of Edward Sapir in Language, Culture, and Personality*. Ed. D.G. Mandelbaum. Berkeley: U of California P, 1949. 509–21. Print.

———. "Culture, Genuine and Spurious." *American Journal of Sociology* 29 (1924): 401–29. Print.

———. "The Dainty and the Hungry Man." *Dreams and Gibes*. Boston: Gorham Press, 1917. 35–37. Print.

———. "Death." Typescript. William Cowan's Typescript in Edward Sapir Papers, Library, American Philosophical Society, Philadelphia. 1917. 35. Print.

———. "To Debussy: 'La Cathédrale Engloutie'." *Dreams and Gibes*. Boston: Gorham Press, 1917. 57. Print.

———. "Delilah." *Dreams and Gibes*. Boston: Gorham P, 1917. 32–33. Print.
———. "Del Inferno." *The Pagan* 3.3 (1918): 22–23. Print.
———. "Dirge." *The Dial* 83.3 (1927): 208. Print.
———. "Distant Strumming of Strings, Vague Flutings, Drum." *The Canadian Forum* (Nov. 1924): 53. Print.
———. "Dream Journey." *The Canadian Forum* (Feb. 1927): 148. Print.
———. "Dreams." *The Canadian Forum* (Sept. 1923): 366. Print.
———. "Dream of the Dead." *The Canadian Forum* (Jan. 1926): 118. Print.
———. *Dreams and Gibes*. Boston: Gorham P, 1917. Print.
———. "The Dumb Shepherdess." *Poetry: A Magazine of Verse* 16.4 (July 1920). Print.
———. "An Easter Day." *Dreams and Gibes*. Boston: Gorham P, 1917. 59–60. Print.
———. "Emily Dickinson, a Primitive." Rev. of *The Complete Poems of Emily Dickinson: The Collected Works of Edward Sapir. Vol. 3: Culture*. Eds. Regna Darnell and Judith T. Irvine. Berlin: De Gruyter, 1999. 1001–6. Print.
———. "Epitaph of a Philosopher." *Dreams and Gibes*. Boston: Gorham P, 1917. 17. Print.
———. "Epitaph of a Soldier." *Dreams and Gibes*. Boston: Gorham P, 1917. 30. Print.
———. "[Excerpt from] Preliminary Report on the Language and Mythology of the Upper Chinook." *The Collected Works of Edward Sapir. Vol. 4: Ethnology*. Eds. Regna Darnell and Judith T. Irvine. Berlin: De Gruyter, 1994. 293–95. Print.
———. "Everlasting Sun." Typescript. William Cowan's typescript in Edward Sapir Papers, Library, American Philosophical Society, Philadelphia. 1920. 121–22. Print.
———. "A Fear." Typescript. William Cowan's typescript in Edward Sapir Papers, Library, American Philosophical Society, Philadelphia. 1917. 26. Print.
———. "The Firmament Advises Man." *The Stratford Monthly* 3.2 (1924): 106. Print.
———. "French-Canadian Folk-Songs." *Poetry: A Magazine of Verse* 16.4 (July 1920): 175–76. Print.
———. "God." *Contemporary Verse* 9.3 (1920): 34. Print.
———. "God Blows a Message." *Poetry: A Magazine of Verse* 39.2 (1931): 81.
———. "The Halt of Summer." *Queen's Quarterly* 30 (July–Sept. 1922): 24.
———. "On Hearing Plaintive Jazz by Radio." Typescript. William Cowan's Typescript in Edward Sapir Papers, Library, American Philosophical Society, Philadelphia. 1924. 159–60. Print.
———. "The Heuristic Value of Rhyme." *The Collected Works of Edward Sapir. Vol. 3: Culture*. Eds. Regna Darnell and Judith T. Irvine. Berlin: De Gruyter, 1994. 922–25. Print.
———. "How You Were More Beautiful than Dusk." *The Canadian Forum* (1926): 407. Print.
———. "I Came to Sing Over Your Hair." Typescript. William Cowan's Typescript in Edward Sapir Papers, Library, American Philosophical Society, Philadelphia. 1926. 197. Print.
———. "I Cannot Say." Typescript. William Cowan's Typescript in Edward Sapir Papers, Library, American Philosophical Society, Philadelphia. 1920. 122. Print.

——. "Indian Legends from Vancouver Island." *The Collected Works of Edward Sapir. Vol. 4: Ethnology*. Eds. Regna Darnell and Judith T. Irvine. Berlin: De Gruyter, 1994. 525–26. Print.

——. "Indian Tribes of the Coast [of British Columbia]." *The Collected Works of Edward Sapir. Vol. 4: Ethnology*. Eds. Regna Darnell and Judith T. Irvine. Berlin: De Gruyter, 1994. 369–95. Print.

——. "The Indians of the Province [of British Columbia]." *The Collected Works of Edward Sapir. Vol. 4: Ethnology*. Eds. Regna Darnell and Judith T. Irvine. Berlin: Mouton de Gruyter, 1994. 335–45. Print.

——. "Involvement." *The Menorah Journal* (July 1928): 50. Print.

——. "To Joseph Conrad." *Queen's Quarterly* 30 (July–Sept. 1922): 22. Print.

——. "The King of Spain's Daughter and the Diver." *Poetry: A Magazine of Verse* 16.4 (July 1920). Print.

——. "The King of Thule." *The Nation* 115.2977 (1922): 96. Print.

——. "King Solomon." Manuscript. Edward Sapir Papers, Library, American Philosophical Society, Philadelphia, 1921. Print.

——. *Language: An Introduction to the Study of Speech*. New York: Harcourt, Brace and Company, 1921. Print.

——. "The Learned Jew." *Dreams and Gibes*. Boston: Gorham Press, 1917. 20–21. Print.

——. "Letter to Harriet Monroe of April 5, 1919." Manuscript. Poetry: A Magazine of Verse Records 1895–1961. Special Collections Research Center, U of Chicago P. Box 21, Folder 34. Print.

——. "Letter to Harriet Monroe of Aug. 1, 1919." Manuscript. Poetry: A Magazine of Verse Records 1895–1961. Special Collections Research Center, U of Chicago. Box 21, Folder 34. Print.

——. "Letter to Harriet Monroe of Dec. 6, 1919." Manuscript. Poetry: A Magazine of Verse Records 1895–1961. Special Collections Research Center, U of Chicago. Box 21, Folder 34. Print.

——. "Letter to Harriet Monroe of July 5, 1919." Manuscript. Poetry: A Magazine of Verse Records 1895–1961. Special Collections Research Center, U of Chicago. Box 21, Folder 34. Print.

——. "Letter to Harriet Monroe of June 10, 1920." Manuscript. Poetry: A Magazine of Verse Records 1895–1961. Special Collections Research Center, U of Chicago. Box 21, Folder 34. Print.

——. "Letter to Harriet Monroe of Mar. 23, 1925." Manuscript. Poetry: A Magazine of Verse Records 1895–1961. Special Collections Research Center, U of Chicago. Box 21, Folder 35. Print.

——. "Letter to Harriet Monroe of Oct. 23, 1918." Manuscript. Poetry: A Magazine of Verse Records 1895–1961. Special Collections Research Center, U of Chicago. Box 21, Folder 34. Print.

——. "Letter to Harriet Monroe of Oct. 28, 1918." Manuscript. Poetry: A Magazine of Verse Records 1895–1961. Special Collections Research Center, U of Chicago. Box 21, Folder 34. Print.

——. "Letter to Ruth Fulton Benedict of Aug. 26, 1924." Manuscript. The Papers of Margaret Mead, Library of Congress, Manuscript Division. T4/1

——. "The Lexicographer." Typescript. William Cowan's Typescript in Edward Sapir Papers, Library, American Philosophical Society, Philadelphia. 1924. 148–50. Print.

———. "Love." *Dreams and Gibes*. Boston: Gorham P, 1917. 54. Print.
———. "Lovers' Night." *The Measure* 53 (July 1925): 9. Print.
———. "The Man of Letters." *Dreams and Gibes*. Boston: Gorham P, 1917. 15. Print.
———. "Maples." Typescript. William Cowan's Typescript in Edward Sapir Papers, Library, American Philosophical Society, Philadelphia. 1917. 37. Print.
———. "Mary, Mary, My Love." *Poetry: A Magazine of Verse* 14.5 (Aug. 1919): 248–49. Print.
———. "The Measurer." *The Canadian Forum* 3.36 (Sept. 1923): 366. Print.
———. "Memory." *The Canadian Forum* 6.68 (1926): 246. Print.
———. "The Metaphysician." *Dreams and Gibes*. Boston: Gorham P, 1917. 16. Print.
———. "Miriam Sings Three Hymns." *The Canadian Forum* 5.52 (Jan. 1925): 110. Print.
———. "The Mislabeled Menagerie." *Dreams and Gibes*. Boston: The Gorham P, 1917. 9–10. Print.
———. "The Moon's Not Always Beautiful." *The Double Dealer* (1921): 130. Print.
———. "Music." *The Measure* 47 (Jan. 1925): 11. Print.
———. "Music Brings Grief." *The Nation* (July 28, 1926): 85. Print.
———. "The Musical Foundations of Verse." *The Collected Works of Edward Sapir. Vol. 3: Culture*. Eds. Regna Darnell, Judith T. Irvine, and Richard Handler. Berlin: Mouton de Gruyter, 1999. 930–44. Print.
———. "The New Religion." Typescript. William Cowan's Typescript in Edward Sapir Papers, Library, American Philosophical Society, Philadelphia. 1920. 116. Print.
———. "Nocturnal Comfort." Toni Flores, "The Poetry of Edward Sapir." *Dialectical Anthropology* 11 (1986): 165. Print.
———. "Note on French-Canadian Folk-Songs." *Poetry: A Magazine of Verse* 16.4 (July 1920): 210–13. Print.
———. "Notes on the Takelma Indians of Southwestern Oregon." *The Collected Works of Edward Sapir. Vol. 4: Ethnology*. Eds. Regna Darnell and Judith T. Irvine. Berlin: De Gruyter, 1994. 251–92. Print.
———. "Observations on the Sex Problem in America." *American Journal of Psychiatry* 8 (1928): 519–34. Print.
———. "The Oil-Merchant." *The Canadian Forum* 4.40 (Jan. 1924): 111–12. Print.
———. "The Old Maid and the Private." *Dreams and Gibes*. Boston: Gorham P, 1917. 30–31. Print.
———. "To One Playing a Chopin Prelude." Typescript. William Cowan's Typescript in Edward Sapir Papers, Library, American Philosophical Society, Philadelphia. 1918. 64. Print.
———. "Our Love." *Dreams and Gibes*. Boston: Gorham P, 1917. 55. Print.
———. "A Pair of Tricksters." *Queen's Quarterly* 31.2 (1923): 183. Print.
———. "The Parting." Typescript. William Cowan's Typescript in Edward Sapir Papers, Library, American Philosophical Society, Philadelphia. 1918. 54. Print.
———. "Poetry." Typescript. William Cowan's Typescript in Edward Sapir Papers, Library, American Philosophical Society, Philadelphia. 1918. 51. Print.
———. "Poet's Coterie." *Voices* 4.2 (1924): 45. Print.

———. "The Preacher." Typescript. William Cowan's Typescript in Edward Sapir Papers, Library, American Philosophical Society, Philadelphia. 1920. 127–28. Print.

———. "This Age." *The Canadian Forum* 3.36 (Sept. 1923): 366–67. Print.

———. "When the Greens of the Field Are Shot with Gold." *The University Magazine* 18 (Feb. 1919): 80. Print.

———. "When Love Came." *Palms* (Jan. 1929): 105–6. Print.

———. "The Prince of Orange." *Poetry: A Magazine of Verse* 16.4 (July 1920): 176–79. Print.

———. "The Professor." *Dreams and Gibes*. Boston: Gorham P, 1917. 16. Print.

———. "Promise of Summer." *The Double Dealer* (July 1924): 160. Print.

———. "The Rain." *Dreams and Gibes*. Boston: Gorham P, 1917. 63. Print.

———. "Rain-Storm." *The Pagan* 4.3–4 (1919): 48–49. Print.

———. "Realism in Prose Fiction." *The Dial* 62 (1917): 503–6. Print.

———. "To a Realistic Poet." Typescript. William Cowan's Typescript in Edward Sapir Papers, Library, American Philosophical Society, Philadelphia. 1919. 94. Print.

———. "To a Recruiting Girl." *Dreams and Gibes*. Boston: Gorham P, 1917. 26. Print.

———. "[Religion of the] Vancouver Island Indians." *The Collected Works of Edward Sapir. Vol. 4: Ethnology*. Eds. Regna Darnell and Judith T. Irvine. Berlin: Mouton de Gruyter, 1994. 511–24. Print.

———. "To a Returned Soldier." *The Canadian Forum* (Sept. 1922): 753. Print.

———. "Revery Interrupts Time." *Palms* (Mar. 1926): 183–84. Print.

———. *The Sapir-Kroeber Correspondence: Letters Between Edward Sapir and A. L. Kroeber, 1905–1925*. Ed. Victor Golla. Berkeley: Survey of California and Other Indian Languages, 1984. Print.

———. "Sayach'apis, a Nootka Trader." *The Collected Works of Edward Sapir. Vol. 4: Ethnology*. Eds. Regna Darnell and Judith T. Irvine. Berlin: De Gruyter, 1994. 481–506. Print.

———. "Oh Say You Are Not Dead." Typescript. William Cowan's Typescript in Edward Sapir Papers, Library, American Philosophical Society, Philadelphia. 1924. 158–59. Print.

———. "The Sermon on the Mount." Typescript. William Cowan's Typescript in Edward Sapir Papers, Library, American Philosophical Society, Philadelphia. 1920. 119. Print.

———. "The Siding." *The Canadian Forum* 5.58 (July 1925): 307. Print.

———. "Signal." *Poetry: A Magazine of Verse* 27.4 (1926): 175–76. Print.

———. "The Snow." Typescript. William Cowan's Typescript in Edward Sapir Papers, Library, American Philosophical Society, Philadelphia. n.d. 210. Print.

———. "Snowstorm in the Dusk." *The Pagan* 3.10 (1919): 15. Print.

———. "The Social Organization of the West Coast Tribes." *The Collected Works of Edward Sapir. Vol. 4: Ethnology*. Eds. Regna Darnell and Judith T. Irvine. Berlin: De Gruyter, 1994. 427–50. Print.

———. "Some Aspects of Nootka Language and Culture." *The Collected Works of Edward Sapir. Vol. 4: Ethnology*. Eds. Regna Darnell and Judith T. Irvine. Berlin: De Gruyter, 1994. 323–34. Print.

———. "A Song for Lovers." Typescript. William Cowan's Typescript in Edward Sapir Papers, Library, American Philosophical Society, Philadelphia. 1919. 106. Print.

———. "Song Recitative in Paiute Mythology." *The Collected Works of Edward Sapir. Vol. 4: Ethnology.* Eds. Regna Darnell and Judith T. Irvine. Berlin: De Gruyter, 1994. 541–58. Print.

———. "The Soul of Summer." *Poetry: A Magazine of Verse* 14.5 (Aug. 1919): 248. Print.

———. "Spring Light." Typescript. William Cowan's Typescript in Edward Sapir Papers, Library, American Philosophical Society, Philadelphia. n.d.210. Print.

———. "The Stenographer." *Dreams and Gibes.* Boston: Gorham P, 1917. 24–25. Print.

———. "Before the Storm." *Dreams and Gibes.* Boston: Gorham P, 1917. 62. Print.

———. "Summer in the Woods." *Dreams and Gibes.* Boston: Gorham P, 1917. 60–61. Print.

———. "The Tawny Hills." Typescript. William Cowan's Typescript in Edward Sapir Papers, Library, American Philosophical Society, Philadelphia. 1920. 114. Print.

———. "Three Folk-Songs of French Canada." *Queen's Quarterly* (Jan.–Mar. 1922): 286–90. Print.

———. "Three Hags Come Visiting." *Poetry* 27.4 (1926): 176–77. Print.

———. *Time Perspective in Aboriginal American Culture: A Study in Method.* Ottawa: Government Printing Bureau, 1916. Print.

———. "Time's Wing." *The Nation* (Jan. 21, 1925): 71. Print.

———. "Tom." *Canadian Courier* (Dec. 7, 1918): 7. Print.

———. "The Twilight of Rhyme." *The Dial* 63 (1917): 98–100. Print.

———. "War." *The Pagan* 3.6 (1918): 13. Print.

———. "The Water Nymph." *Dreams and Gibes.* Boston: Gorham P, 1917. 38–42. Print.

———. "We Others." Typescript. William Cowan's Typescript in Edward Sapir Papers, Library, American Philosophical Society, Philadelphia. 1918. 61–62. Print.

———. "White as the Snow." *Poetry: A Magazine of Verse* 16.4 (July 1920). Print.

———. "Winter Approaches." Typescript. William Cowan's Typescript in Edward Sapir Papers, Library, American Philosophical Society, Philadelphia. 1917. 36. Print.

———. "Why Cultural Anthropology Needs the Psychiatrist." *Psychiatry* 1 (1938): 7–12. Print.

———. "Women Play Mandolines Before Night." *The Measure* 47 (Aug. 1921): 10. Print.

———. "Worms, Wind and Stone." *The Measure* 51 (1925): 9. Print.

———. "Zuni." *Poetry: A Magazine of Verse* 27.4 (January 1926): 178. Print.

Sapir, Edward, and Morris Swadesh. *Native Accounts of Nootka Ethnography.* Bloomington: Indiana UP, Research Center in Anthropology, Folklore, and Linguistics, 1955. Print.

———. *Nootka Texts: Tales and Ethnological Narratives, with Grammatical Notes and Lexical Materials.* Philadelphia: Linguistic Society of America, 1939. Print.

Sarett, Lew R. "About Council Talks." *Poetry: A Magazine of Verse* 15.2 (Nov. 1919): 98–99. Print.

Schweighauser, Philipp. "An Anthropologist at Work: Ruth Benedict's Poetry." *American Poetry from Whitman to the Present*. Eds. Robert Rehder and Patrick Vincent. Tübingen: Gunter Narr, 2006. 113–25. Print.

———. "Faire du neuf, autrement: la poésie de Margaret Mead." Trans. Éléonore Devevey. *Anthropologie et poèsie*. Eds. Vincent Debaene and Nicolas Adell. Spec. issue of *Fabula LHT* 21 (2018): 35 pars. Web. Aug 22, 2022.

———. "Of Syncretisms, Foils, and Cautionary Examples: Ruth Fulton Benedict's Ethnographic and Poetic Styles." *Revisiting Style in Literary and Cultural Studies: Interdisciplinary Articulations*. Eds. Jasmin Herrmann et al. New York: Peter Lang, 2019. 193–205. Print.

———. "Playing Seriously with Genres: Sapir's 'Nootka' Texts and Mead's Balinese Anthropology." *RANAM: Recherches Anglaises et Nord-Américaines* 50 (2017): 107–21. Print.

———. "Ways of Knowing: The Aesthetics of Boasian Poetry." *Boasian Aesthetics: American Poetry, Visual Culture, and Cultural Anthropology*. Eds. Schweighauser et al. Spec. issue of *Amerikastudien/American Studies* 63.4 (2018): 541–56. Print.

Schweighauser, Philipp et al. "Introduction." *Boasian Aesthetics: American Poetry, Visual Culture, and Cultural Anthropology*. Eds. Schweighauser et al. Spec. issue of *Amerikastudien/American Studies* 63.4 (2018): 431–40. Print.

Sedgwick, Peter. "Cultural Relativism." *Cultural Theory: The Key Concepts*. Eds. Andrew Edgar and Peter Sedgwick. New York: Routledge, 2004. 99. Print.

Seremetakis, C. Nadia, ed. *The Senses Still: Memory and Perception as Material Culture in Modernity*. Boulder: Westview Press, 1994. Print.

Shakespeare, William. "Sonnet 18." *The Complete Sonnets and Poems*. 1609. Ed. Colin Burrow. Oxford: Oxford UP, 2002. 415. Print.

Shankman, Paul. "The Public Anthropology of Margaret Mead: Redbook, Women's Issues, and the 1960s." *Current Anthropology* 59.1 (2018): 55–73. Print.

———. *The Trashing of Margaret Mead: Anatomy of an Anthropological Controversy*. Madison: U of Wisconsin P, 2009. Print.

Shelley, Percy Bysshe. "A Defence of Poetry." *Peacock's Four Ages of Poetry, Shelley's Defence of Poetry, Browning's Essay on Shelley*. Ed. H. B. Brett-Smith. Oxford: Blackwell, 1921. 23–59. Print.

Shklovsky, Victor. "Art as Device." Trans. Benjamin Sher. *Theory of Prose*. Champaign: Dalkey Archive Press, 2009. 1–14. Print.

———. "Art, as Device." Trans. Alexandra Berlina. *Poetics Today* 36.3 (2015): 151–74. Print.

Silverman, Sydel. "The Boasians and the Invention of Cultural Anthropology." *One Discipline, Four Ways: British, German, French, and American Anthropology*. Eds. Fredrik Barth et al. Chicago: U of Chicago P, 2005. 257–74. Print.

Simmel, Georg. "Christianity and Art." *Essays on Religion*. Ed. Horst Jürgen Helle. New Haven: Yale UP, 1997. 65–77. Print.

Singh, Nikhil Pal. "Liberalism." *Keywords for American Cultural Studies*. Eds. Bruce Burgett and Glenn Hendler. 2nd ed. New York: New York UP, 2014. 153–58. Print.

Smedal, Olaf H. *Making Place: Houses, Lands, and Relationships Among Ngadha, Central Flores*. Diss. U of Oslo, Oslo, 1994. Print.

Sorby, Angela. *Schoolroom Poets: Childhood and the Place of American Poetry, 1865–1917*. Hanover: U of New Hampshire P, 2005. Print.
Spurgeon, Charles Haddon. "The Rent Veil." The Spurgeon Center, 1888. Web. Sept. 22, 2020.
Stewart, Susan. *Poetry and the Fate of the Senses*. Chicago: U of Chicago P, 2002. Print.
Stocking, George W., Jr., ed. *American Anthropology, 1921–1945: Papers from the American Anthropologist*. Lincoln: U of Nebraska P, 2002. Print.
———. "The Ethnographic Sensibility of the 1920s and the Dualism of the Anthropological Tradition." *The Ethnographer's Magic and Other Essays in the History of Anthropology*. Madison: U of Wisconsin P, 1992. 276–341. Print.
———. "Introduction: Thoughts Toward a History of the Interwar Years." *American Anthropology, 1921–1945: Papers from the American Anthropologist*. Ed. Stocking. Lincoln: U of Nebraska P, 2002. 1–74. Print.
———. "Paradigmatic Traditions in the History of Anthropology." *Companion to the History of Modern Science*. Eds. Robert C. Olby et al. London: Routledge, 1989. 712–27. Print.
———, ed. *Race, Culture, and Evolution: Essays in the History of Anthropology*. Chicago: U of Chicago P, 1968. Print.
———, ed. *Romantic Motives: Essays on Anthropological Sensibility*. Madison: U of Wisconsin P, 1989. Print.
———. *Victorian Anthropology*. New York: Free P, 1987. Print.
Strout, Cushing. "Personality and Cultural History in the Novel: Two American Examples." *New Literary History* 1.3 (1970). Print.
Taussig, Michael. *Mimesis and Alterity: A Particular History of the Senses*. New York: Routledge, 1993. Print.
Tedlock, Dennis. "Zuni Religion and World View." *Handbook of North American Indians*. Ed. Alfonso Ortiz. Washington: Smithsonian, 1979. 499–508. Print.
Teslow, Tracy. *Constructing Race: The Science of Bodies and Cultures in American Anthropology*. New York: Cambridge UP, 2014. Print.
Thacker, Andrew. "Canada: Introduction." *The Oxford Critical and Cultural History of Modernist Magazines. Vol. 2: North America 1894–1960*. Eds. Peter Brooker and Thacker. Oxford: Oxford UP, 2009. 599–601. Print.
———. "Poetry in Perspective: The Mélange of the 1920s: *The Measure* (1921–6); *Rhythmus* (1923–4); and *Palms* (1923–30)." *The Oxford Critical and Cultural History of Modernist Magazines. Vol. 2: North America 1894–1960*. Eds. Peter Brooker and Andrew Thacker. Oxford: Oxford UP, 2009. 320–46. Print.
Thomas, David Hurst. "Margaret Mead as a Museum Anthropologist." *American Anthropologist* 82.2 (1980): 354–61. Print.
Tietjens, Eunice "The Tepid Hour." *Poetry: A Magazine of Verse* 14.5 (Aug. 1919): 247. Print.
Tompkins, Jane. *Sensational Designs: The Cultural Work of American Fiction, 1790–1860*. Oxford: Oxford UP, 1985. Print.
Torgovnick, Marianna. *Gone Primitive: Savage Intellects, Modern Lives*. Chicago: U of Chicago P, 1990. Print.
Tyler, Stephen A. "Post-Modern Ethnography: From Document of the Occult to Occult Document." *Writing Culture: The Poetics and Politics of Ethnography*.

Eds. James Clifford and George E. Marcus. Berkeley: U of California P, 2011. 122–40. Print.

Tylor, E. B. *Primitive Culture: Researches into the Development of Mythology, Philosophy, Religion, Art, and Custom.* Vol. 2. London: John Murray, 1871. Print.

Tynianov, Yuri. "On Literary Evolution." *Readings in Russian Poetics.* Eds. L. Matejka and K. Pomorska. Cambridge: Harvard UP, 1971. 66–78. Print.

Untermeyer, Louis, ed. *Modern American Poetry: A Critical Anthology.* 4th rev. ed. New York: Harcourt Brace, 1930. Print.

Voget, Fred W. "History of Anthropology." *Encyclopedia of Cultural Anthropology.* Eds. David Levinson and Melvin Ember. Vol. 2. New York: Henry Holt, 1996. 567–79. Print.

Waldenfels, Bernhard. *Phenomenology of the Alien: Basic Concepts.* Trans. Tanja Stähler and Alexander Kozin. Evanston: Northwestern UP, 2011. Print.

Walker, Cheryl. *The Nightingale's Burden: Women Poets and American Culture Before 1900.* Bloomington: Indiana UP, 1982. Print.

Welsch, Wolfgang. "Aesthetics Beyond Aesthetics." *Practical Aesthetics in Practice and Theory.* Ed. Martti Honkanen. Proceedings of the XIIIth International Congress of Aesthetics, Lahti 1995. Helsinki: U of Helsinki P, 1997. 18–37. Print.

———. *Ästhetisches Denken.* 6th ed. Stuttgart: Reclam, 2003. Print.

———, ed. *Die Aktualität des Ästhetischen.* Munich: Fink, 1993. Print.

Wendt, Albert, and Sophie Foster. "American Samoa." *Encyclopædia Britannica.* February 16, 2017. Web. March 21, 2018.

Wenger, Tisa J. "Modernists, Pueblo Indians, and the Politics of Primitivism." *Race, Religion, Region: Landscapes of Encounter in the American West.* Eds. Fay Botham and Sara M. Patterson. Tucson: U of Arizona P, 2006. 101–14. Print.

Weston, Jessie L. *From Ritual to Romance.* Garden City: Doubleday, 1957. Print.

Williams, Raymond. "Structures of Feeling." *Marxism and Literature.* Oxford: Oxford UP, 1977. 128–35. Print.

Wimsatt, William K., and Monroe R. Beardsley. "The Intentional Fallacy." *Sewanee Review* 54.3 (1946): 468–88. Print.

Woolf, Virginia. "Character in Fiction." *Virginia Woolf: Selected Essays.* Ed. and introd. David Bradshaw. Oxford: Oxford UP, 2008. 37–54. Print.

Wordsworth, William. "Preface." *Lyrical Ballads: 1798 and 1802.* Oxford: Oxford UP, 2013. 95–116. Print.

Young, Virginia Heyer. "Benedict, Ruth F." *Theory in Social and Cultural Anthropology: An Encyclopedia.* Eds. R. Jon McGee and Richard L. Warms. Los Angeles: Sage, 2013. 64–68. Print.

Index

Note: Page locators in *italics* indicate a figure.

Adams, Léonie 17, 57
Adorno, Theodor W. 28
aesthetics: definition of 3, 33, 36, 81, 86; early/original 16, 82; Sapir 115
alterity: cultural 3, 5–8, 10–11, 22, 28, 39, 153; *see also* otherness; poetic 3, 153
American: anthropologist 1; Indian 104; poetry 7, 103; poets 27, 103; society/culture 5–6, 37, 41, 44, 71–3, 110; youth 72–3, 80
American Anthropological Association 73
American Association for the Advancement of Science 73
Americanism 5, 37, 46, 152
American Samoa 2, 4, 6, 76–9, 81
Anderson, Amanda 154
Anderson, Mark 150–2
Anderson, Sherwood 104
Anglo-American 20, 36
anthropological: research 1, 28, 56, 58, 60, 87, 90; work 8, 20–1, 70, 82, 86, 109, 132, 136–7
Anthropologist at Work, An (Benedict) 2, 20–3, 25, 27, 29, 33, 38, 46, 85, 90
anthropology: cultural 2–3, 17, 70, 103, 105, 122, 148, 152; sensory 3, 82; visual 1, 56, 69, 82, 144
art: as means of expression 4, 17, 36; culture and 36, 102; love of 18; negativity of 28, 35; poetry and 61–2
Aronoff, Eric 110–11

Bali 144
Balinese Character (Bateson/Mead) 8, 69, 75–6, 81, 144, *145*–6, 147, 149
Ball, Hugo 64–5
ballads 101, 105
Barbeau, Marius 106–7
Barthes, Roland 21, 147
Bateson, Gregory 8, 69, 74, 76, 81, 144, *145*, *146*, 147–9
Bateson, Mary Catherine 85, 89
Baumgarten, Alexander Gottlieb 3
Beardsley, Monroe R. 22
Benedict, Ruth Fulton 16–55, 57, 63, 90, 109
Bennett, Paula Bernat 86
Berryman, John 67
Biblical narrative 33, 87, 107
Boas, Franz 1, 6, 9n.2, 15n.20, 39, 62, 90, 93n.13, 104n.15, 104n.16, 150–1
Boasian: anthropology, use of 45, 56; concept of culture, changing 1, 5, 62–3, 75, 125, 147–50; poetry of 21–2, 81–2, 85, 90; traditional forms 6–7, 9
Bogan, Louise 17, 56
Böhme, Gernot 3
Bourne, Randolph 105

Caffrey, Margaret M. 18
Cassirer, Ernst 43–4
cautionary examples 6, 39, 44, 46, 48
Christian: mythology 30, 47–9; pagan practice 37–8; traditional 59, 66, 88
Clifford, James 28, 133, 148–9

colonialism 78–81, 151
Coming of Age in Samoa (Mead) 1, 3, 34, 42, 48, 70, 72, 80, 83, 95
Corbin Henderson, Alice 20, 103–4
counterculture 105, 107, 110, 151–2
Crapanzano, Vincent 148–9
creation, as myth 33–4, 60, 110, 148
Croce, Benedetto 86
cross-cultural comparison: Benedict 36, 40, 44, 46, 48; Mead 73
cultural: anthropologist 57, 122, 132; authenticity 110; criticism 109, 111; other(s) 2, 5, 7–8, 28–9, 31–2, 75, 137, 153; relativist 8, 36, 63, 152
cultural critique: Benedict 31, 43, 45–6; Mead 56, 70, 75, 87; mythical 30–1, 48, 87; Sigourney 86

Dial (magazine) 2, 25, 90, 100, 109, 111–12
Dillon, Elizabeth Maddock 86
Dobson, Joanne 86
Dobu, island of 39–40
Doctorow, E.L. 131–2
Dowthwaite, James 22, 110–12, 116–17

Eliot, T.S. 6, 57–62, 67–9, 103, 109, 116
epistemology 5, 40, 59, 61–3, 73, 85, 131
essay(s) 16, 21, 36, 68, 70, 88, 104
ethics 7, 131
ethnographer 49, 122–3, 131, 149, 151
ethnographic: knowledge 120, 130, 132–3; poems 8, 38, 78, 81, 86, 90, 108, 118, 137; research 113, 137
evolutionists 61–3, 153
expectations 45, 67
expression: cultural 48, 62, 91; emotional 8, 38–9, 56, 63, 85, 114; modernist 30, 109, 115; progressive 23, 131; sensory 31, 66

Fischer, Michael M. 148
foils 6–7, 41, 56, 70, 110; *see also* cautionary examples
folk songs 102, 104; *see also* Sapir
Ford, Henry 131

Frank, Florence Kiper 118
Frazer, James George 40, 60

Geertz, Clifford 149–150
genre 120
Gruber, Jacob W. 106

Hallowell, Irving 17
Handler, Richard 22, 82, 109–10, 114–16
Harris, J. Rendel 60
Harris, Joel Chandler 104
Hegeman, Susan 83, 110–11
Hertel, Ralf 135
Howes, David 134
human liberalism 151

immediacy 31, 43–4, 81, 115
Indigenous: community(ies) 60, 119–20, 134; persons 79, 120, 122, 128, 133, 144, 150
innovation 56, 68, 76, 150
intellectual 8, 21, 73, 84–5, 100
intentional fallacy 9, 22, 147
Intentional Fallacy (Wimsatt/Beardsley) 21, 147
Iser, Wolfgang 32

Jobson, Ryan Cecil 151–2

King, Charles 150–2
Kluckhohn, Clyde 17
Kroeber, Alfred 46, 108
Kwakiutl (Pacific Northwest Indian) 6, 39–41, 44, 46, 147

Leclerc, Georges-Louis 39
Letters from the Field (Mead) 22, 136
Levinas, Emmanuel 28
liberalism: Boasian 9, 151–2; political 154
Lowell, Amy 16–18, 57, 108, 110–11
Lowell, James Russell 104
Lowie, Robert H. 108
Lyrical Ballads (Wordsworth) 86

Manganaro, Marc 37, 110–11
Marcus, George E. 148
Matthews, F.H. 45
McLuhan, Marshall 18, 81

Mead, Margaret: 56–99; early works 69, 85; make it new 56, 63, 75; poetry/sonnets 7, 56, 63, 65–7, 71, 85, 89, 101; on sensory experience 8, 78, 82, 136; visual anthropologist 1, 4, 69–70, 82
Measure (magazine) 2, 20, 22, 57, 90, 100
media 58, 69–70, 76, 81–3
Menand, Louis 68
Millay, Edna St. Vincent 8, 17, 56
modernism 16, 19, 32, 75, 101; *see also* Benedict; Sapir
modernist: movement 2, 4, 104, 118; revolution 101, 120; writers 6, 63, 66, 108–9, 111–12, 115
Monberg, Torben 132
Monroe, Harriet 8, 27, 68, 101, 103, 108
Montesquieu, Charles de 61
Morgan, J.P. 131
Morgan, Lewis Henry 40, 61
mythology: Christian 30, 34; Greek 19, 66; Indigenous 119

Nation (magazine) 2, 20, 90, 100
Native Americans 7, 151
New Republic (magazine) 2, 90, 100, 112

O'Donnell, Charles L. 117
Ojibwa (people) 36
Olson, Charles 86
otherness 19, 28, 32

Papua New Guinea 2, 39
Patterns of Culture (Benedict) 1, 17, 34, 37, 39, 42, 46–8, 70, 83, 135, 147
perception; habitual 35–6, 43; sense/sensory 3, 8, 35, 81, 134, 138;
Plessner, Helmuth 3
poems, traditional expression of 6, 8, 18, 56, 86, 108, 114, 118, 120
poetic license 8–9
Poetry magazine 20, 28, 57, 100–2, 105–6, 108
poetry, modernist 18–19, 102, 104, 116–18, 127
Pound, Ezra 8, 57, 67–8, 75, 101, 109–10, 111, 115–16

primitivism 19, 38, 42, 49, 62, 102, 104, 108
private/public divide 8, 86

Quebec, folk songs 8, 102, 108, 120, 152

racial: consciousness 103, 151–2; inequality 6
Rancière, Jacques 3, 81
Reichel, A. Elizabeth 2, 22, 34, 70, 102, 111–12, 134–5
ritual 44–5, 59, 87, 123, 125, 135

Samoan(s) 4–5, 7, 48, 71, 79–80, 83
Santayana, George 16
Sapir, Edward: essays of 106, 111–14, 120, 127–30; folk songs 8, 102–6, 108; modernism, contribution to 108–9; poetic license 100, 127–8, 131, 147; poetry of 26–7, 85, 112, 118, 131, 133, 136; on sensory experience 134; work of 101, 119, 121, 128, 134
Shakespeare, William 89
Shelley, Percy Bysshe 28, 30
Shklovsky, Victor 4–5, 28, 30, 34–5, 113, 153
Sigourney, Lydia Huntley 16
Silverman, Sydel 75
Simmel, Georg 28
Singh, Nikhil Pal 153
Singleton, Annie 17, 20, 27
slavery 132, 151, 153
social sciences 32, 48, 83
Stewart, Susan 35–6, 66, 81, 136
Stocking, George 42
Strout, Cushing 131–2

Teasdale, Sara 17
Thaxter, Celia 16
Tietjen, Eunice 117
Tompkins, Jane 85–6
Trump, Donald J. 152
truth value for fiction 131
Tyler, E.B. 40
Tyler, Stephen A. 132–3
Tylor, Edward Burnett 60–2

Untermeyer, Louis 17, 56

Waldenfels, Bernhard 5
Waste Land (Eliot) 7, 58, 60, 67, 107, 110, 116
Welsch, Wolfgang 3
Wheeler Wilcox, Ella 16
Williams, Raymond 131–2
Williams, William Carlos 57, 101
Wimsatt, William K. 21–2, 147
Woolf, Virgina 16
Wordsworth, William 86

World War (I–II) 65, 73
Writing Culture (Marcus) 8, 28, 70, 80, 122, 132–3, 148–50
Wylie, Elinor 17

Zuni (poem) 8, 108, 120, 134, 136–7
Zuni Mythology (Benedict) 135
Zuni Pueblo 29–30, 34, 39–44, 70, 134